Integration of Refugees into the
European Education and Labour Market

Louis Henri Seukwa (ed.)

Integration of Refugees into the European Education and Labour Market

Requirements for a Target Group Oriented Approach

Bibliographic Information published by the Deutsche Nationalbibliothek
The Deutsche Nationalbibliothek lists this publication in the Deutsche Nationalbibliografie; detailed bibliographic data is available in the internet at http://dnb.d-nb.de.

Library of Congress Cataloging-in-Publication Data

Integration of refugees into the European education and labour market : requirements for a target group oriented approach / Louis Henri Seukwa (ed.).
    pages cm
    ISBN 978-3-631-64152-1
    1. EQUAL (Program) 2. Refugees—Employment—Government policy—European Union countries. 3. Refugees—Education—Government policy—European Union countries. 4. Labor policy—European Union countries. 5. Education and state—European Union countries. I. Seukwa, Louis Henri
    HD8378.5.A2I565 2013
    331.6'2094—dc23

                                                        2013017072

ISBN 978-3-631-64152-1

© Peter Lang GmbH
Internationaler Verlag der Wissenschaften
Frankfurt am Main 2013
All rights reserved.
Peter Lang Edition is an Imprint of Peter Lang GmbH.

Peter Lang – Frankfurt am Main · Bern · Bruxelles · New York · Oxford · Warszawa · Wien

www.peterlang.de

Contents

General introduction

Louis Henri Seukwa

Background

Handling the political, economic and social consequences of flight and migration has been a major challenge for many countries in Europe. This challenge finds its expression in contradictions on refugee-related topics. While on the one hand it is regarded as a social security problem, as a threat to a nation's prosperity and a burden for the welfare system, migration – and thus flight as one form of migration – is on the other hand also viewed as a way to ensure the competitiveness and viability of these countries given the demographic change and the ageing of the population and the challenges coming along with it, such as imbalances in the pension system and a skills shortage. These contradictions to be observed in European refugee and migration policies, which are usually based on defending the security and economic interests of nation states, are intensified by the goal set by the EU member states to apply humanistic ideals such as human rights and democratic principles to the group of refugees. The requirements for equality associated with them, that is the non-discrimination against a particular group in the fight for access to and control over resources that are generally considered by the society as being of material and symbolic value – and thus as desirable – are hard to reconcile with the common practice of giving priority to the interests of the national. This narrow view adopted in migration policy, which is tailored to the interests of the EU states, tends to ignore the global interdependencies of the causes of flight. One of the main push factors for flight and migration movements worldwide is the global structural imbalance caused by the rich countries of the north through the excessive exploitation of natural and human resources to the disadvantage of the poor countries of the south.

With the EU Council Directive 2003/9/EC of 27 January 2003, laying down minimum standards for the reception of asylum seekers as well as for the promotion of access to education and of participation in employment and VET, at EU level an important signal was sent to the member states regarding the recognition of asylum seekers and refugees as subjects of integration, and hence subjects of education – regardless of whether they have a secure residence status. Explicitly including the group of refugees in the EQUAL programme of the European Union can, in this context, be seen as the intention to fulfil the aim as formulated in the directive to harmonize reception standards as well as to promote access to education and participation in employment and VET in the integration policies of the member states. From 2001 to 2007 EQUAL made it possible, to experiment with new ways to fight against discrimination and inequalities across Europe – in the labour market in particular. For the first time in the history of the European Union, the group of asylum seekers and refugees had been explicitly considered in an employment programme trough EQUAL.

Despite the success of this programme, praised alike by the EU Commission and the individual countries involved for the implementation of its operational and strategic results (in particular, in the European Thematic Group 5, focusing on asylum seekers and refugees), EQUAL as a participant-oriented programme – i.e. one that designed its activities on basically all levels around the direct benefit of the participants – was not restarted after 2007. It thus remained an experimental programme, much to the disadvantage of a transfer of best practices developed in the model projects in sustainable structures.

Even though one of the most important strategic programme goals was to ensure the horizontal and vertical mainstreaming of the innovations developed here for sustainability purposes, the question of what happened to the many EQUAL network initiatives, the so-called development partnerships for the promotion of vocational and educational integration of asylum seekers and refugees, remains open. Whether these networks, which had been organized on a local, regional, national and transnational level, could be transformed into sustainable structures after the experimental phase to prepare the target group for the labour market is not sure. Also, the question as to the vocational future of the many participants who benefit from the EQUAL programme remains unanswered, i.e. the question of whether they could be brought into employment and if so, in what way and in which area of the labour market their integration took place, whether it was the formal, non-formal or informal sector.

Up to today, no systematic ex-post evaluation on the sustainability of the EQUAL measures has been carried out to determine if the target group-specific integration models devised and tested in the different development partnerships of the countries could be transferred into permanent structural integration measures. Neither has there been a post-study to follow up on the participants and on the effectiveness of their career development after EQUAL.

Study questions and objectives

In this context the idea for this project was born. The project, though, is not supposed to evaluate the EQUAL programme from the perspective outlined above. It rather aims at analyzing the results achieved by EQUAL with respect to the harmonization of reception standards, as formulated by the EU Council Directive, and the promotion of access to education and participation in employment and VET in the integration policies of the member states. Based on case studies in four European cities, the question of access to education and training programmes as well as to the labour market for refugees and asylum seekers was examined, while also highlighting the conditions for the success of such measures. The project thus aims at investigating the question of in what way and under which (legal, political, structural and individual) circumstances the vocational preparation and integration of this extremely disadvantaged group of migrants can be successful in Europe. What role can be ascribed to their biographies, which are characterized by transnational mobility, and thus to the specific competences they bring with them in the process of vocational preparation and integration? These questions follow up on the goals of the Leonardo da Vinci programme to develop innovations and assure quality in the vocational education of a group of people which is extremely marginalized in the European context that is for instance the group of refugees and asylum seekers.

Regarding the sometimes significant historical, economic and structural differences between the European cities whose VET integration structures as well as their functioning from the perspective of refugees and asylum seekers are examined and compared here, questions are raised on the countries' ability and willingness to implement such harmonization measures as laid down by the EU Council Directive in integration policies, bringing up issues of compatibility as well the gap between theoretical ambitions and the reality of harmonization. The circumstances under which harmonization is possible are thus to be investigated on an empirical basis.

All these questions are linked to specific theoretical assumptions on the vocational integration of refugees and asylum seekers, reflecting the particular perspective of the partners involved in the project. These will be summarized in the following.

Theoretical approaches

The resources approach: Regarding the extremely difficult situation of asylum seekers and refugees in basically all European countries, refugee research has, up to now, primarily focused on the legal, social and structural mechanisms of discrimination with respect to the integration in the receiving countries as well as on individual deficits as a drawback (cf. Radtke/Gomolla 2002, Neumann et al. 2003, Brekke 2004). As a matter of consequence most practical projects are deficit-oriented in their approach to integration, and the majority of the offers based on these approaches focus on compensating the deficiencies asylum seekers may have, whether linguistic, mental, physical, cognitive, cultural, social or material. This project, however, is based on a firm resources perspective towards integration structures and the group examined here.

Resources perspective on structures: This perspective has been methodologically operationalized in the project through social space analysis of the research unit "city". It is based on the theoretical assumption that the spatial distribution of what Pierre Bourdieu calls "structural capital", that is the quantitative and qualitative availability of valuable infrastructures, institutions and services, constitutes one of the most important structuring dimensions of the social space (cf. Schroeder 2002). Due to the spatialization of the different forms of capital (economic, cultural, social and symbolic), specific *capital configurations* are to be observed in urban quarters, resulting from the given local objective conditions including housing conditions and the availability of jobs, social and healthcare services etc. "As a social and physical location, residential areas provide an average probability of acquiring material and cultural goods and services available at a given time" (Bourdieu 1991, p. 31). It is these forms of capital varying across social spaces – the material conditions which are unequally distributed – that condition the residents' development potential and their scope of action, thus their acquiring ability, and that define their access to and control over educational, vocational and labour market resources.

Based on this assumption, in all four cities examined here a comprehensive survey of the existing structural resources was conducted, focusing on VET-related institutions of integration (i.e. institutions preparing for the labour market), while also addressing the question of accessibility and usefulness of these structural resources for refugees and asylum seekers when considering the specific needs and requirements of this target group.

Resources perspective on refugees: It is mainly unfavourable associations that pervade the dominant social construction of asylum seekers, labelling them with negative, hence stigmatizing attributes such as "criminals", "sluggards", "parasites" or "illegitimate beneficiaries of social services", and they are even viewed as "victims" by social and educational workers and other so-called "mentors" or "helpers". Also, due to the fact that their biographies are usually characterized by several traumatic experiences including their precarious situation in the receiving countries as a whole, refugees tend to be essentially regarded as helpless beings and victims. The project EduAsyl, however, takes a different approach and assumes that due to their primary socialization in different contexts of their countries of origin as well as due to their transnational biographies and experiences of

10

flight, these young people are equipped with various competences acquired in the formal, non-formal and informal education sector. Systematically considering these existing individual resources and competences shall thus be the theoretical basis for examining the success of any kind of education, social pedagogy or social work as well as labour market support programme which aims at reducing the individual effects of the structural disadvantages refugees face. This contributes among others to preventing the downgrading of refugees in the formal and non-formal education and VET systems of the receiving European countries, which is usually the result of a wrong assessment of their qualifications and competences, as well as the unnecessary prolongation of the time this target group spends in the education system.

Lifelong learning and life-wide learning: In turn, the advantages of making use of the resources already available, inter alia by including the qualifications and competences acquired in the countries of origin and during the flight in integration-related work, are obvious. The transnational experience of flight under quite adverse conditions can thus be viewed as a biographical resource which may manifest itself in resilience capabilities regarding all the challenges which go together with the existing conditions of a refugee in everyday life.

Moreover, the capitalization of all learning experiences made by the refugee in the *course of time* in integration work also contributes to promoting lifelong learning for this target group – despite biographical breaks and disruptions related to the flight. Focusing on the plurality of (educational) places (formal, non-formal, informal), which may serve as learning locations before and during the flight, constitutes, furthermore, a contribution to *life-wide learning*.

With this term we want to highlight the localization of education, that is to say that *place* is fundamentally constitutive for educational content and for the competences resulting from it. In this way, alongside the formal and non-formal sector, the informal sector as a *place* for education, and thus for competence acquisition, gains in significance. The combination of these three educational locations or sectors is decisive in order to get a comprehensive overview of all the resources migrants bring with them in the context of their transnational biographies. As empirical studies on the relation between the formal and informal sector with regard to the issue of transfers of competencies in migration situations have shown, the distinction between different sectors (formal, non-formal, informal) in which educational experiences prior to flight were made by the refugees and thus competencies acquired is irrelevant when it comes to use of these competencies in the migration context of Europe (cf. Seukwa 2007). This is due to the fact that many competences acquired in the informal sector in the countries of origin as well as in transit countries (linguistic and calculating abilities, farming, negotiation or selling and handicraft skills etc.) are also of use in the formal education sector in Europe. This indicates that the qualitative difference between both sectors regarding their contents is less significant than commonly assumed. The decisive difference, however, lies rather in the conditions under which experiences are made and competences are acquired. The formal education sector has a legal character and is either under direct control of the state or funded most of the time at least partly by the state when under control of independent institutions. It is usually only to be accessed through clearly regulated admission formalities, while the educational method is strictly defined and structured.

The informal sector, in contrast, tends to develop on the margins of society in many countries, especially in those of the "South". It comprises people of all ages and both genders that have very little share in the different "forms of capital". In the context of these countries, the informal sector is an important place of action for the disadvantaged majority of the population, which demonstrates their ability and will to survive through transgression – despite and beyond all forms of heteronomy. Since this sector requires disobedience, violations of the law and subversive creativity as paradigms of liberation, which are constantly practiced by the people "from below", a nuanced look at the difference between the legal and the illegal as distinguishing factor between the formal and informal sector is necessary. It is the relativity of the distinction, in combination with the similarity of the educational contents in both sectors, which make the transfer from one sector to the other easy despite the change in context.

Employment biographies and life situations – the Capital theory: VET research has shown that the vocational integration of disadvantaged adolescents and adults is most successful when their whole life situation is stabilized through appropriate educational intervention (Baur et al. 2004). While previously, educational work focused on vocational qualification and training, assuming that this would create the conditions for social integration, today it is the stability in the individual life situation that is regarded as prerequisite for successful vocational integration. Thus, if the success of vocational support programmes is to be evaluated, it is simply not enough to focus exclusively on the educational pathways and the employment biographies of the participants. The successful completion of such educational programmes, along with the possibility of entering training or work, depends on the forms of handling the difficult life situations refugees have to face. Their financial situation, their residence status and other law-related issues, the stability of their social relations, their civil competences, their housing and health conditions as well as the forms of their recreational activities are significant dimensions that have an impact on the success of an educational support programme.

"The social situation of an individual is dependent on different dimensions, which are not to be reduced to the financial aspect. Apart from the material circumstances, factors such as education, employment or unemployment, housing conditions, separation, single parenthood, social networks etc. have an impact on the life situation. The term refers to the whole social interconnections, in which people make use of their material and immaterial possibilities. The life situation determines people's development potential and the possibility to live their life the way they chose without losing self-respect". (cf. Engels 2006, p. 109 ff.).

We thus assume that there is a close – albeit not causal – relation between the life situation of an individual and his/her possibilities to ask for and to acquire *education* (cf. Voges et al. 2003). With regard to considerations made by the sociologist Pierre Bourdieu, we understand education as a product of individual possibilities of access to and control over different forms of economic, social and cultural capital (Bourdieu 1983). According to Bourdieu, the life situation of an individual is determined by the specific quantity (volume) and configuration of the types of capital: economic capital, which can directly be converted into money; cultural capital, which manifests itself in certificates or educational degrees and may pay off in the form of a well-paid job; social capital, which is made up of different types of useful social relations and also has significant influence on the social positioning and social status of the individual. From this perspective, it can be shown that the educational and employment careers of refugees develop under quite adverse conditions, since their access to "capital" is extensively restricted. Basically no form of capital can be accessed without restriction or is available without control. Their "acquisition potential" for different types of capital, i.e. their capacity to shape their educational career and to realize their aims in life, is in fact minimal, and in many cases their specific "capital configurations" allow for nothing more than to aim at individual self-realization under highly precarious conditions for years. The legal, physical, economic and social capital available to them is insufficient to be able to act "profitably" in the fields of education, training and employment. That some individuals are able, despite the most adverse conditions, to earn educational degrees and to find employment, deserves greatest respect. That others have resigned – who would blame them for it?

Research methods

Based on these theoretical perspectives, the empirical data have been analyzed in the city reports on the vocational integration of the study group in the four European cities of research (Florence, Glasgow, Hamburg, Gothenburg[1]).

---

1   The Swedish partner – Göteborgsinitiativet, an NGO working in the field of social support and training for asylum seekers and refugees – has, due to internal financial problems, opted out

The city approach: As research locations, cities and metropolitan areas in the countries involved have been chosen. The decision has been made for research-pragmatic reasons, since cities and metropolitan areas are centres of attraction for refugees and migrants, for the simple reason that the possibilities to find a job or training or to study are better there. They are also destinations for asylum seekers or newly arrived immigrants which migrate in the context of family reunion. Apart from better opportunities to find employment, the existence of networks of ethnic communities plays a significant role in the cities, since these support structures serve as bridges to integration. The same is true for family connections already present in the cities. As the influx of migrants and refugees leads to an increase in the diversity of the urban population, municipal integration policies need to respond to the demands of the different population groups, providing them with equal opportunities for integration and promoting the peaceful coexistence between the local population and the migrants. In order to do so, most cities are equipped with qualitatively and quantitatively well-established integration structures (cf. Gag/Schroeder 2011).

In these four cities, data have been collected, from the structural perspective, on the VET institutions existing in the formal and non-formal sector. Following the target group-oriented approach, data have been collected, from the perspective of the study group, on the functioning of the existing structures and their accessibility for asylum seekers and refugees as well on the recognition and usefulness of their transnational biographies as a resource for vocational integration. For that purpose, problem centred face to face interviews with six asylum seekers and refugees were conducted in each city, collecting data on their transnational biographies and the competences and qualifications they bring with them. Also, data on the way these competences are utilized or not in the VET institutions of the receiving countries were of interest, including the individual expectations regarding integration and future prospects of the people interviewed. The evaluation and analysis of the data was bundled in city reports. These are coherent and consistent analyses based on the VET structures available, the individual biographies and the concrete reception and integration situation of the asylum seekers and refugees. In the analysis and presentation of the study results, each city has its own focus – depending on the contextual background with respect to relevant legal and political conditions, the institutional

from the project in February 2011. Thanks to the intervention from a flanking EU programme, the European Social Fund, also represented as a silent partner in the partnership, a way to finance and finalize the Swedish reporting and participating in the project was nevertheless found. Swedish participation from that on was fully financed by the Swedish ESF Council, Management Authority for the European Social Fund in Sweden, and the budget completely separated from the budget of the LdV project.

14

context of the VET systems (regarding their availability and accessibility for the asylum seekers and refugees) as well as the integration practices as applied by the institutions and refugees.

Summary of the outcomes

The city report of Florence, entitled "The paradox of being a recognized refugee in Italy: living in an open prison, Florence, Tuscany", thus focused on a very specific problem of the city and provincial territory of Florence, whose main characteristic is the absence of far-reaching policies on the right of asylum with regard to recognition of status, reception and integration. Consequently, recognised refugees (single individuals and families) face a life of precarious social and living conditions, unemployment, lack of concrete possibilities for adult education, training or professional requalification. The most visible (and *symbolic*) characteristic of this situation are the *"Occupied Public Buildings"* (abandoned public buildings – hospitals, schools, railway stations, offices, etc.), in which many people of our target group, single individuals and families, have been living for the past 10 years.

The city report of Glasgow, entitled "A life in limbo: barriers to VET and labour market integration for asylum seekers awaiting for the granting of 'Leave to Remain'", focuses on the plight of asylum seekers as they wait for the cogs of the decision-making process to slowly come to a conclusion. The length of this wait and policies that exclude access to vocational education and paid employment deny asylum seekers full integration into Glaswegian society, with the consequence that there may be an impact on emotional and financial well-being that exacerbate the trauma of what has happened in their lives before and the trauma of finding themselves in a new country. Through the biographies of refugees and asylum-seekers featured here, the report analyzes their personal experiences and coping strategies. The report also looks at the formal and non-formal structures that are in place to support refugees and asylum-seekers with a focus on practices that try to help in the integration into VET and the labour market as well as the challenges they face. In the report, the following question is posed: Are the principles of integration in Glasgow really different from the reality of barriers to integration faced by asylum seekers in the present political climate?

The Hamburg city report, entitled "Vocational integration of refugees and asylum seekers in Hamburg – roundabout routes from model to structure" reflects exclusion and inclusion mechanisms of formal and non-formal educational programmes in Hamburg, while focussing on the factors and concepts which improve refugee-sensitive vocational integration work in that city. It shows how useful medium and/or long-term regular financial support of model and experimental projects in the field of vocational integration of refugees and asylum seekers is for the sustainability of innovations, i.e. their transfer from experimental projects into regular structures, thus changing progressively, in a positive sense, the political discourse as well as the administrative practices regarding the vocational integration of this disadvantaged group in Hamburg. However, these positive changes also bring with them some challenges regarding, for instance, the systematic inclusion in regular VET structures where refugees and asylum seekers have been excluded until now. In order to help the local Hamburg VET institution to tackle this inclusion and diversity management challenge successfully, a concept of refugee monitoring in educational and VET systems was developed; (see "Refugee Monitoring"). And a description and comments on first steps in implementation of such a Refugee monitoring concept in Hamburg was made with a focus on the situation of young refugees in the Hamburg transitional system from school to vocation and recommendations

The city report of Gothenburg, entitled "The reception and introduction of asylum seekers and new arrivals in Gothenburg: Successes and failures in the development of a new system", describes the new national system for examining asylum applications and goes on to analyze the reception of asylum seekers and refugees in Gothenburg, the second biggest city in Sweden. The system primarily supports new arrivals in finding employment, but does not sufficiently deal with the impact of needs such as housing, family reunion, medical and psychological treatment as well as specific needs of traumatized refugees on the successful integration of this target group into the VET system and the labour market. The report shows both possibilities and difficulties within the system and closes with a number of recommendations.

Based on these particularities of the VET and labour market integration systems and practices for refugees and asylum seekers in the four cities of research, bad, promising and good practices as well as recommendations for the integration of refugees into the European education and labour market have been formulated, on a local as well as on a European level. Latest i.e. the recommendations on European Level takes advantage from the outcomes of the case studies and draw consequences which might help technicians and stakeholders in the field of VET for asylum seekers and serve as evidence base for policy drives at EU level.

Cities Reports

I.
The paradox of being
a recognized refugee in Italy:
Living in an open prison, Florence, Tuscany

Margherita Buchetti, Rita Cardini, Daria Franceschini, Chiara Trevisan,
Maria Omodeo Nicola Solimano, Claudia Zaccai

Chapter 1: General Introduction – National Asylum Framework in Italy

The first and the most important law concerning the right of asylum in Italy is the Constitution of the Italian Republic, article 10. A constitutional principle that still is not enforced in the ordinary legal order:

> The Italian legal order complies with the rules of international law generally recognized. The legal condition of the foreigner is regulated by the law in accordance with the international law and treaties. The foreigner who cannot exercise his/her democratic liberties granted by the Italian Constitution has the right of asylum in the territory of the Republic according to the conditions established by law. It is forbidden the extradition of the foreigner for political crimes.

In 1990, the Law n. 39/90, "Norme urgenti in materia di asilo politico, di ingresso e soggiorno dei cittadini extracomunitari e di regolarizzazione dei cittadini extracomunitari ed apolidi già presenti nel territorio dello Stato", (Urgent legal measures in the field of political asylum, of entry and residence of non-EU citizens and of regularization of non-EU citizens and stateless peolple that already are in the territory of the State), abolished the geographical reserve to the Geneva Convention of 1951 – that limited in Italy the recognition of refugees coming uniquely from Europe – and provided a set of rules that regulated the asylum matter only in part.

With the law of 28th February 1990, n. 39, the Italian State finally ratified completely the Geneva Convention of 1951, that entirely became law of the Italian State.

In September 2002, the law was again modified with the approval of the Law L. 189/02, "Modifica alla normativa in materia di immigrazione e di asilo" (Amendment of the set of rules in the field of migration and asylum), implemented only in 2005 with the "Decreto del Presidente della Repubblica 16 Settembre 2004, n. 303, Regolamento relativo alle procedure per il riconoscimento dello status di rifugiato" (Decree of the President of the Republic, September 2004, 16, n. 303, concerning the procedure for the recognition of the refugee status).

These amendments brought many changes to the law of the 25th July 1998 n. 286, "Testo unico delle disposizioni concernenti la disciplina dell'immigrazione e norme sulla condizione dello straniero", (Measures concerning migration and the condition of foreigners), that is the general law in matters concerning migration in Italy, but it also changed the set of norms on asylum (cf. art.31 e 32). In fact the most important changes about asylum matters concerning the procedure for asking and obtaining the status of refugee under the Geneva Convention.

It is interesting to note that this law influenced considerably asylum matters, in particular through the decentralization of the asylum procedure and the institution of some Territorial Commissions, that have to examine the instances of recognition of international protection. These Commissions are now in several north and south Italian cities and they are made up of government officials and representatives of the Local Authorities. A representative of UNHCR participates *de jure* to the work of these Commissions.

These Commissions are directed and coordinated by the National Commission for the Right of Asylum, once the only organism to have functions of recognition of the refugee status in Italy.

It is, however, in the three-year period 2005 – 2008, with the reception of the European law in asylum matters, that in Italy an important legislative reform on the right of asylum takes shape.

In 2005 the "Directive 2003/9 with minimum standards on the reception of asylum seekers in the member States" was been implemented with the Legislative Decree "Implementation of the directive – D.lgs. 140/2005" that establishes the norms on reception of foreigners asking the recognition of the refugee status on the national territory.

Then the Directive 2004/83/CE of the Council on "Minimum rules on the attribution of the refugee status or of persons otherwise in need of international protection to non-EU citizens or stateless people, as well as minimum rules on the contents of the recognized protection" has been implemented with the Legislative Decree 19/11/2007 n. 251 so-called *Decreto Qualifiche*. This Decree establishes the criteria that Italy, as a member State, must use in order to decide if an asylum seeker has the right to international protection and which kind of protection he/she has to receive, if the refugee status or a kind of subsidiary protection.

Whereas with the Legislative Decree 28/01/2008 n. 25 so-called *Decreto Procedure*, modified and integrated by the Legislative Decree of the 3rd October 2008, n. 159 was implemented by the Directive 2005/85/CE on "Minimum rules for the procedures applied in the Member States in order to recognize or to revoke the refugee status". With this set of laws some minimum rules for the procedure applied in order to recognize and revoke the refugee status have been introduced. In fact these two decrees modify these issues in a substantial way but, despite the changes made in order to regulate the entire asylum field and to improve the situation of refugees and asylum seekers in Italy, an organic law that guarantees those asking protection in Italy the access to a solid system of protection, assistance and integration is still necessary. Italy still remains the only EU country where there are no organic policies and a national system of reception, protection and integration. Furthermore this situation would reduce the operative difficulties both for the local administrations and for the private-social sector that work in the field of assistance and safeguard of the rights of people under international protection.

In response to these problems, in April 2001, the UNHCR, the Home Office and the National Association of the Italian Cities (ANCI) created and implemented the National Asylum Program (PNA), inserted in the Law n. 189/2002 in the System of protection for asylum seekers and refugees (SPRAR). With the institutionalization of this system, a coordination structure, the Central Service of Information, Promotion, Consultancy, Monitoring and Technical Support to the Local Authorities was set up. Among the aims of this Program there was the constitution of a reception network in order to accompany the asylum seekers all during the status recognition *iter* and the predisposition to intervene in support for the refugee integration.

In fact the SPRAR is a network of Local Authorities that – in order to implement "integrated reception" projects – have access to available resources, of the National Fund for Asylum Policies and Services.

On a territorial level the Local Authorities, with the support of the Third Sector, guarantee an "integrated reception" that goes beyond the only distribution of board and lodgings, offering also in a complementary way information services accompaniment, assistance and orientation, through the building up of individual paths of socio-economic integration.

Several tasks concern the Central Service such as the monitoring of the presence on the territory of people asking or having the status of international protection; the creation, the maintenance and the constant updating of a data bank of the interventions implemented at the local level for people asking or having the status of international protection; the dissemination of information on good practices; technical assistance to the Local Authorities, as well as the predisposition of reception services; support to the information services and orientation carried out in the governmental centers for asylum seekers.

SPRAR Report – 2010

In order to read correctly the data concerning the activities of SPRAR, it is necessary to remember the extraordinary number of arrivals in the year 2008 that determined a growth of the reception needs in Italy during the following two year period, as it is equally important to remember the events in 2011. In fact the migration fluxes from Tunisia and Libya of the last months have had a strong impact on the claims of international protection and, consequently, on the reception system for refugees and asylum seekers in Italy.

The SPRAR reception network at a national level

Moreover, during the two year period 2008-2010 some general considerations about the changes of the characteristics of the asylum seekers and refugee population who arrived in Italy in this period are interesting. We noted mainly the emersion of a significant number of situations, indicated by both the territorial and the governmental reception centers, concerning physical and psychological conditions, serious disabling diseases of people also victims of violence and torture. This important increase of vulnerability situations made the research of places with specific services inside SPRAR complex, most of all for those presenting problems connected to mental disease.

Therefore in total the System of protection has 3.146 places that, during 2010, guaranteed the reception of 6.855 beneficiaries, both asking or having the status of international protection. From this point of view, analyzing the accommodation of SPRAR in the Regions, we note that the primacy of reception goes to Lazio – 1.580 receptions, 22.39% for a total number of places of 466 – (where the reality of Rome doubtless create a difference) and then Lombardia 1.163 receptions, 16.48% for a total number of places of 254, Sicilia 807 receptions, 11,44% for a total number of places of 469, Puglia 499 receptions, 7,07% for a total number of places of 314 and Emilia Romagna 439 receptions, 6,22% for a total number of places of 255.

Whereas Toscana is present with only 307 receptions, 4,35% for a total number of places of 173.

Brief socio-demographic profile of people received in SPRAR network

Analyzing the most important characteristics of the 6.855 people received in the SPRAR network in 2010, the data which emerged during the previous years on gender, age and family members wasconfirmed. These elements, even if in a general way, identify the "beneficiary type" as being a young single man (5.209), between 18 and 40 years old (about 3000).

In 2010 the first five nationalities were Somalia, Eritrea, Afghanistan, Nigeria and Iraq, that remain almost unchanged compared to the previous years – 2007-2010.

The significant presence of people coming from the Horn of Africa, region from where, as it has already been underlined in the past, is constant because of the flow of forced migrations.

Moreover it is interesting to note the paths of arrival in Italy. The people received in SPRAR came mostly by sea (60%), 15% through an airport frontier, 9% from an overland frontier, whereas 5% arrived from EU countries or came back in Italy under the 2nd Dublin Regulation.

A statistical pattern

In 2008 in Italy a significant increase of the asylum requests occurred, in line with the European standards (30.300). Many of those presenting a request arrived mainly by sea. In 2009, the number of asylum requests decreased drastically, this decrease depends also on the restrictive policies carried out in the Canal of Sicily by Italy and Libya, as the rejection on high seas. From 2008 to 2009 the asylum requests fell by half (17,600). In 2010, this trend continued with 8,200 requests classifying Italy at the 14th place for destination among the 44 industrialized countries. This change is due to the ratification of the "Treaty of friendship, partnership and cooperation" with Libya approved by the Parliament in February 2009, that determined the intensification of the frontier controls in order to contrast irregular migration with a significant decrease of the arrivals by sea and consequently of the international protection instances.

In fact at the end of 2010, the refugees living in Italy were circa 56 thousand, whereas the number of the new asylum instances sent to the Territorial Commissions were lower than the previous year by 31%, that is 12.1217.

During 2010, most of the people who presented a request for protection came from Africa (4.284), Europe (4.018) and Asia (3.560). In particular, besides the asylum request presented by ex-Yugoslavian citizens or Kurds coming from Iraq and Turkey by sea or overland in Italy through the Italian-Slovenian boundary, also in the last year as in the previous three year period the majority of the instances was made by citizens escaping from Africa e and Asia mainly through trajectories that connect the sub-Sahara to the Mediterranean sea.

In particular people escaping from conflicts or persecutions who arrived in Italy to present an international protection request in 2010, came mainly from, in decreasing order, ex-Yugoslavia (2.249), Nigeria (1.632), Pakistan (1.115), Turkey, Afghanistan, Iraq, Ghana, Iran, Ivory Coast and Bangladesh.

Compared to the two year period 2008/2009 the numbers of migrants escaping from the Horn of Africa and Bangladesh decreased significantly.

The most part of recognitions of the refugee status concerned, for the year 2010, citizens coming from Eritrea (418), Afghanistan (224), Turkey (204), Iran (199), Palestine (191) e Iraq (144), that are also in part the priority addressees of the concession of subsidiary protection. In fact, to the citizens coming from Afghanistan, Eritrea and Iraq this form of safeguard has been recognized, and also to Pakistanis and Somalis. Whereas the proposal of humanitarian protection was formulated in a more consistent way for people asking protection coming from ex-Yugoslavia (1401), Nigeria (313), Turkey, Pakistan, Liberia and Ghana, the most number of negative results concerned citizens coming from Nigeria (1.595), followed by Ghanaians and Somalis.

Despite the limitations of the European law on the possibility of moving away in another country of the EU, many refugees leave Italy – also in certain cases immediately after the recognition of protection in Italy. Concerning this situation, it is interesting to note that a majority of the returnees so-called Dublin in Italy is constituted by people to whom a form of protection in Italy was recognized and then they presented a new asylum instance in another member State.

The rights of people asking International Protection

- **Legal Assistance:** they can request legal assistance, during the judicial appeal and obtain the recognition of the expenses on State relief.
- **Health care:** once obtained the permit of stay for a request of international protection, they have the right to be enrolled in the National Health Service.
- **Lodgings:** they are lodged in Reception Centers for People asking International Protection (CARA) during identification and/or during the exam of the request. At the end of the reception period (from 20 to 35 days) and having obtained the residence permit for a request of international protection, they must leave the Centers.
- **Training:** In the Centers Italian language courses are sometimes offered. For minors enrollment in schools is facilitated.
- **Subsidy:** Asylum seekers who have the requirements to benefit of a reception place, but who have not found a SPRAR or CARA reception possibility, can request for financial help.

- **Work:** if the Commission for the recognition of the refugee status does not issue a decision on the request within six months from its presentation and if the delay is not imputable to the people asking protection, the Italian law provides for the renewal of the residence permit for six months and it allows the asylum seeker to work until the conclusion of the status recognition procedure.

The typologies of residence permits for international protection in Italy

- Refugee status under the Convention of Geneva of 1951 – The residence permit has a duration of 5 years and it is renewable at each expiry.
- **Subsidiary Protection** is given to a non-EU citizen or stateless person, who has not the requirements to be recognized as a refugee, but founded reasons exist to believe that if he/she went back to his/her country of origin, or in the country he/she had his/her habitual residence, he/she would run the effective risk of being subjected to seriuos damage. **The residence permit** for subsidiary protection has a duration of three years. At the moment of its renewal, it can be converted into a residence permit for work reasons, if the request of conversion is presented before the expiry of the previous permit; the applicant has a document of identity: passport or a travel document; the applicant has a work contract or an autonomous activity.
- **Humanitarian Protection,** in case the Commission, even if it does not approve the request of international protection, believes that grave humanitarian reasons exist: **The residence permit** for humanitarian reasons has the duration of one year and it can be converted in a residence permit for work reasons at the same conditions indicated for the international protection.

The rights of people under international protection in Italy

- **The right to health care** guarantees the same treatment recognized to the Italian citizen for both social assistance and health care.
- **Work** – concerning subordinated work, autonomous work, enrollment to a professional register, professional training and internship on the work place they have the right to have the same treatment as Italian citizens.
- **Travel documents** – can freely circulate on the national territory. In order to travel outside Italy, only refugees are given a Travel Document with a duration of five years and renewable.

- **Family unity** – The family members who on an individual basis do not have the right to international protection have in any case the same rights recognized as the holder of international protection status.
- **Family reunification** – it is possible to ask for family reunification permission when married; the children underage, whether born within or outside the marriage, are not married, provided that the other parent, if in life, has given his/her consent; – dependent children of age who cannot provide for their essential life needs because of their state of health; dependent parents who do not have an appropriate family support in the country of origin.
- **Education** – the minor has the right to education, as the Italian citizens, in particular during school age (from 6 to 16 years old). The adults have the right to education and professional training according to the laws established for foreigners who regularly stay in Italy.
- **Attending university** – access to the universities is permitted to foreigners who regularly stay in Italy on equal terms with Italian citizens.
- **Housing** – the participation to the notices for the allocation of public residential housing on equal terms with Italian citizens.

The Toscana Region 2012: The migration phenomenon

During the years, besides the traditional migratory presences coming from the Asiatic continent (the city of Prato is home to one of the biggest Chinese communities of Italy), the neo-communitarian population from East Europe has increased, whereas the arrivals from countries like Morocco and the Philippines, that have reached now a consistent migratory seniority have slowed down (therefore their numbers increase mainly with new births and family reunification).

The migratory phenomena in Tuscany is essentially different at a provincial level, in fact Florence, Regional capital, absorbs by itself 30% of the regional total as well as, it is important to underline, a significant presence of almost 12% in the Province of Prato. Also in the Provinces of Arezzo, Pisa, Pistoia and Lucca the number of migrants are well over the 25 000 presences, whereas those of Livorno, Massa Carrara and Grosseto record much lower presences.

In Tuscany between 2005 and 2010 the foreign population recorded a growth of 69% with a greater increase in 2007 (17,4%) and in 2008 (12,5%). In the same period the percentage of the foreign population on the resident population increased constantly, passing from 6% in 2005 to 9,7% in 2010.

For all the five considered years, the three numerically most significant nationalities in the Tuscany territory were, in a decreasing order, Albania, Romania and Chinese Republic. For all of them a percentage increase during the five considered years; in particular the number of people of the Rumanian community grew most of all arriving at a total of circa 217% with a significant peak in 2007 (87,5%). The Chinese community increased less than the Albanian one during all the period considered (37,8% against circa 45%) and however a new strong increase is recorded in the last two year period (9,5% and 11%).

The gender analysis shows a substantial parity of the number of men and women compared to the total of the foreign population; in 2005 it was precisely 50% whereas during the next years a weak female prevalence is recorded and in 2010 it is at 52, 7% against 47,3% of the male presences. If we read the data in light of the several nationalities, it is possible to note that the female prevalence is given by the Rumanian and Albanian communities whereas the Chinese Republic is characterized by a male prevalence.

The presence of foreign minors compared to the total of foreign residents does has not had substantial changes during the six considered years varying from 21, 2% in 2005 to 20,7% in 2010. Whereas, if considered in connection with Italian minors, the foreign minors percentage increases constantly and in a relevant way from 8,6% in 2005 to 13,3% in 2010.

Consequently, another interesting data shows the increase of foreign minors that in the five years period 2005/2010 is 65% against 1,7% of the same period for Italian resident minors.

Between 2005 and 2008 the residence permits issued in Tuscany compared to the number of permits issued in Italy increase very little passing from 7,5% in 2005 to 8,5% in 2006 and in the two years after, it stops at 8,4%.

If we compare the national data concerning the released permits with the regional one, we note a percentage increase of the latter above the national data (45,8% compared to 31% during the five years period in exam). Concerning the number of permits released for asylum, asylum request and humanitarian reasons, these increased between 2005 and 2008 by 304,7% at a regional level, a percentage greater than the medium national increment stopped at 258,4%; on the contrary, the permits for work reasons increase by 16,4% in Tuscany, whereas they decrease in Italy by 2,3%.

In Tuscany the concessions of Italian citizenship status in the last five years recorded an increase very near to the national one (129,6% against the national 130%), but the percentage of foreigners who have citizenship compared to the total of resident foreigners is very low and it appears almost stable passing from 0,9% in 2005 to 1,2% in 2010.

The reception system for asylum seekers and refugees in Tuscany

In Tuscany from 2008, the Local Authorities that are in the SPRAR network increased by one unit; each of them heads a project for ordinary beneficiaries.

Between 2007 and 2011 the financed places decreased by 2,5%, with a maximum peak of 224 places in 2008. Concerning the financial source, inly in 2008 12,5% places were financed with extraordinary funds. On the contrary, if we consider the beneficiaries of the places, in Tuscany all the places financed during the five years considered are dedicated to ordinary beneficiaries.

The beneficiaries of the SPRAR system in Tuscany

If we examine the number of people received, between 2007 and 2010 a decrease of 5% is recorded and it concerns only the represented category, that is the ordinary beneficiaries category. If we connect the number of places with the number of people received, it was possible to evince the medium time of reception in the SPRAR centers. From this analysis, it results that between 2007 and 2010 there was a substantial balance in the medium time of permanence in the centers (224 days in 2007 and 233 in 2010); 2009 is the year when we can note a greater time of stay (249 days).

Chapter 2: A survey of Reception Centers for young asylum seekers and refugees in the City and Province of Florence

Introduction

Concerning the European project EduAsyl, our working group, during a first step of research, has dealt with the mapping of the reception centers for asylum seekers[1] or people under international protection[2] in the Florentine territory. This study

---

1   The asylum seeker is a person who has crossed an international frontier and who makes, in another State, an asylum request for the recognition of the refugee status. His/her request is examined by the authorities of that country. Until the decision moment concerning his/her request, he/she is considered an asylum seekers. Not all the asylum seekers are then recognized as refugees. [Source: United Nations High Commissioner for Refugees – www.unhcr.it].

2   For people under international protection we consider those who have the refugee status and those who are under subsidiary or humanitarian protection. The refugee is a person who, for a founded fear of persecution "for reasons of race, religion, nationality, membership to a determined social group or political opinion, is outside the country where he/she is citizen and cannot or because of that fear does not want avail himself/herself of the protection of that country". [Source: Con-

has had as aims both the analysis of the "reception conditions" of people under international protection, adults and minors in the City and the Province of Florence, and the exam of the integration policies carried out by the different reception centers for this specific category of migrants.

In order to carry out this Mapping we have considered both the reception centers of the City of Florence, divided into districts, and the centers of the remaining provincial area. A further distinction has been done between the centers for adults and families and those for Unaccompanied Foreign Minors and Unaccompanied Minor Asylum Seekers. The latter group, even if it represents a smaller segment of this universe, in any case it shows the most vulnerable and fragile group of young people. The protection of the minor's "superior interest" is always in conflicts with migration policies of control.

Moreover we have surveyed the occupied buildings and we have decided to focus our study research on them. In fact, the precariousness situation and the living conditions of asylum seekers, refugees and people under International protection, that is people escaping from persecutions, wars and calamitous events in their origin countries and therefore migrants for humanitarian reasons and with a legally and recognized status by the Italian State, need a specific concern.

2.1 The methodology of work

After having observed that a mapping including all the reception centers, both those involved in the *SPRAR* program (National System of protection for asylum seekers and refugees)[3] and those not involved in this program, had never been

---

vention of Geneva of 1951 about the refugee status]. The subsidiary protection is useful to give a status to foreigners who, even if they are not in the definition of refugee under the Convention of 1951, because an individual persecution is without foundation, need anyway of protection because, in case of repatriation in the country of origin, would be subjected to a grave damage because of armed conflicts, generalized violence and/or massive violations of human rights. The subsidiary protection was codified on a European level and it entered in the Italian system in 2008.

Until 2008 in Italy, as in other EU countries, the concession of the subsidiary protection was not provided for. Those who were not in the refugee definition, but would be in danger in case of repatriation, can benefit of a residence permit for humanitarian reasons. The definition of humanitarian protection is remained in a residual way in the Italian system, even if it foresees minor rights than the subsidiary protection and the refugee status. [Source: United Nations High Commissioner for Refugees – www.unhcr.it].

3   First Italian public system that is widespread throughout Italy for the reception of asylum seekers and refugees under Convention, with the involvement of central institutions and Local Authorities, depending on a shared responsibility between Home Office and Local Authorities. The law n. 189/2002 introduced the SPRAR and the coordinating organization of the System, that is the "Central Service Bureau of information, promotion, consultancy, monitoring and technical sup-

carried out, our working group needed to precede a quantitative analysis of this phenomena to the qualitative phase shared with the other countries involved in this project. Therefore, after a first research on web, we contacted the directors of the several reception centers in the Florentine territory, and then we have surveyed only those which receive our research target. In fact, it was necessary to look first at the reception centers that give lodgings both to Italians and foreigners, and after, through phone conversations, we located the specific centers taken into consideration. The information provided in order to carry out this mapping have been collected both through a direct contact with the center, and through repeated phone conversations. Then, the collected material was analyzed and elaborated according to the specific goals of this research.

2.2 The quantitative analysis and the distribution of the reception centers on the territory (last update: December 31, 2010)

The statistical data was obtained to the date of December 31, 2010. The reception centers have been divided into those which are official, and that receive adults and families or unaccompanied minors asylum seekers, and those which are occupied buildings. It was necessary, then, a further distinction between the centers of the City of Florence and those of the remaining provincial area.

In the table n. 1 are presented the aggregated data concerning the 289 asylum seekers or people under International Protection surveyed in the Florentine territory. As we can see, 59 people live in occupied buildings. Most adults and families involved in reception programs inside reception centers live in the area of the City of Florence, whereas only 37 are received in centers outside the metropolitan area. Unaccompanied minor asylum seekers are only 4.

---

port to Local Authorities" (entrusting ANCI – The National Association of Italian Cities – to manage these services). *SPRAR* is a network of Local Authorities that accede, according to available resources, to the National Fund for policies and asylum services, in order to carry out "integrated reception" projects. At the territorial level the Local Authorities, with the support of the Third Sector, guarantees "integrated reception" interventions that are not limited the distribution of board and lodging, with complementary activities such as:
– Information,
– Accompaniment,
– Assistance and counseling, through the setting-up of individual paths towards economic and social integration.

Table 1: *Number of asylum seekers or people under International Protection in the reception centers*

Centers for adults and families	n° of people
Villaggio La Brocchi	20
1 Mini Alloggio	2
1 Mini Alloggio	5
3 Mini Alloggi	10
Centro Polifunzionale	130
Villa Pieragnoli	55
Centro Santa Lucia	2
San Michele a Rovezzano	2
TOTAL	**226**
TOTAL IN THE CITY OF FLORENCE	**189**
TOTAL IN THE REMAINING PROVINCIAL AREA	**37**

Occupied buildings	n° of people
Occupation of via Bardelli	2
Kulanka	50
Occupation of Poggio Secco	5
Ex Ospedale militare Monte Oliveto	2
OCCUPIED BUILDINGS	**59**

Centers for Unaccompanied Minor Asylum seekers	n° of people
Comunità Ed. Alberto	1
Centro Mercede	1
Comunità Don Zeno	2
TOTAL	**4**

Concerning the nationality, as we can observe in table n. 2, most people come from Somalia, Eritrea and Ethiopia.

Table 2: Number of asylum seekers or people under International Protection divided by nationality[4]

Nationality	n° of people
Afghanistan	7
Armenia	3
Azerbaijan	4
Ivory Coast	2
Eritrea	21
Ethiopia	14
Kosovo	7
Lebanon	5
Nigeria	2
Pakistan	5
Somalia	203
Togo	1
Turkey	10
TOTAL	**284**

Concerning the status of International Protection, most people has subsidiary protection and they are received in the "Centro Polifunzionale". 45 people are recognized as Refugees under Convention and 80 are asylum seekers. These latter are received within the *SPRAR* program in the "Villa Pieragnoli" and "Villaggio La Brocchi" centers and in the three mini lodges managed by *ARCI*.

---

4   In this Table there are 54 more people if compared to data of Table n. 1 because, since the beginning of April 2010, in the "Centro Polifunzionale" 54 people were discharged.

Table 3:   *Number of people by legal status and reception center for adults and families and Unaccompanied Minor Asylum Seekers (occupied buildings are not included)[5]*

Centers	Refugees Under Convention	Asylum seekers	Subsidiary Protection	Humanitarian Protection	TOTAL
Casa S. Lucia	2	0	0	0	2
Villa Pieragnoli	0	55	0	0	55
San Michele A Rovezzano	2	0	0	0	2
Centro Polifunzionale	30	0	151	3	184
Villaggio La Brocchi	0	20	0	0	20
1 Mini Lodging	2	0	0	0	2
1 Mini Lodging	5	0	0	0	5
3 Mini Lodgings	2	5	3	0	10
Comunità Alberto	1	0	0	0	1
Centro Mercede	1	0	0	0	1
Comunità Don Zeno	0	0	2	0	2
TOTAL	45	80	156	3	284

2.3 Mapping reception centers and integration programs for asylum seekers and refugees in The Florentine territory

2.3.1   The reception centers for adults and families under International Protection in the City of Florence

In the City of Florence there are five districts. For any of these we have identified where are localized the reception centers that receive our research target, visualizing them on a map.

---

5   In this Table there are 54 more people if compared to data of Table n. 1 because, since the beginning of April 2010, in the "Centro Polifunzionale" 54 people were discharged.

2.3.1.1 District 1: Historic center

As we can see in the Figure 1, in the district 1 of Florence we have surveyed three centers: the "Casa Santa Lucia", the "Casa San Felice" and the "Albergo Popolare".

Figure 1: Map of District 1 (Q1) of the City of Florence

The "Casa Santa Lucia" is a reception center that receives women and mothers with their children and its managing body is the "Associazione progetto S. Agostino". The time of stay in this center changes according to the individual project usually set up together by client, center and Integrated Services for the Territorial Social Assistance. Two women from Somalia, both refugees under Convention, are received in this center according to the data obtained to the date of December 31, 2010. The reception services provided by this center are the supply of board and lodging, whereas an information center, a social secretariat, a career counseling, some Italian language, computer and VET courses are provided concerning the integration activities.

The "Casa San Felice" is a reception center which is managed by the same body of the "Casa Santa Lucia" and which receives mothers with their children. It is a center opened in 1990 and it offers reception for 8 mothers and 9 children

(0-3 year-old) with inside a nursery for worker-mothers. The time of stay in this center changes according to the individual project, as the "Casa Santa Lucia". According to the data to the date of December 31, 2010 there were no asylum seekers or refugees in this center.

The "Albergo Popolare Fioretta Mazzei" is managed by the "Azienda Pubblica ai Servizi alla Persona (A.S.P)", Educatorio della S.S. Concezione called «Fuligno». The "Albergo Popolare", a center of the City of Florence for the reception of marginalized people, both Italian and foreigners, is a big structure that includes many buildings. This center offers different typologies of reception:

– Short reception: for 18-65 year-old male citizens who live in the City of Florence. In this center there are 63 beds. People can stay here for three months with the possibility of extending their stay for a further 3 months. People can accede to this center through a program of the Local Social Service arranged with the socio- educational service of the Public Administration;
– First reception – night reception: for marginalized people. There are 40 beds: 32 beds in case of first reception; 5 beds in case of emergencies, according to the discretion of the direction; 3 beds in case of "pronto intervento sociale";
– Special area – night reception: it can receives 22 marginalized citizens (over the age of 55) who live in the City of Florence, according to an individual project set up by the Integrated Services for the Local Social Assistance;
– Mini Lodgings: there are 8 lodgings for handicapped persons and 10 lodgings for marginalized people. People can accede to the Mini Lodgings through a list set up by a special social commission.

Data concerning people received to the data of December 31, 2010 is not available, but it can give hospitality to refugees under Convention and asylum seekers. The reception services and the "integrated reception" activities provided by this center are: lodging, room and toilet cleaning service, nursing service, personal assistance services, breakfast and canteen service, laundry service, wardrobe service, educational service.

2.3.1.2 District 2: "Campo di Marte"

In the district 2 of Florence, as we can see in the Figure 2, we surveyed two centers.

Figure 2: Map of District 2 (Q2) of the City of Florence

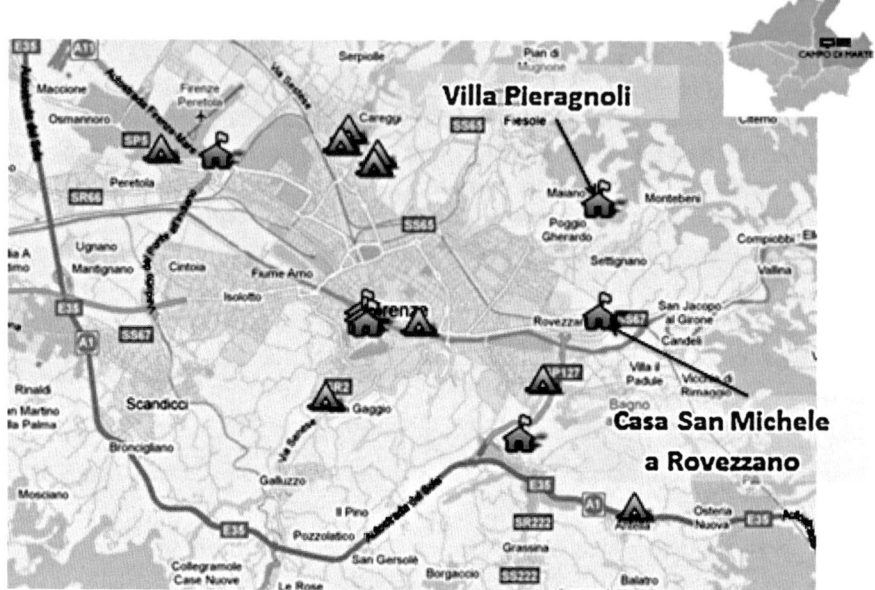

"Villa Pieragnoli" is a reception center, included in the *SPRAR* program, for refugees under Convention and asylum seekers. The project "Villa Pieragnoli" has been promoted in 2001 by the "Caritas Diocesana", in collaboration with the City of Florence and the "Associazione Accoglienza Toscana". It is organized only for asylum seekers and refugees who arrive, in large numbers, in our country to escape from war situations or persecutions. The managing bodies are "Caritas" and "Arci".

To the date December, 2010 the center received 55 asylum seekers from different countries who can stay in this center for 6 months, that can be extended according to the *SPRAR* program.

Concerning the reception and integration activities, besides lodging, board, clothing and a pocket money of 2 € a day, there is a health service counseling, an information and assistance service to deal with bureaucratic-administrative questions, mediation e interpreting, Italian language courses and job counseling, integration support in the labor market, lodging search support, legal counseling, integration of minors in local schools, homework help, socialization workshops for minors.

As we can see in the Graph n. 1, most people come from Somalia.

Graph1: Number of people received by nationality – Villa Pieragnoli

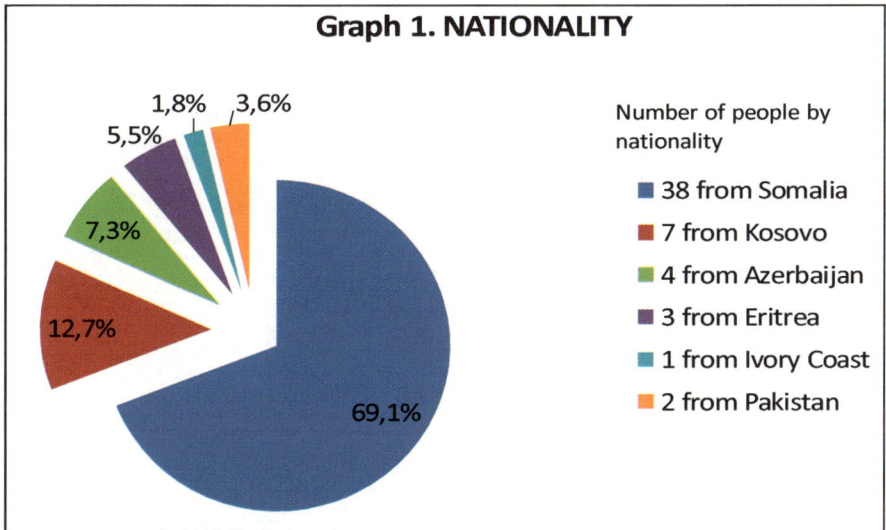

"San Michele a Rovezzano" is a reception center managed by the "Caritas Diocesana". It can receive marginalized women (with children or on their own), who live in the City of Florence. The time of stay in this center can change according to the individual project, usually set up together by client, center and Integrated Services for the Territorial Social Assistance. From the data obtained to the date of December 31, 2010, this center receives two women with status of refugees under Convention from Somalia (one of them is a minor and the other one is a 30-35 year-old). The integration services and activities are: integration support into the labor market, lodging search support, school integration of children, day nursery service, homework help, internal pediatric service for non-residents, minor integration in recreation projects and activities.

2.3.1.3 District 5: "Rifredi"

In the district 5 of the City of Florence, as we can see in the Figure n. 3, we surveyed only one center: the "Centro Polifunzionale".

Figure 3: Map of District 5 (Q5) of the City of Florence

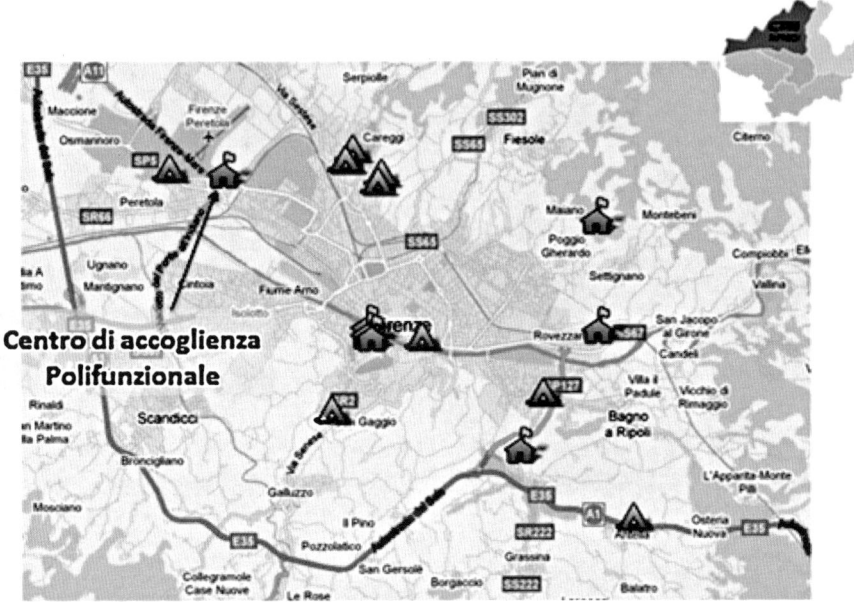

The "Centro Polifunzionale", is born in April 2010 and it is managed by the "Cooperativa Il Cenacolo" involved in the "Consorzio per la Cooperazione e la Solidarietà" (Co&So). This center is promoted by the City of Florence within a convention signed in November 24, 2009 with the Home Office under the art. 15 of "L. 7 August 1990", n. 241, for the carry out in the City of Florence of a reception and support system to the social and cultural integration of asylum seekers and people under International Protection.

This center receives only asylum seekers, refugees under Convention, humanitarian and subsidiary protection (men, women and families with children). It has 130 beds. From the beginning of the project (April 2010) it has received 184 people, 14 of them have been discharged between April and June, 17 between June and September, 23 between October and December.

The "Centro Polifunzionale" does not guarantee only the provision of reception services (as three meals a day, beds in dormitories, provision of underclothes, information and assistance to deal with bureaucratic-administrative problems, psychological assistance, renewal or change of residence permits, but also "integration reception" services (as Italian courses and school integration of children, mediation and interpreting, VET courses and integration into the labor market, collaboration with the local social services socializing activities, legal counseling, pocket money of 2 € a day).

Graph 2: Number of people by nationality

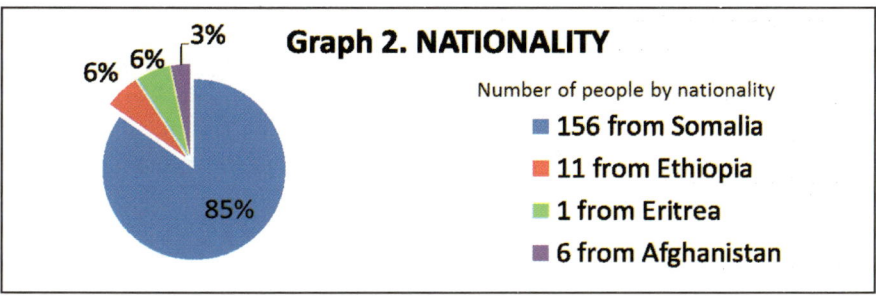

Graph 3: Number of people by gender

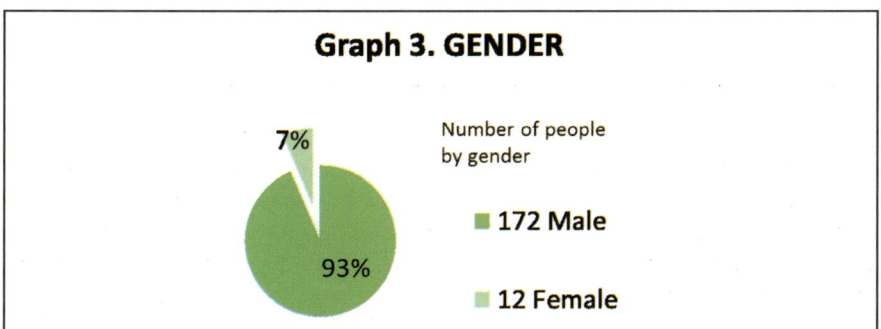

Graph 4: Number of people by legal status

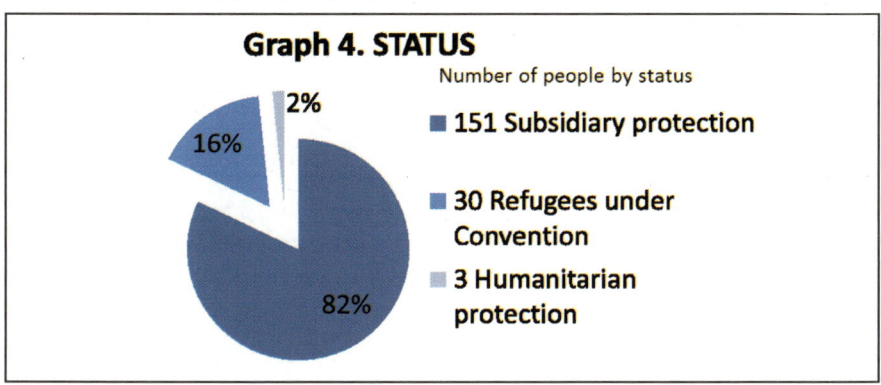

As we can observe in Graphs 2-4, most people received in this center come from Somalia (85%) and it belongs to male sex (93%). Concerning the legal status, as we can see in Graph n. 4, all the people received are under International Protection and most people of these (82%) are under Subsidiary Protection and (16%) refugees under Convention.

2.3.2 The centers for adults and families under International Protection in the remaining provincial area

In this area we have located both reception centers, and mini lodgings ("Mini Alloggi"), that is typologies of integration reception structured in mini independent flats which receive our research target in a protected situation.

Figure 4: Map of the Province of Florence

The "Villaggio La Brocchi", a system of reception for refugees and asylum seekers, has been carried out in the City of "Borgo San Lorenzo", after the renovation of a property of the "Istituto degli Innocenti" of Florence. It is involved in the *SPRAR* program and it is managed by the association "Progetto Accoglienza".

40

According to *SPRAR* program, the time of stay of the people that this center receives is six months and can be extended.

Concerning the integrated reception activities, besides the services of lodging, board, clothing and daily pocket money, this structure offers:

- Ceramics workshops and gardening;
- Enrolment to Italian courses for adults in local secondary schools;
- Integration into the labor market counseling;
- Psychological and psychiatric assistance and health care;
- Lodging search support.

According to our data (last update: December 31, 2010), there are 20 asylum seekers from different countries (5 men, 5 women and 10 minors, from Turkey (4), Ethiopia (3), Lebanon (5), Armenia (3) e Eritrea (5).

The association "Progetto Accoglienza" manages, therefore, a mini lodging in "Luco di Mugello", which receives a family from Turkey(Kurdistan) with three children with the status of refugees, and the "Casa Madre dei Semplici" in Scarperia, that at the moment of our survey was closed for renovation, but it can receive refugees under Convention and asylum seekers. It has 15 beds.

In Scarperia there is another mini lodging. This flat is managed by the "Casa di Accoglienza Scarperia", instituted by a group of volunteers and receives a larger target, that is marginalized people for a maximum period of a year. To the date of December 31, 2010 there were a woman asylum seeker and a female child asylum seeker from Eritrea. There are ad-hoc integration and reception activities, according to the needs of the people received. The flat is in use since 1992.

"ARCI" manages, for the *SPRAR* program, 3 mini lodgings in "Bagno a Ripoli" which receives 10 people (5 asylum seekers, 3 people under Subsidiary Protection and 2 refugees under Convention.

Graph 5: Number of people by nationality – 3 mini lodgings

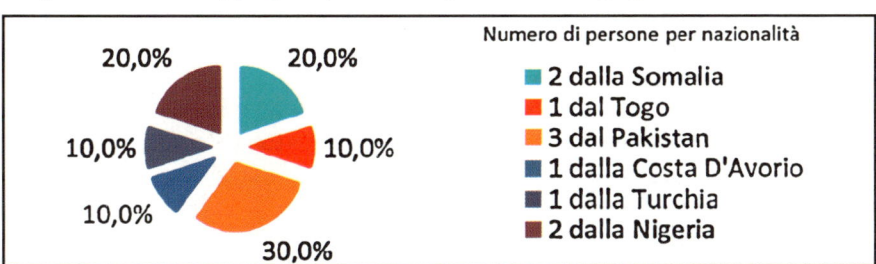

The paths for the integrated reception activities are personalized for each person. Beneficiaries are received in flats managed in a collective way which consist in the organization of counseling programs for local services and assistance for the access to healthcare and education services (Italian lessons for adults and school integration for minors). Moreover, beneficiaries can enjoy professional counseling and training or professional requalification courses. It is expected to support people in job and lodging search. Furthermore this structure offers legal protection (each beneficiary is helped in administrative questions concerning the issue of the residence permit or refugees status) and psychological support.

2.3.3   Unaccompanied minors asylum seekers

In 2010 the requests in Europe were 258.945 (52.725 in France, 48.490 in Germany, 31.875 in Sweden, 26.130 in Belgium whereas only 10.050 in Italy.

The situation and the asylum procedure in Italy

It is a localized system that make reference both to the Territorial Commissions and to the following decrees: with the Legislative Decreto 28/01/2008 n. 25 so-called *Decreto Procedure*, modified and integrated by the Legislative Decree 3rd October 2008, n. 159 is actuated the Directive 2005/85/EC about "Minimum rules for the procedures applied in the Member States in order to recognize and revoke the refugee status" and the Legislative Decree 19/11/2007 n. 251 so-called *Decreto Qualifiche* that establishes the criteria that Italy, as a Member State, must use to decide if an asylum seeker has the right to international protection and which form of protection he/she have to receive, if the refugee status or a form of subsidiary protection.

The most important points of the procedure for the recognition of a minor with a refugee status:

- The access to procedure with priority times
- The tutor (nomination and procedure times)
- The regulation of Dublino. If the asylum seeker is an unaccompanied minor, the Member State where a family member lives is competent for the exam of the asylum request, if this is for the best interest of the minor. In default of a family member, the Member State where the minor presented the asylum request is competent. (art. 6, Reg. EC 343/2003)
- Referral at a specialized institution.

The set of rules of reference foresees some guarantees for the minors:

1. necessary assistance provided for the minor who expressed his/her will to present a request;
2. the assistance of the tutor in any phase of the procedure for the exam of the request;
3. when the request is presented by an unaccompanied minor, the authority that receives it suspends the procedure and gives immediate communication to the tribunal for minors and to the tutelary judge for the opening of the protection and for the tutor nomination. The tutelary judge during the 48 hours after the police commissioner communication provides for the tutor nomination. The tutor takes immediate contact with the police headquarters for the confirmation of the request.
4. The Territorial Commission examines in a priority way the request, in accordance with the fundamental principles and the guarantees foreseen by the law, when the request is presented by an applicant belonging to the vulnerable people categories indicated by the legislative decree 2005, n. 140 that establishes the rules on reception of foreigners applying for the recognition of the refugee status in the national territory (minors included).

Therefore the set of rules in this field asks for a ready identification and referral, as well the age determination. In this case, if some doubts about the age remain, the unaccompanied minor can, in any phase of the procedure, be subjected, with the consent of the minor or of his/her legal representative, to medico-sanitarian not invasive verifications in order to verify his/her age. If the verifications effectuated do not consent the exact determination of the age with the benefit of doubt, as well the auto-declaration, the Dublin procedure needs a multidisciplinary approach.

The reception system for asylum seekers and refugee plays an important role. In fact the authority that receives the request informs immediately the Service of the protection system for asylum seekers and refugees – SPRAR – for the integration of the minor in a centers operating in the protection system area. In case that it is not possible the immediate integration of the minor in such centers, the assistance and reception of the minor are temporally assured by the public authority of the city where the minor is.

The reception centers for Unaccompanied Minor Asylum Seekers in the
      Province of Florence

In the City of Florence the social services do not make a distinction between
unaccompanied foreign minor[6] and unaccompanied minor asylum seekers[7] as
foreseen by the "EU directive on unaccompanied minor asylum seekers of
December 7, 2006". This directive want to reinforces the assistance of unaccompanied minor asylum seekers by State institutions and, therefore, in art. 1
determines that, upon arrival, they be duly informed on their rights and on the
existing legal opportunities. After the tutorial judge has assumed the protection
of the minor, the latter is immediately assigned to the National System of protection for asylum seekers (and not to other institutions), in order to prevent
the minor from being involved in exploitation networks or the risk he might
remain without legal protection. Indeed, the system of protection has an
amount of places that are assigned every year to vulnerable categories and it is
competent and instructed to help the minor to integrate in a new cultural context. Therefore, we had to contact all the Educative Communities that receive
unaccompanied foreign minor and then we had to locate, among them, those
which receive our research target.

The unaccompanied minors asylum seekers received by the City of Florence
during 2009 have been 215. 81 of them have been arrived at the beginning of this
year. If there are not any particular cases after a period at a Centre of First Reception, minors are moved to an Educative Community. The unaccompanied
minor asylum seekers received in the City of Florence are only 4 and they live in
3 educative communities, as we can see in the Figure n. 5.

---

6   An "unaccompanied foreign minor" is the minor (present in the State territory) not having
     Italian citizenship or the citizenship or other EU countries, who, not having applied for asylum,
     is present in the territory of the State for different reasons, lacking protection and legal tutorship
     by his/her parents or by any other adult who is legally responsible for him/her according to the
     law in force in the Italian legal system." Decree of the Italian Prime Minister, December 9,
     1999, n. 535.
7   An unaccompanied minor asylum seeker is "...the minor present in the State territory who
     having a well-founded fear of being persecuted for reasons of race, religion, nationality, mem-
     bership to a particular social group or for their political opinion, is outside of the country of his
     nationality and is unable or, owing to such fear, is unwilling to avail himself of the protection of
     that country, and applies for the recognition of refugees status. (Directive 2004/83/EC on
     Minimum Standards for the qualification and status of third-state nationals or stateless persons
     as refugees or as persons who otherwise need international protection).

Figure 5: Map of the City of Florence

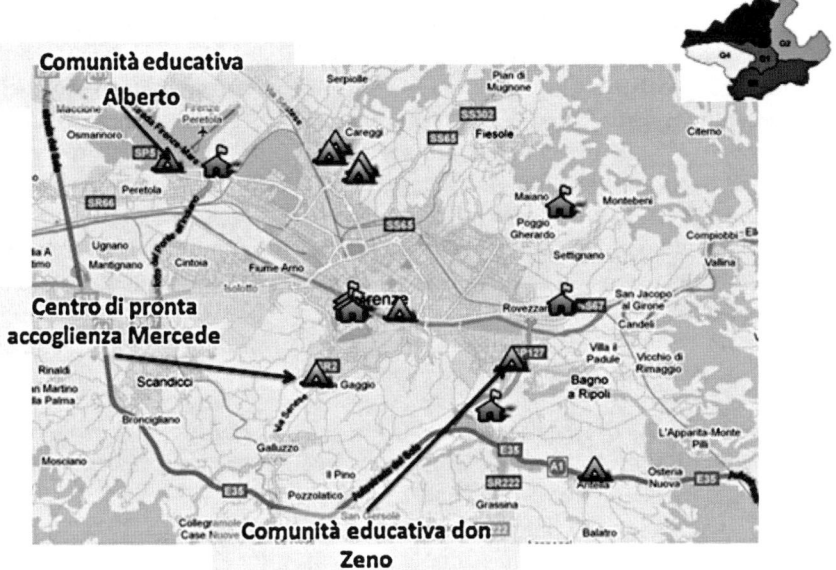

The "Centro di pronta accoglienza Mercede" and the "Comunità Educativa Don Zeno" are both managed by the "Padri Mercedari" and receive minors and adolescents in social distress.

The first one receives to the date of December 31, 2010, an unaccompanied minor asylum seeker (male) from Somalia. The time of stay in this structure changes according to the individual project. For unaccompanied foreign minors under the Criminal Tribunal depends on the typology of the offence. Unaccompanied foreign minors usually can stay 180 days with the possibility to go on a project of medium/long duration until the age of eighteen. This center, besides the organization of internal activities, as post school, homework help and recreational activities, presents some external "integrated reception" activities, as some Italian courses, the possibility of a 150 hours training course with the aim to accede to the final year of Italian middle schools, some projects in collaboration with local sports associations or with social theatre associations.

The Educative Community receives to the date of December 31, 2010 two male with subsidiary protection from Somalia. The time of stay in this structure depends on what is foreseen by the individual project, until the age of eighteen. Usually a reception period of 4/5 months is expected in the Centre of first reception and later reception in the Educative Community. The integrated reception activities are both internal, as the homework help, and external, as school integration and professional counseling.

The "Consorzio Zenit" manages the "Comunità educativa Alberto". This structure receives minors and adolescents in social distress as well and the time of stay changes according to the individual project usually set up together by client, center and Integrated Services of Territorial Social Assistance. To the date of December 31, 2010 it receives a male asylum seeker from Afghanistan, who turned 18 years old in 2011. The integrated reception activities include homework help, psychological support in collaboration with social services, support for administrative regularization, some activities on caring for themselves, orderliness and neatness and group activities with the aim of encouraging cohesion among different nationalities.

2.3.4 The occupied buildings in the Province of Florence[8]

We have located 4 occupied buildings in the Province of Florence with circa 59 people under humanitarian and subsidiary protection or refugees under Convention from Somalia, Eritrea, Ethiopia and Turkey (Kurdistan).

At "Kulanka" to the date of December 31, 2010 live circa 50 male people, but the number of beds available is only 20. People are 17-50 year-old, with only a minor, and come from Somalia. They are all under International Protection, in particular circa 5 are refugees under Convention, 40 are under Subsidiary Protection and 5 under Humanitarian Protection. The structure is self-managed by the Somalia "Società di Mutuo Soccorso Abucar Moallim" and offers an intercultural center.

The reception activities include a bed in dormitory and shared toilet. The integration activities carried out by volunteers are: Italian and computer courses, intercultural meetings and debates, support for the integration into the labor market, healthcare and legal assistance and legal.

---

8   Last update on occupied buildings (September 30, 2011): we have later included the building located in "Via Slataper", an occupation begun in June 2011. Here circa 94 people under international protection live, and among them about the half come from Somalia, the others come, mainly, from Eritrea, Ethiopia and Liberia. Most people are men. There are circa ten children from 0-5 years old and some women, three of them are pregnant.

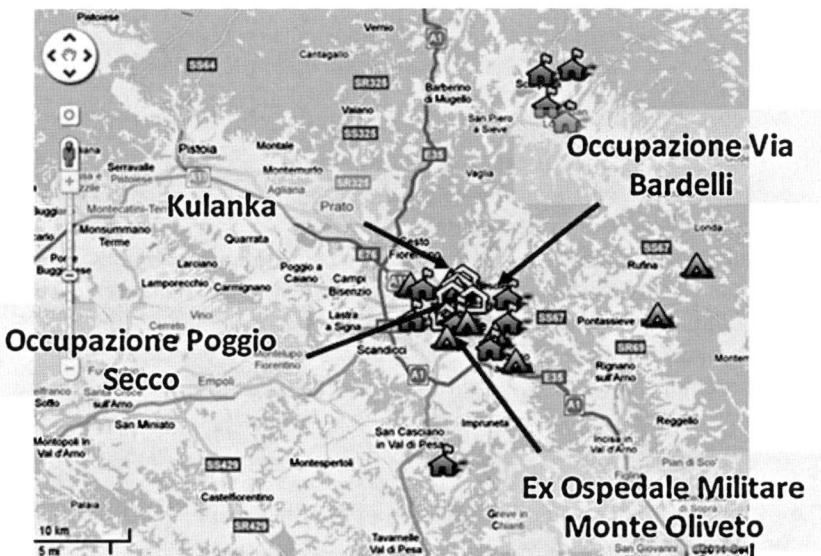

"Kulanka" is the only occupation that foresees some paths of integrated reception and not strictly a bed. In the occupied building in "Via Bardelli" 2 male people (25-30 year-old) live from Eritrea. In the occupied building "Poggio Secco" a family from Turkey (Kurdistan) lives with three minors and all the members of this family have a recognized status of refugee under Convention. Finally, in the ex-military hospital "Monte Oliveto", to the date of December 31, 2010, 2 male refugees from Ethiopia live.

2.3.5 The foreign minor asylum seekers

In 2010 the requests in Europe were 258.945 (52.725 in France, 48.490 in Germany, 31.875 Sweden, 26.130 in Belgium whereas only 10.050 in Italy.

The situation and the asylum procedure in Italy

It is a localized system that make reference both to the Territorial Commissions and to the following decrees: with the Legislative Decreto 28/01/2008 n. 25 so-called *Decreto Procedure*, modified and integrated by the Legislative Decree 3rd October 2008, n. 159 is actuated the Directive 2005/85/EC about "Minimum rules for the procedures applied in the Member States in order to recognize and revoke the refugee status" and the Legislative Decree 19/11/2007 n. 251 so-called *Decreto Qualifiche* that establishes the criteria that Italy, as a Member

State, must use to decide if an asylum seeker has the right to international protection and which form of protection he/she have to receive, if the refugee status or a form of subsidiary protection.

The most important points of the procedure for the recognition of a minor with a refugee status:

- The access to procedure with priority times
- The tutor (nomination and procedure times)
- The regulation of Dublino. If the asylum seeker is an unaccompanied minor, the Member State where a family member lives is competent for the exam of the asylum request, if this is for the best interest of the minor. In default of a family member, the Member State where the minor presented the asylum request is competent. (art. 6, Reg. EC 343/2003)
- Referral at a specialized institution.

The set of rules of reference foresees some guarantees for the minors:

- necessary assistance provided for the minor who expressed his/her will to present a request;
- the assistance of the tutor in any phase of the procedure for the exam of the request;
- when the request is presented by an unaccompanied minor, the authority that receives it suspends the procedure and gives immediate communication to the tribunal for minors and to the tutelary judge for the opening of the protection and for the tutor nomination. The tutelary judge during the 48 hours after the police commissioner communication provides for the tutor nomination. The tutor takes immediate contact with the police headquarters for the confirmation of the request.

The Territorial Commission examines in a priority way the request, in accordance with the fundamental principles and the guarantees foreseen by the law, when the request is presented by an applicant belonging to the vulnerable people categories indicated by the legislative decree 2005, n. 140 that establishes the rules on reception of foreigners applying for the recognition of the refugee status in the national territory (minors included).

Therefore the set of rules in this field asks for a ready identification and referral, as well the age determination. In this case, if some doubts about the age remain, the unaccompanied minor can, in any phase of the procedure, be subjected, with the consent of the minor or of his/her legal representative, to medico-sanitarian not invasive verifications in order to verify his/her age. If the verifications effectuated do not consent the exact determination of the age with the benefit of doubt, as well the auto-declaration, the Dublin procedure needs a multidisciplinary approach.

The reception system for asylum seekers and refugee plays an important role. In fact the authority that receives the request informs immediately the Service of the protection system for asylum seekers and refugees – SPRAR – for the integration of the minor in a centers operating in the protection system area. In case that it is not possible the immediate integration of the minor in such centers, the assistance and reception of the minor are temporally assured by the public authority of the city where the minor is.

Chapter 3: Life stories

Introduction

In the second phase of our research study, we submitted 12 questionnaires to refugees and people under International Protection who live in an occupied building of Florence. The main goal consisted in a first study on the paths of life of refugees and asylum seekers, so that it was possible to identify the problems these persons have in the City of Florence and the remaining provincial area and to focalize our attention on them, in order to have a more precise idea of the life condition of these people.

We built the questionnaire working up on these questions: demographical context (sex, age, civil status, citizenship, religion …), the journey (countries crossed in order to arrive in Italy, countries where they lived, etc.), education and training (educational qualification, linguistic knowledge, professional training, etc.) and work (during all the different phases of their life).

Then we went personally to the occupied buildings and contacted some refugees and asylum seekers that live there and were available to answer our questionnaires, after explaining the aims of our survey. Sometimes, people with a better understanding of Italian language helped us during the submission of the questionnaires with a linguistic and cultural mediation.

In this first phase of our work, we did not consider, in our questionnaires, sex, age and citizenship of these people. All the questionnaires were submitted at the beginning of June 2011[9] to 12 people of Somali, Eritrean, Ethiopian, Liberian and Sudanese origin, who lived in the occupied building of "via Slataper" – Florence. All the 12 people were under International Protection (refugees, subsidiary or humanitarian protection), therefore we are talking about people with a recognized legal status in our country.

---

9   The questionnaires had the duration of circa 20-30 minutes.

From our questionnaires we evinced that these people arrived in Italy by sea, in Sicily. Many of them lived in other countries of North Europe, but they were forced to come back to Italy because of the European legal framework in force.[10]

Moreover many people who answered our questionnaires arrived when they were still minors, but despite that nobody was recognized as an unaccompanied minor asylum seeker. To our question "Why did you not say that you were a minor?" they answered: " I wanted my documents to work as quickly as possible".

Concerning work, from our questionnaires it is evident that seldom, if ever, men found a regular work (they found only casual, seasonal and irregular works) in Italy. On the contrary, the women worked often as carers, living with the assisted person.

After the analysis of this information, we decided to focalize our attention on people in precarious living conditions. The occupied buildings are a symbol of the situation of refugees and asylum seekers living in Florence, because almost all of them, besides similar experiences in reception Centers have had or have an experience of living marginality.

Among the communities that live in our territory we chose to focalize our analysis on the Somali one: it represents in fact in the Florentine territory an important reality since many years and nowadays we can observe that in the occupied buildings the Somalis represent the majority. Therefore we submitted 6 in-depth interviews[11] (to 3 men and 3 women – 23/35 years old) who live in the occupied building of "via Slataper" – Florence.

These interviews gave us a deeper knowledge of the living conditions of these people (background, journey, training, work, housing, health, expectations, etc.), in order to focalize the analysis on further aspects inherent to the training/educational and working experience of refugees and asylum seekers. All that with the aim to understand what are the factors that facilitate the access and those, on the contrary, that are an obstacle for the access in the formal/informal training and in the labour market.

So we built the pattern of the interview with in depth questions building on the questionnaires in order to inquire into: the demographic context, the journey and the mobility in Italy and in Europe (when, where, for how long, housing, the reason of their leaving), training and education (language level, language courses, educational qualifications and professional training in Italy and Europe),

10 According to the Dublin II Regulation (EC Regulation n. 343/2003 of the Council, February 18, 2003), the first country where the asylum seeker entered in the European Union is responsible for the asylum request. The asylum seeker is bound to that country even if it does not offer him reception and integration possibilities.

11 Each interview lasted circa 1 ½-2 hours.

experiences in the paths of first and second reception in Italy, experiences in the occupied buildings, work (both in the country of origin and in the destination country).

From the analysis of the interviews we re-built the biography of every interviewee, focalizing our attention on the journey to Italy and the mobility in Italy and Europe, on the family and cultural background, on the professional and working path, on the Italian courses L2, on the obstacles for the access to National Education and Training System (Vet) and to the labour market, and on the living precariousness.

Farida, Zahra and Maisa are the three Somali women interviewed, Bassam, Amir and Hassan are the three men.

The three Somali women interviewed are:

Farida was born in Somalia, in Mogadishu. She doesn't know her birth date, but the Italian authority wrote on her documents that she was born on the 1/1/1983. She obtained from Italy the status of refugee under Convention. She left Somalia, pregnant, in 2009 and after travelling for about three months through Ethiopia, Sudan and Libya she arrived in Lampedusa. After a few days, she was transferred to the CARA (Reception center for asylum seekers) of Pian del Lago (near Caltanisetta, Sicily), where she applied for asylum and where her daughter Marabì was born. In 2010, ended the 6 months of reception, she entered in the CARA of Borgo Mezzanone, near Foggia, Puglia, where she spent two months until the arrival of her documents. She decided to go to Norway because she couldn't stay in the center any longer and because she applied for an other place to sleep in without receiving any answer. In February 2010 Farida arrived in Norway with her daughter Marabì, applying again for asylum. They spent the first days in a center for asylum seekers, but shortly afterwards the Norwegian authorities found them a place to stay in an apartment with other asylum seekers and people under International Protection. She received 700 Euros every month and her rent was paid. Furthermore, she worked as a cleaner in one of these reception centers, receiving about 100 Euros every 15 days. This was possible because her daughter Marabì joined straightaway a nursery. After 1 year and 8 months, the Norwegian authorities found her finger prints and F. was obliged to go back to Italy with Marabì, with the promise of a place to stay by the Italian authorities. Back in Italy and arrived in Florence, she applied to enter in one of the centers for the second reception (*Centro Polifunzionale*), but she declares she couldn't find an available place. She was obliged to occupy some buildings with other people under International Protection until she stayed in the one she actually lives in at the moment.

Zahra was born in Somalia, in Mogadishu, in 1980. She has Subsidiary Protection. She left her country in 2007 and, passing through Ethiopia, Sudan and Lybia, she arrived in Lampedusa (Italy) in 2008 with a boat. After some days in Catania (Sicily), she arrived at the CARA (Reception center for asylum seekers) in Salinagrande (Sicily), where she stayed for about 5 months. Obtained her documents, she left this center and went near Lecce (Puglia), where she stayed for about 9 months. After moving to several Italian cities (Torino, Reggio Emilia, Bologna; Bergamo; Milano and Siena) in order to look for a job which she has never found, she decided to go to Norway. Always housed by friends, during 2010 she lived for short periods in Norway, Holland, Denmark and Sweden. In 2011 she came back to Italy, in Florence, where now she is living in an occupied building.

Maisa, is 29 years old, she is Muslim and she was born in Galohaio, Somalia. She has Subsidiary Protection. She took one year and half to arrive in Italy. She arrived with the boat in 2007 in Sicily, in Ragusa. She stayed one month in a CARA (Reception Center for Asylum Seekers) in Trapani, where she applied for her documents. Once she obtained the documents, she went to a CARA in Cassino (Frosinone) where she stayed for 7 months more. In 2009 she went to Norway and she asked again for Asylum, but she could stay there only one year and 5 months because Norwegian authorities found her fingerprints and she had to leave the country. In 2010 she lived in a friend's house. At the moment she is living in an occupied building.

The three Somali men interviewed are:

Bassam, who is Muslim, was born in Mogadishu, Somalia, in 1976. He is under Humanitarian Protection. He left Somalia in 1996 and he lived for 5 years in Nairobi, Kenya, housed by his cousin. In 2001 he moved to Egypt where he stayed for three years, before coming to Italy. After being some days in Niger he went to Lybia, where he was arrested and imprisoned for 15 days. In July 2003 he arrived in Lampedusa by boat. From there he was moved to CARA (Reception Center for Asylum Seekers) in Crotone, Calabria, where he stayed for a months, obtaining all documents, he decided to leave from Italy and to ask again for Asylum in Sweden. After 6 months the Swedish authorities found his fingerprints and he had to come back to Italy.

Amir, who is Muslim, was born in Somalia, in 1987. He is a refugee under Convention. After leaving Somalia in December 2006, he lived for about 2 years in Ethiopia and in Eritrea. In July 2008 he went to Sudan and spent 10 days at a "passeur's home" waiting to pass through the Sahara in order to arrive in Lybia. After arriving in Lybia, he was imprisoned in Kufra and in Bengasi and he succeeded to come out under the payment of 600 dollars. Then he went to Tripoli.

During the crossing of the Mediterranean sea, near the Maltese coast, the engine failure caused the death of 70 people out of 100. The Maltese guard coast came to their help to repair the engine in order to arrive in Italy, convincing them not to stay in Malta because they would have passed 6 months in prison. Amir and the other 30 survivors were able to arrive in Sicily, on 14 August 2008. In the CIE (Center of identification and expulsion) of Pozzallo (Sicily) he was identified and he was able to request for Asylum. After 2 months he was moved to a CARA (Reception Center for Asylum Seekers) of Comiso, Ragusa, Sicily, where he remained 8 months waiting for his documents. In June 2009, he arrived in Tuscany, where there is a quite big Somali community and well rooted. For more than 2 years he has been living in occupied buildings, because he asked to enter in a reception center of the city of Florence but he is still waiting for an accomodation.

Hassan was born in Somalia in 1989, but when he arrived in Italy, the Italian authorities wrote the 1st of January 1991, because he didn't understand their questions. He has Humanitarian Protection. He arrived, then, in Italy at 19 years old, but he declared that he was a minor in order to obtain all benefits. He left Somalia in 2007 and he passed through Ethiopia, Sudan and Lybia. He arrived in Lampedusa (Sicily) by boat after about one month. He arrived in Italy because it was the nearest place in Europe. He declared that in Lybia and Sudan he couldn't live because they don't have an Asylum system. He passed 2 weeks in a CPA (First Reception Center) in Lampedusa (Sicily), where he was brought in a Reception Center for minors near Agrigento, Sicily, where he stayed until he was 18 years old. He tried to ask the Province of Rome to obtain accomodation, but they didn't find anything so he had live under a bridge for about one month. At the end of 2008 he went to Terni (Umbria), where he worked, with a regular contract for 9 months in a steel mill. In 2010 he decided to go to Sweden where he asked for Asylum. There he received financial aid to pay the rent and pocket money of 250 Euros per month. After 3 months, the Swedish authorities found his fingerprints. He had to leave the country and go to Norway. Then he went again to Sweden and after a police control he had to come back to Italy. From March 2010 he lives in an occupied building. He decided not to go in a Second Reception Center because he preferred to maintain his independence, since he did not need to be assisted. He declared in fact in these centers there is a control on times of entrance and of going out and he would be obliged to follow a life imposed by others.

53

3.1 The journey to Italy and mobility in Europe

We noted that all our interviewees arrived in Italy, landing in Sicily.

Zahra, Farida and Bassam for example arrived in Lampedusa (Sicily) after crossing some African countries. Bassam, who now is under International Protection, tells us of having left Somalia in 1996 and he lived in Nairobi, Kenya, for 5 years, housed by his cousin. In 2001 he moved to Egypt where he stayed for three years, before coming to Italy. After being some days in Niger, he went to Lybia, where he was arrested and imprisoned for 15 days. Also Amir tells us of having been imprisoned, after his arrival in Libya, in Kufra and in Bengasi and he succeeded to come out under the payment of 600 dollars, arriving then in Tripoli. Farida (one of the three women interviewed) left Somalia, pregnant, in 2009 and after traveling for about three months through Ethiopia, Sudan and Libya, with a journey similar to those of Hassan and Zahra, she arrived in Lampedusa.

Very significant is the story of the journey by sea of Amir. In fact, during the crossing of the Mediterranean sea, near the Maltese coast, the engine failure caused the death of 70 people out of 100. The Maltese guard coast succoured them and helped them to repair the engine in order to arrive in Italy, convincing them not to stay in Malta because they would have passed 6 months in prison. Therefore they decided to carry on their journey to Sicily.

So we can evince that for most of them, the countries crossed to arrive in Italy from Somalia are Eritrea, Ethiopia e Libya.

Concerning the mobility in Europe, Zahra tells us of having lived during 2010 for short periods in Norway, Holland, Denmark and Sweden looking for a work, always housed by friends. In 2011 she came back to Italy.

Farida, after arrival in Lampedusa, was transferred to the CARA (Reception center for asylum seeker) of "Pian del Lago" (near Caltanissetta), where she applied for asylum and where her daughter was born. In 2010, after 6 months of reception, she entered in the CARA of "Borgo Mezzanone", near Foggia, where she spent two months until the arrival of her documents. She decided to go to Norway because she couldn't stay in the center any longer and because she applied for another place to sleep in without receiving any answer. In February 2010, Farida arrived in Norway with her daughter, applying again for asylum. As Farida tells us, they spent the first days in a center for asylum seekers, but shortly afterwards the Norwegian authorities found them a place to stay in an apartment with other asylum seekers and people under International Protection. She received 700 euro every month and her rent was paid. Furthermore, she worked as cleaner in one of these reception centers, receiving about 100 euro every 15 days, while her daughter joined straightaway a nursery. After circa a year and a half, the

Norwegian authorities found her finger prints and Farida was obliged to go back to Italy with her daughter, with the promise of a place to stay by the Italian authorities. Back in Italy and arrived in Florence, she applied to enter in one of the centers for Second Reception of the city (PACI), but she declares she couldn't find an available place. She was obliged to occupy some buildings with other people under International Protection until she stayed in the one she actually lives in at the moment.

Also Bassam stayed for a month in CARA in Crotone and here he obtained a residence permit of three months. After staying for a short period in Rome and obtaining all documents, he decided to leave from Italy and to ask again for Asylum in Sweden. Here he tells us of his stay for 6 months, living in an apartment with other 6 people and receiving some state aids for the payment of his rent, besides 250 euro each month as pocket money. When the authorities found his fingerprints he was obliged to come back to Italy, but after several years of experiences in some reception centers and occupied buildings he lived two years in Poland and, for short periods in Norway and Holland. Back in Italy in 2008 he lived in precariousness living conditions under a bridge or in some occupied building of the Florentine territory.

On the contrary, Hassan arrived in Italy at 19 years old, but he declared that he was a minor in order to obtain all benefits. He arrived in Italy because it was the nearest place in Europe. He declares that in Libya and Sudan he couldn't live because they do not have an Asylum system. HE passed 2 weeks in a CPA (First Reception Center) in Lampedusa (Sicily), where he was brought in a Reception Center for minors near Agrigento where he stayed until he was 18 years old. He tried to ask the Province of Rome to obtain accommodation, but they did not find anything so he had to live under a bridge for about one months. At the end of 2008 he went to Terni (Umbria), where he worked, with a regular contract for 9 months in a steel mill, then the contract was not renewed.

In 2010 he decided to go to Sweden where he asked for Asylum. There he received financial aid to pay the rent and a pocket money of 250 Euro per month. After 3 months, the Swedish authorities found his fingerprints. He had to leave the country and go to Norway. Then he came again to Sweden and after a police control he had to come back to Italy.

From March 2010 he lives in an occupied building. He decided not to go in a Second Reception Center because he preferred to maintain his independence, since he did not need to be assisted. He declared in fact that in these centers there is a control on times of entrance and of going out and he would be obliged to follow a life imposed by others.

The journey to Italy and the mobility in Europe: Farida

Country	Year	How long	Accomodation	Why she went away
Ethiopia	2009			
Sudan	2009			
Libya	2009			
Italy	2009	The journey from Somalia to Italy lasted 3 months		
Norway	February 2010	1 year and 8 months	The first days in a hotel for asylum seekers, then in an appartment with other people	The authority found her fingerprints
Italy (Florence)	?			

The journey to Italy and the mobility in Europe: Bassam

Country	Year	How long	Accomodation	Why he went away
Kenya (Nairobi)	1996	5 years (until 2001)	Cousin's home	
Egypt	2001	3 years (until 2003)		
Niger	2003	Some days		
Libya	2003	About one month (June)	Arrested by the Libyan police. Imprisoned for 15 days.	
Crotone (granting of residence permit for three months)	2003	1 month	CARA (Crotone) They slept inside the containers	Having the residence permit for 3 months, after his arrival in Italy, he received 750 Euros, since during those 3 months he was not able to work.
Roma (granting of other documents)	2003			
Sweden (asking for Asylum)	2003 October	6 months	In an apartment with 6 people. Granting benefits for the rent, more than 250 Euros per month	Found his fingerprints
Crotone	2004	Some days	At the railway station	The 25/04/2004 he partecipated in a demostration in front of the police head-quarters in order to

Country	Year	How long	Accomodation	Why he went away
				ask for the residence permit: he was beaten by a police-man not in uniform
Torino	2004	15 days		
Palermo	2004	4 months	Caritas	
Firenze	2005		In an occupied building – 150n people	Granted the residence permit for 1 year
Firenze	2005	6 months	"Villa Pieragnoli" project (SPRAR)	6 months
Bologna	2005		Housed by his cousin	
Firenze	2007		In an occupied building	
Poland	2007	2 years		
Norway	2007	25 days		
Holland	2008	1 month		
Italy (Florence)	2011		Under the bridge of Peretola and then in an occupied build-ing (Via Slataper)	

The journey to Italy and the mobility in Europe: Hassan

Country	Year	How long	Accomodation	Why he went away
Ethiopia	2007	3 days	In the home of a friend	
Sudan	2007	2 days	In a pension	
Libya	2007	21 days	In a rented apartment in Trip-oli with other people with whom he had crossed Sahara	
Sweden (Asylum request)	2010	3 months	For the first 2 days in a hotel for asylum seekers, than in an apartment with another person who had International Protec-tion	They found his fin-gerprints. He escaped to Norway in order not to return to Italy
Norway	2010	3 months	Was living with a friend	
Sweden	2010	21 days	Was living in a Center for repatriation. It was a con-trolled Center and he could not escape	The police informed him that he was excluded from the Swedish protection system because he had been expelled
Italy (Florence)	?			

The journey to Italy and the mobility in Europe: Zahra

Country	Year	Accomodation
Ethiopia	2007	
Sudan	2007	
Libya	2008	
Norway	2010	Hosted by friends
Holland	2010	Hosted by friends
Norway	2010	Hosted by friends
Denmark	2010	Hosted by friends
Florence	?	

The journey to Italy and the mobility in Europe: Amir

Country	Year	How long	Accomodation
Ethiopia	December 2006	8 months	In a rented house with friends in Addis Ababa
Eritrea	July 2007	4 months	In a rented house with friends
Ethiopia	November 2007	8 months	In a rented house with friends
Sudan	July 2008	10 days	At a "passeur's home"
Sahara	July 2008	8 days travelling	
Libya (Kufra)	July 2008	3 days	Imprisoned, the police authorities ask for 300 dollars to let him out. He paid and was moved to another prison in Bengasi
Libya (Bengasi)	July 2008	4 days	Also in Bengasi the police authorities asked for 300 dollars to let him out and to arrive in Tripoli. He paid and finally he moved to Tripoli
Tripoli	July 2008	2 weeks	
Holland	2009	20 days	Hosted by friends
Holland	February 2010	20 days	In a family's home
Florence	?		

3.2 Family context and cultural background

Farida, Zahra, Maisa, the three interviewed women, are married with children. **Zahra** tells us that she lives in Italy with her husband who has just come back from Norway. She has four children in Somalia, but they could not rejoin them in Italy yet. **Farida** has five children, but only the last one lives in Italy, where she was born.

Amir has nine brothers and sisters, some of them were able to leave their country, the others are still living in Somalia. It seems that their father collaborated with the government of Siad Barre and for this reason he was killed. We do not know exactly what kind of persecution **Amir** suffered, but in order to avoid death, he decided to leave Somalia as the other bigger brothers. After four years from his arrival in Italy he is still waiting for family reunification with his mother.

Bassam is married and has two children in Somalia. His father died when he was three years old and his mother put him in a military college because she was not able to take care of him.

Living in occupied buildings

Farida tells us of her last experience in the occupied building of "via Slataper" of Florence: "I feel almost good in this structure, I've a room where I can stay quietly with my daughter. I feel free, I don't have a schedule to go in and out, nobody controls my life. I can decide for myself and my daughter. Furthermore the other people we live with help us a lot. The biggest problems are related to the threat of clearing out and the difficulty to get a residence permit in an occupied space".

Also **Zahra** tells us to feel quite good in this structure and says: "Here we are about 100 people from different nationalities and sometimes our life in common is not so easy, because we all have our problems and difficulties, but we are happy that we have a place to sleep and to cook. Once I tried to live in a Reception center, but it was not comfortable. I have had lots of different experiences in my life. I have lived in lots of different places. I have known many people. I don't want to be in a center where others take decisions for you, where you cannot have a normal life and where you cannot even offer tea in your room when a friend of yours come to visit. I am not a person who needs to be assisted". Also **Amir** tells us that in the precarious situation in which he is living (without work, without a home and without the possibility to build social relationships), he thinks often of the "ghosts" of his past. Ali says: "I feel quite good, even though I live in a room with other two people, there are no showers, there are no kitchens, but only small kitchenette. We are many people, men, women, children, Somalis,

Eritreans, Ethiopian, Liberians, each of us with our problems and sometimes some tense situations arise, but I think it is normal in the conditions we live".

Besides **Maisa**, who lives for the first time in an occupied building, the others interviewed had several experiences like this in Florence in the last years, after they had been in some center of first or second reception.

Bassam says. "The only real problem here is that the City of Florence wants to stop our occupation and we risk living under a bridge".

Living in an occupied space: Hassan

Italian City	When	For how long	Lodging	Why they left
Lampedusa	2007	2 weeks	CPA	
Agrigento (Provincia)	2007	Until september 2008	Family Center	It was a home for minors. When coming of age they had to leave whitin 15 days
Roma	2008	20 days	A few days in an occupied center and then under a bridge	He went to many City municipalities and to the Province of Rome to ask for accomodation (a bed) but he never received any reply
Terni	End of 2008	Until mid 2010 (9 months)	In a friend's home	When his contract ended it was not renewed. The same happened to many other colleagues who were working with him
Firenze	Since March 2010	Until today	Various occupations	

3.3 Wishes for the future

Maisa, Amir and Farida would like to go back to Norway. **Farida** in fact tells us that when she was living there, she could send some money to the other children who are still living in Somalia. Here she can only survive. In Italy she expected to live in dignity, to find a house, work, to send her daughter to school, to send some money to the family who remained in Somalia. All this has been impossible. Her relatives remained in Somalia and can't believe that the situation for **Farida** and her daughter in Italy is almost worse than in Somalia. Her family made big efforts to gather money for her voyage, and now it's very painful for Farida to say that their hopes are broken.

60

Amir: "I would like to live in Italy because I get along well with the people over here. The problems are the politicians. We cannot live without a house, work, we cannot get married and we cannot have children. It is also very difficult to think of studying, participating in VET training courses, because if you don't have a roof under which to sleep or any food to eat because maybe you spent all morning in queues in front of the police Station and the canteen shut down, well everything else becomes less important. Even in the Centers for the Second Reception one does not live well. You cannot cook, but you have to eat spaghetti and tomato everyday. You have exit and entrance hours, you must behave as they impose you to do. All this of course if you want to remain in their project".

Also Zahra thought to find a different situation in Italy, on the contrary, she tells us of the many difficulties, first of all concerning the problems to find a place where she can live and find work. She says: "Also in Somalia there were no jobs, but at least I had something to eat. I had a small piece of land where I could grow fruit and vegetables for me and for my family. If I could, I would go back to Somalia, because there life for us would be better. Since I cannot go back to Somalia, I would like to live in Norway, where there is the possibility to work. I would like to work in a food shop, as I have done for many years in Somalia."

Bassam and Hassan would like to live in Italy because they feel well with Italian people, but both of them criticize the Italian policies. **Bassam** says that in Italy there is less racism than in Northern Europe countries, as Sweden. **Hassan** tells "I would like to live in Italy because I get along well with the people over here. The problem are the politicians. We cannot live without a house, work, we cannot get married and we cannot have children. It is also very difficult to think of studying, participating in VET training courses, because if you don't have a roof under which to sleep or any food to eat because maybe you spent all morning in queues in front of the Police Station and the canteen shut down, well everything else becomes less important. Even in the Centers for the Second Reception one does not live well. You cannot cook, but you have to eat spaghetti and tomatoes every day. You have exit and entrance hours, you must behave as they impose you to do. All this of course if you want to remain in their project".

Chapter 4: The VET system in Italy

Introduction

NATIONAL LLL STRATEGY

MAIN OBJECTIVES AND PRIORITIES OF THE NATIONAL LLL STRATEGY	MAIN ACTIONS/MEASURES TO ACHIEVE THEM AND VET RELATED ASPECTS
Development of **key competences for lifelong learning** in the wider context of building up a framework for vocational qualifications, also according to European guidelines (Recommendation of 23 April 2008 on the constitution of EQF and recommendation of 9 April 2008 on ECVET)	– Constitution of a **Technical Board** for the building of a *"National System of minimum training standards, of recognition and validation of competences and training standard"*, set up by the initiative of the Ministry of Labour, Health and Social Policies, with the aim of promoting a wider access to the opportunities of development of competences for employability and active citizenship. The "Technical Board" involves institutional actors (Ministry of Labour, Ministry of Education, Universities and Research, Regions and Autonomous Provinces and Social Partners, together with the technical support of ISFOL and Tecnostruttura) and the main objective is the building of a *"National Standard System"* constituting the main structure of the future National Qualification Framework. – Adhesion to **PIACC 2008-2013** (*Programme for the International Assessment of Adult Competencies*), an international survey managed by OCSE to which ISFOL will participate on behalf of the Ministry of Labour, aimed at evaluating and assessing adult population competencies.
Continuous commitment by the Ministry of Labour towards the improvement of the accreditation system as a major tool to assure high quality VET standards, also following what has been established in the Proposal of Recommendation of European Parliament and the Council on the quality of VET.	– Set up of a new accreditation system, implemented by the Ministry of Labour (approved in March 2008, by State-Regions Conference and published in the Italian official Journal / *Gazzetta Ufficiale* on the 23/01/2009) through the adaptation of regional tools. The regions, through the 2007-2013 Operational Programmes of the European Social Fund, have committed to supporting the perfection of the system according to a precise timetable agreed with the EU Commission.

MAIN OBJECTIVES AND PRIORITIES OF THE NATIONAL LLL STRATEGY	MAIN ACTIONS/MEASURES TO ACHIEVE THEM AND VET RELATED ASPECTS
Reinforcing the attractiveness of VET systems and make them respondent to labour market needs; promoting training initiatives for employed workers and improvement in the quality of training offered; training and placement of young people in the labour market.	– Institution of the "Italian Reference Point for Quality (established in 2006, providing information to the main stakeholders in relation to the activities of the European Network for quality in Education and Professional Training), which includes the participation of Ministry of Labour, Ministry of Education, Regions, Social Partners and VET institutions' representatives) supplying active support for the developments of the network programme and promoting the use of methods for developing quality – Definition of professional, training and recognition and certification standards for skills, which represents a priority for the National Operating Programmes (PON) and for 2007-2013 ESF planning. The technical committee activated by the Ministry of Labour, with the participation of the Ministry of Education, Universities and Research (MIUR), in collaboration with Regions and Social partner, is developing an initial set of minimum professional standards at a national level. – Strengthening the role of apprenticeship contracts (as defined by Law 276/2003) as a link between education and the business world, underscoring the role of firms and trainers and considering apprenticeship a "high level training", giving employers the possibility of implementing agreements with universities.
Improve continuing training for teachers as a tool to increase quality of VET provision; development of skills and competences for teachers/trainers.	Development of the "Permanent System for on line training" (Sistema permanente di formazione on line- SFP on line), promoted by the Ministry of Labour, and implemented through the technical assistance of ISFOL and ItaliaLavoro. (i.e. for Toscana Region: http://www.progettotrio.it/trio/) The aim of the project consists on supporting the reform processes ongoing in Italy within the systems of Education, Vocational Training and Labour market, ensuring a proper supply of ICT-based continuing training, addressed to qualify or re-qualify all the human resources involved in the provision of education, training and employment services.

MAIN OBJECTIVES AND PRIORITIES OF THE NATIONAL LLL STRATEGY	MAIN ACTIONS/MEASURES TO ACHIEVE THEM AND VET RELATED ASPECTS
Reorganization of Employment Services, exploiting the role of the public sector as the "director" of employment services at the level of the organization of the entire labour market	Improving Employment Services capacity for properly providing assistance, increasing the relationship between Permanent Employment Centres (CPIs) and professional training. With the exercise of the authority delegated by Law 247/2007 with respect to Employment Services, CPIs will be a tool for managing the active labour market policy measures.

Policy development in the main vet policy areas

Law no. 3 of 2001, reformed the Title V of the Constitution, in particular new article 117 distributes the legislative power as follows:

- the State has exclusive legislative power over a specific series of subjects, including the definition of the general rules on education and of the basic provisions concerning civil and social rights to be guaranteed all over the national territory;
- the Regions have exclusive legislative power on all subjects not expressly reserved to the State legislation by the Constitution, like vocational education and training;
- as for certain subjects, which are expressly listed, the Regions have concurrent legislative power; it means that they have law making power in the respect of general rules, fundamental principles and essential benefits reserved to the State legislation; education falls within the concurrent legislation; in this respect, the regional legislation should respect school autonomy.

In view of this framework, it is worth noting the significant commitment of the regional administrations with regard:

- to strengthening the education and training system in order to elevate its quality;
- to ensure certification or qualification to the greatest number of people possible.

The most significant example of shared responsibility includes the National Strategic Framework for Cohesion Policy 2007-2013 and its practical implementation. In fact the 2007-2013 National Strategic Framework (*Quadro Strategico Nazionale* – QSN) includes education among the "public service objectives".

The Regions are also contributing to the objectives via co-financing initiatives to leverage human capital involving the European Social Fund, and Regional Operational Programme (ROPs.). In this regard, the accent is placed on the qualification of the education and training system in order to raise the public's skills level and to reduce, particularly in the Convergence objective area, the ratio of young people dropping out of school. The priority in question has been addressed differently in the two Convergence and Competitiveness areas in light of the different possible measures available under the European Social Fund's Regulations.

In the Competitiveness objective Regions, the initiatives are primarily focused on the targets most exposed to the risk of dropout (e.g. immigrants). In the Convergence Regions, a specific, dedicated objective is contemplated, and initiatives complementary to those initiated at a national level have been planned through specific Operational Programmes. The emphasis is thus placed on improving the quality of the school system through instructional programmes for teachers (to raise skills levels) and for students (to make it possible for young people to earn a diploma or professional training and education certification).

In order to allow a better activation of integrated guidance services, ISFOL – on behalf of the Ministry of Labour, is setting up a number of guidance initiatives focused mainly on the southern regions (Convergence Objective) in order to promote the development of a national guidance system, considering regional disparities but, at the same time, ensuring effectiveness and efficiency of services (please, for a wider framework for guidance and counselling, refer to theme 8).

Strategies for the professional development and vocational retraining of teachers and trainers operating in the Vocational Education and Training and adult education systems have been financed mainly under the ESF NOPs and ROPs. Training initiatives addressed to trainers are mainly intended to provide an essential contribution towards strengthening skills and competences with respect to: new learning methodologies and new expertise related to training credit and competence certification; use of new technologies for the development of educational settings; e-learning; accreditation of guidance/VT bodies; and design of tailored-made training pathways.

To update and improve teachers and trainers' skills, a project based on a 'blended' methodology has been set up in collaboration with the Italian MLPS, Regions, Universities, Isfol and Social Partners. The aim is to foster the updating and retraining of VT practitioners by creating and experimenting a vocational training course within the three-year degree course in education sciences.

Validation of non formal and informal learning is at the core of the socio-institutional debate and to this regard there have been implemented several validation experiences acquired in regional local and sectoral context in the framework of specific pathways. Some Regions (Basilicata, Emilia Romagna, Piemonte, Provincia Autonoma di Trento, Veneto and Valle d'Aosta) have defined policies and strategies towards the validation of non-formal and informal learning for the recognition of training credits inside specific formal learning pathways or for the acquisition of official qualifications.

Legislative framework for CVET

The right to «training and vocational improvement of workers» is expressly set by the Italian Constitution (1948); in defining the distribution of responsibilities between the State and the Regions, it assigns these latter with exclusive jurisdiction in the vocational training field.

Reform law 53/2003 introduced 'lifelong learning' among the principles and directive criteria of the education and training system. For its implementation, the reform law provided a programmatic plan to fund 'interventions for the development of higher level technical education and training and adult education'.

The local training bodies have consultancy and promotion functions. Following the guidelines established at national level, the Regional Authorities' tasks include the identification of medium- and long-term objectives through the analysis of training needs, activity-administrative management, monitoring and evaluation of the training-activities' efficiency and effectiveness. Thus, the Regional Authorities are exclusively responsible for both initial and continuing-vocational training, and, on occasions, this power is exercised by delegating or transferring a number of functions to the Provincial Authorities.

A first step towards recognition of training as a strategic resource for all people, in particular for young people, workers, and enterprises, is the approval of Law 236/93, which allowed launching the structuring of a national continuing-training system. With the Labour Agreement signed by the Government and the Social Partners in September 1996, a real strategy of innovation of the system was envisaged. With specific reference to initial vocational education and training, among the Agreement's objectives are worthy of note:

- the overall increase of the schooling level (quantitative and qualitative) by raising the compulsory schooling age and introducing the right to training;
- the consolidation of an integrated system for the certification and recognition of training credits;
- the definition of a system of permanent recognition of the quantity/quality of the training supply.

Consistent with the indications of the above Agreement, Law 196/97 has introduced:

- the identification of requirements for the "accreditation" of training providers to be entrusted with managing the activity; to the re-launching of apprenticeship training;

66

- the introduction of "guidance" and "training" practical work or experience;
- the definition of criteria for skill certification and the creation of a system for the credit recognition.

The next step was the introducing of Law 53/00 (recognizing the right to training leave for workers) and Law 388/00 (amended by Law 289/02) which established the Fondi interprofessionali (joint interprofessional funds) supporting continuing training. Financed by a contribution of 0.30% of the wage bill paid by employers, these funds support company, sectoral and regional training plans, supplementing the regional authorities' work in the continuing training system. These funds are managed by the social partners and supervised by the Ministry of Labour and Social Policy.

Institutional framework: CVET

Continuing Vocational Education and Training in Italy consists of the following elements:

- lifelong learning activities for the acquisition of basic, general and pre-vocationally-oriented skills;
- lifelong learning activities for the enhancement of cultural background, and the attainment of skills for social life and active citizenship;
- continuing training activities for the updating and re-qualification of the workers' vocational skills.

[These definitions don't have the status of recognition at a legal level. In recent years, a number of changes have been made to promote a coherent system for financing and managing continuing vocational education and training (CVET) and general adult education initiatives in Italy. The aim has been to establish a more coherent supply structure to achieve the objectives of employability, active citizenship, social inclusion and personal development. It is not an easy task to provide a complete description of the continuing vocational education and training system in Italy because it is quite complex and fragmentary since it is based on a variety of instruments referring to a policy and legislative scenario in constant evolution over recent years. In Italy there isn't yet a national law on CVET.]

Upper secondary educational (general and vocational)

The "Moratti Reform" (Law 53/2003 reforming the education and training system) has organized the second cycle in two channels:

- the licei (lycée) system, for which the State is responsible, lasting five years, at the end of which students take the State examination paving the way for university entrance;
- vocational education and training system, for which the regional authorities are responsible, lasting at least three years, and leading to the award of a certificato di qualifica professionale (vocational qualification certificate) recognized nationally and within Europe. The qualification can be used to enter the labour market or to enter post-qualification courses leading to the award of an upper secondary vocational diploma. This diploma is required for entry into pathways of "Istruzione e formazione tecnica superior" (IFTS – higher technical education and training) or, after attending a supplementary year, for entry into universities.

The second cycle of education (secondo ciclo di istruzione) includes the following types of institutes:

- Liceo classico (classical upper secondary school);
- Liceo scientifico (scientific upper secondary school);
- Liceo linguistico (linguistic upper secondary school);
- Liceo socio-psico pedagogico (upper secondary school with a sociological- psycological- and pedagogical orientation).

They are attended by pupils aged 14-19, and the Liceo artistico (artistic upper secondary school) attended by pupils aged 14-18/199. These are the schools foreseen for general upper secondary education.

Vocational upper secondary education includes:

- technical education, i.e. istituto tecnico (technical school), attended by pupils aged 14-19;
- vocational education, i.e. istituto professionale (vocational schools) pupils aged 14-19; and
- istituti d'arte (art schools), attended by pupils aged 14-17/19.

Both in the licei and in the technical institutes, the overall length of study is 5 years, except for the liceo artistico, which offers a course of study of 4 years plus an additional year. Vocational institutes offer courses lasting either 3 or 5 years.

The image below shows the difference between the pupils with non-Italian citizenship and with Italian citizenship, learning in upper secondary schools (Italian Ministry of Education data):

Fig. 2: Studenti con cittadinanza italiana e non per tipo scuola secondaria di secondo grado. A.s. 2010/11

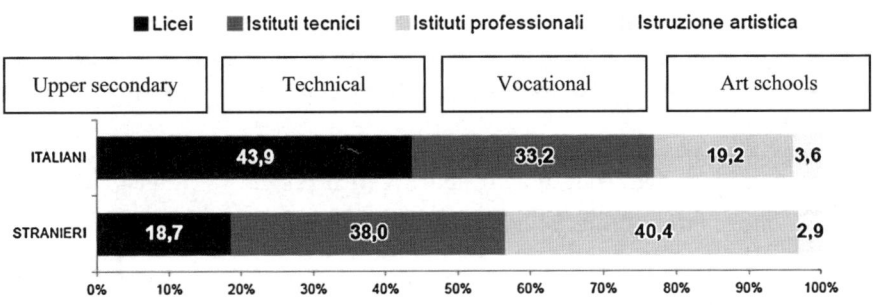

Fonte: Miur – Fondazione Ismu

According to D.Lgs. 297/1994, education offered by the licei specialising in classical and scientific studies aims at preparing students to university studies, whereas education offered by the liceo specialising in arts subjects aims at teaching art, independently from its industrial applications. Financial law 2007, which has provided for the extension of compulsory education up to 10 years (16 years of age), has at the same time established that the first two years of upper secondary education are aimed at the acquisition of knowledge and competences common to all types of education and training (general and vocational). These knowledge and competences have been included in the Decree no. 139/2007, issued for the implementation of the extension of compulsory education and are organised into 4 'cultural areas': languages, mathematical, scientific-technological, historical-social. Knowledge and competences are then the basis for building learning pathways aimed at acquiring key competences that can help students for their adult lives and for the lifelong learning. Key competences are: learning to learn, planning, communicating, collaborating and participating, acting autonomously, problem solving, creating connections and relations, acquiring and interpreting information. According to the same Decree, technical education aims at preparing to carry out technical and administrative functions as well as some professions in the trade, services, industry, building, agriculture, navigation and aeronautics sectors.

Vocational education and training system, for which the regional authorities are responsible, lasts at least three years, and leading to the award of a certificato di qualifica professionale (vocational qualification certificate) recognised nationally and within Europe. The qualification can be used to enter the labour market or to enter post-qualification courses leading to the award of an upper secondary vocational diploma. This diploma is required for entry into pathways of istruzione e formazione tecnica superiore (IFTS – higher technical education and training) or, after attending a supplementary year, for entry into universities.

Vocational education aims at providing a specific theoretical and practical preparation to carry out qualified functions in the trade, services, industry, artisanship, agriculture and navigation sectors. Art education aims at preparing to artistic work and production according to the local industry tradition and typical row materials.

As for the redefinition at the national level of the aims and general objectives, it is necessary for both educational pathways (general and vocational upper secondary education), to wait for the possible amendments to D. Lgs. 226/200510.

At the end of the upper secondary school (general and vocational upper secondary education), students take a state examination. Those, who successfully pass the examination obtain an upper secondary school leaving diploma, which allows them to continue their studies at a higher level.

The certificate mentions the branch and duration of their studies, the subjects and courses included in the curriculum in addition to the total duration of the course, the grade awarded in written tests and in the oral examination, along with their school credits and training credits. The training credits are awarded based on the pupil's experience outside of school in different aspects of social life.

The certification models are drawn up by the Ministry of education. Diplomas and certificates are written in four Community languages so that they can be understood in the different countries of the EU.

Initial vocational training

Initial Vocational Training (Formazione Professionale Iniziale – FPI), is offered by the recognised formative agencies operating nationwide. The FPI provides for:

- First-level (or basic) training pathways, addressed to those who have completed the first cycle of education (2.4.). These paths have a three-year length and lead to the obtainment of a regional qualification certificate or to the qualification diploma;
- Second-level training pathways addressed to those who have completed the upper secondary level of education or who have obtained a first-level vocational qualification;
- Apprenticeship.

Law 30/2003 has introduced some reforms in the apprenticeships system, now organised as follows:

- an apprenticeship aimed at the fulfilment of the right/duty to education and training: young people who have reached 16 years of age can be enrolled for

all the fields of activity. The contract lasts a maximum of three years and is aimed at helping students obtain a vocational qualification;
- a profession-oriented apprenticeship: students aged between 18 and 29 years can be enrolled.

Depending on the type of qualification to be obtained, the collective contracts define the duration of the contract which, however, cannot be less than two years or more than six years. There is also a minimum quota of 120 hours of formal worker training (internal and external); an apprenticeship enabling the student to obtain a second level diploma (within the Initial vocational training) or higher education qualifications. It is addressed to students between 18 and 29 years of age.

Post-secondary education (non tertiary)

Post-secondary education and training is organised both in the higher technical education and training system and in the second-level vocational training courses managed by the Regions.

Higher technical education and training system

The Higher technical education and training (IFTS) courses have been instituted through Law of 17 May 1999, no. 144, and are regulated through Interministerial decree of 31 October 2000, no. 436.

Based on the above mentioned provisions, Regions plan the institution of IFTS courses in order to assure integration among educational systems, on the basis of guidelines defined by a National Committee and approved by the Unified Conference.

In 2008, the guidelines for the reorganisation of the whole higher technical education and training system have been issued. This reorganisation is meant at spreading the higher technical and scientific culture and at supporting the development and competitiveness of the economic and productive Italian system. One of the main goals is to make both young people and adults obtain a higher level technical specialisation, together with specific cultural knowledge coming from both the private and public labour market, and referred in particular to small and medium enterprises and to those sectors that are more interested by technological innovations and internationalization of markets.

According to this recent reorganisation, there are two types of offer within the higher technical educational and training system:
- the formative offer and the programmes organised by the Higher Technical Institutes (Istituti Tecnici Superiori, ITS) leading to a higher level technical

diploma in one of the following areas: energy efficiency, sustainable mobility, new technologies in life, new technologies for the 'made in Italy', innovative technologies for arts and cultural activities, ICT. Courses last 4 semesters for a total of 1800/2000 hours and, for specific subjects, up to a maximum of 6 semesters;
- the formative offer of the IFTS courses organised by the Regions. Courses last 2 semesters, for a total of 800/1000 hours, and lead to a higher technical specialisation certificate.

Second level of initial vocational training – the regional VET courses

The VET courses are managed by the Regional Authorities and aim at providing students with specialized training. The curricula are based on vocational skills having a high theoretical, technical, technological and managerial content, also through practical exercises and on-the-job training periods. Post-secondary training can be accessed by those having an upper secondary school-leaving certificate or having an upper secondary-education level, generally unemployed, and wishing to obtain a certificate or a vocational qualification immediately valid on the labor market.

IVET at lower secondary level

Generally speaking IVET is not provided at this level. Lower secondary school, of three-year duration, has only one education pathway common to all students aged between 11 and 14. The curricula include above all general subjects and have not work-based training. Students learn a second European foreign language and further study of ICTs. Admission is free and is subject to the attainment of a primary-school certificate. Legally recognized private lower-secondary schools are entitled to State subsidies and generally require parents to pay tuition fees. Following the schools' organizational and teaching autonomy provided by Legislative Decree 112/98, lessons can be spread over a period of 5 or 6 days per week, usually in the morning. It is also possible to modify both the duration of individual lessons and the weekly timetable depending on local needs and on teaching and educational programmes. On parental request, disabled children are entitled to a support teacher.

At the end of the three-year cycle, students are required to take a State examination in order to obtain a lower secondary school-leaving certificate (Diploma di Licenza Media) and have to continue their studies by enrolling in and attending upper secondary education.

IVET at upper secondary level (school-based and alternance)

Law 53/2003 and D.Lgs. 226/2005 separated the licei system and the vocational education and training system respectively under the state and the regions responsibility.

D.Lgs. 226/2005 established, in fact, that 'All vocational qualifications are under the regions and autonomous provinces responsibility and are exclusively released by the schools and training institutes of the vocational education and training system'. It establishes also that the two systems have equal dignity and that 'it is granted the possibility to pass from the licei system to the vocational education and training system and viceversa, through specific teaching initiatives aimed at offering an adequate preparation for the new study path'.

Specific agreements of the State/Regions unified Conference, upon proposals of the Minister of education in accordance with the Minister of labour and welfare, should have defined correspondence and recognition procedures for credits obtained both in the licei study and in the vocational education and training in view of the possibility of transition between these two systems.

Main economic sectors	Corresponding isced level / orientation	Balance between general and vocational subjects	Balance between school-based and work-based training	Average duration of studies	Transfer to other pathways
catering wellness tourist promotion and reception installation maintenance of electric installations Mechanic	II level	-40% cultural subjects (key competences for citizenship, maths, scientific, technological subjects) -60% vocational training subjects (technological-vocational skills, stage, laboratories)	Depending on the kind of pathways (if provided by schools or training agencies	1100 hours per year	It is made possible by several tools and mechanism at National level, enabling students to transfer to other pathways, maintaining credits earned.

However, in the meantime, Law 40/2007 has established that the second cycle is made up of the upper secondary education system (licei, technical institutes and vocational institutes) and the vocational education and training system.

Furthermore, law allows 15 to 18 year-old students to attend second-level courses through alternation of study and work periods, under the responsibility of schools or training institutions, on the basis of agreements with enterprises or associations of professional classes, public or private bodies, or to attend integrated courses organized at vocational education and training institutes offering study programmes planned by the two systems together. Following the extension of the length of compulsory education to 10 years, up to 16 years of age, the minimum age required to enter the labour market is now fixed at 16 years of age and, therefore, this is also the minimum age limit for starting alternance training activities.

Vocational education

Schools offering vocational secondary education are the following:

- **Technical institutes**: their duration is subdivided into a common basic two-year cycle and a three year cycle with more branches of study and specialisations teaching programs are established by the decrees that authorised experimental projects and are based on strengthening the study of humanities, scientific and technical subjects to the detriment of practical exercises. Programs of the two-year period are the same and change in the three year period according to the different specialisations; subjects of the two-year period, except from religion or alternative subject (optional subject), are Italian, history, foreign language, mathematics, physics, natural sciences, chemistry and geography, and some specialisation subjects (for example, technical drawing in the Industrial technical institute) and practical exercises. As for the three-year period, the subjects typical of the branch of study will be added to the subjects of the two-year period; weekly timetable foresees 32-38 hours, according to the different classes and branches of study.
- **Vocational institutes**: their duration is subdivided into a three-year cycle, leading to obtain a qualification diploma, and, according to Law of 27 October 1969, no. 754, a post qualification two-year cycle (4th and 5th years) that grants admission to the university.

Initial Vocational Training

Initial Vocational Training (FPI), is offered by the recognised formative agencies operating nationwide. The FPI provides for:

- First-level (or basic) training pathways, addressed to those who have completed the first cycle of education. These paths have a three-year length and lead to the obtainment of a regional qualification certificate or to the qualification diploma;

- Second-level training pathways addressed to those who have completed the upper secondary level of education or who have obtained a first-level vocational qualification;
- Apprenticeship.

First-level initial vocational training

First-level initial vocational training (FPI), which is under the competence of the Regions, is intended to provide a qualification to those who have finished the first cycle of education and want to fulfil the compulsory education (16 years of age) within the vocational training, or to acquire a three-year qualification by the 18th year of age (fulfilment of the diritto/dovere). Three-year courses are organised according to two types:

- vocational training courses organised by accredited training agencies and aimed at helping students obtain a vocational qualification certificate. Teachers are employed by the training agencies;
- education courses combined with vocational training modules organised by schools and aimed at the obtainment of the qualifications required by the mainstream education system.

Second-level initial vocational training

Second-level vocational training courses aim at acquiring vocational skills with a high theoretical, technical and managerial content, also through practical work and stages in enterprises. These are full-time courses leading to a second-level vocational qualification.

Italy has a strong vocationally oriented upper secondary education system: around 60% of upper secondary students are enrolled pre-vocational or vocational programmes, notably higher than the OECD average rate of 48%11; as also showed in the table 1 below for general and prevocational programme. Even though historically significantly lagging in terms of the level of education of the population, Italy has made important progress in recent years: the number of students enrolled in Italy's school system – from elementary to upper secondary school – was up by 0.5% for the 2006-2007 academic year. In terms of macro areas, the northern regions experienced a very significant increase of 1.8%; the increase in the central regions was about half of that, or 0.8%; and in the southern regions, the enrolment fell by 0.9%. The growth of the school-age population in the northern and central regions is related to immigration (which has affected the more developed areas of the country).

Type of educational programme	Main economic sectors	Corresponding isced level / orientation	Balance between general and vocational subjects	Balance between school-based and work-based training	Average duration of studies	Transfer to other pathways
Apprenticeship for the fulfilment of the right-duty to education and training	All	3	Variable	Variable	3 years	On the basis of credits recognized
Higher apprenticeship	All	4-5	Variable	Variable	Variable	On the basis of credits recognized
Profession-oriented apprenticeship	All	3-4-5	Variable	Variable	3-6 years	On the basis of the credits recognised

Law 30/2003 has introduced some reforms in the apprenticeships system, now organized as follows:

An apprenticeship aimed at the fulfillment of the right-duty *(diritto/dovere)* to education and training: young people who have reached 16 years of age can be enrolled for all the fields of activity. The contract lasts a maximum of three years and is aimed at helping students obtain a vocational qualification; at the current moment this kind of apprenticeship needs to be implemented by regional administration. This apprenticeship is not yet available for businesses and young people, as the Regions and Autonomous Provinces do not have issued the specific regulation through an agreement with the Ministry of Education. Therefore the apprenticeship contract for those aged less than 18 years is the one designed by the previous Law No. 196/1997 and relevant implementing decrees.

An apprenticeship enabling the student to obtain a second level diploma (within the Initial vocational training) or higher education qualifications. It is addressed to students between 18 and 29 years of age.

A profession-oriented apprenticeship: students aged between 18 and 29 years can be enrolled. Depending on the type of qualification to be obtained, the collective contracts define the duration of the contract which, however, cannot be less than two years or more than six years. There is also a minimum quota of 120 hours of formal worker training (internal and external); This apprenticeship although the contract is not yet available for all companies over the whole national territory, is being gradually implemented both through regulations the collective contracting.

For all the different types of apprenticeships, the definition of the training profiles is referred to the Regions and the institutions involved, according to the type of apprenticeship (Ministries, social partners and universities). The student's Individual Training Plan must be enclosed in the employment contract. This document includes the programme of training that the apprentice will follow throughout the contractual period. In addition, there must be a tutor with sufficient training and competence to monitor the apprentice's progress within the company.

Vocational education and training at post-secondary (non tertiary) level

Post-secondary non-tertiary education and training is organised both in the higher technical education and training system and in the second-level vocational training courses managed by Regions.

In Italy, two different training pathways are available at post-secondary level, (ISCED 4) within the higher technical education and training system, those offered by the Higher Technical Institutes (*Istituti Tecnici Superiori – ITS*), and those offered by the Higher Technical Education and Training (*Istruzione e Formazione Tecnica Superiore – IFTS*).

The above mentioned pathways have been recently reformed through Decree of the President of the Council of Ministers of 25 January 2008. In 2008, the guidelines for the reorganisation of the whole higher technical education and training system have been issued. This reorganisation is meant at spreading the higher technical and scientific culture and at supporting the development and competitiveness of the economic and productive Italian system. One of the main goals is to make both young people and adults obtain a higher level technical specialisation, together with specific cultural knowledge coming from both the private and public labour market, and referred in particular to small and medium enterprises and to those sectors that are more interested by technological innovations and internationalization of markets.

To access courses organised both by the ITS and within the IFTS system, the possession of an upper secondary school leaving certificate is required. Access to the IFTS courses is allowed also for those who are admitted to the last grade of a liceo, as well as to those who do not hold an upper secondary school certificate, upon recognition of their previously acquired competences (school education, training courses, working experience, etc.).

Admission requirements

The possession of an upper secondary school leaving certificate diploma is required to access the courses organised both by the *ITS* (Higher Technical Institutes) and within the *IFTS* system.

Access to the *IFTS* courses is allowed also to applicants in possession of an upper secondary technical qualification (four-year courses), to those admitted to the last grade of a *liceo*, as well as to those who are not in possession of an upper secondary school certificate, upon recognition of their competences (school education, training courses, working experiences, etc.), acquired after the fulfilment of compulsory education.

Minimum and maximum age of students

The courses provided by ITS as well as the *IFTS* courses are addressed both to young people and adults too. Courses are not organised according to age levels.

Registration and tuition fees

IFTS courses and the ITS courses are free of charge and financed through the European Social Fund.

Main training programmes and corresponding levels of study

The professional profiles related to the various pathways have a high level of cultural knowledge, basic skills, cross-curricular as well as deep technical-vocational skills corresponding to the IV EEC level (Decision 85/368/EEC). According to the reorganisation of Higher Technical Institutes (ITS), the courses offered by these institutes aim at meeting the formative needs referred to the following 6 technological areas: energy efficiency, sustainable mobility, new technologies in life, new technologies the 'made in Italy', innovative technologies for arts and cultural activities, ICT.

IFTS courses are planned by the Regions, which are responsible for the training programmes.

Distance learning programmes and corresponding levels of study

The body responsible for the training can organize part of the course by way of distance learning programmes.

Curricula elements (place of delivery, specific competence-based skills to be developed)

ITS courses can be established by the following institutes: a technical or vocational state or non-state upper secondary school, located in the province where the training is organised; a training institute accredited by the Region for the organisation of this kind of training, located in the province which organises the training; a firm/enterprise of the professional sector related to the Higher Technical Institute; a university department or other body in the scientific and technological research area, and a local authority (province, commune, town, consortium of communes in mountain areas).

IFTS courses are planned and provided by minimum four educational institutes: school, vocational training provider, university, enterprise or another public or private subject, formally associated in the form of a consortium.

Programmes of study of both pathways refer to common competences to be acquired like linguistic, scientific and technological competences, or juridical/ legal and economic/financial competences, organizational competences, and competences related to communication at different level, and technical-professional competences related to the specific higher technical professional profile, organised on the basis of the European Union indicators for certificates and qualifications.

The higher technical education and training system offers courses aiming mainly to develop professional specialisations at post-secondary level which meet the requirements of the labour market, both in the public and private sectors, in particular for what concerns the organisation of services, local bodies and productive sectors undergoing deep technological innovations and by the market's internationalisation according to the priorities indicated by the economic planning at regional level.

Assessment

The courses end with a final assessment of the competences acquired. Final assessment is carried out by examination boards made up of representatives of school, university, vocational training and experts from the labour market. The Regions can define how to set up the examination boards and they are also responsible for the issue of general indications related to the final assessment of the acquired competences and to the relevant certification, in order to issue titles/ qualifications to be recognized at national and European level.

Certification

According to the recent reorganisation of this sector, courses offered by Higher Technical Institutes (ITS) lead to the attainment of a Diploma of high level technician, while *IFTS* courses, organised by the Regions, lead to the attainment of a Certificate of high level technical specialisation. Both of them give access to public competitions.

The reorganisation of the system for Higher Technical Education and Training (IFTS) which constitutes a measure aimed at strengthening post-secondary training not of an academic nature; the value of the professional-technical process is also being enhanced by the contribution of the educational hubs set up by the Regions to ensure acquisition of the skills needed for local economic development.

Major characteristics of formal CVET

In Italy continuing learning may be provided by different institutions; even thought sometimes these structures do not set a learning supply specifically addressed to workers, the participation of the world of work is considerably high. In particular:

- Universities and Research Institutes;
- Upper Secondary schools in collaboration with other formative structures;
- Training Agencies as qualified by regional administrative bodies;
- Non qualified training/vocational guidance structures (they cannot release a formal certifications);
- Training enterprises.

Adult education centres (centri territoriali permanenti)

The Ministry of Education Order No. 455 of 29 July 1997, *Educazione in età adulta – Istruzione e Formazione* set up the "Adult Education Centres" (*Centri Territoriali Permanenti – CTP*), defined as "places for interpreting needs, designing, co-ordinating, activating and governing education and training initiatives [...], as well as for the collection and dissemination of documentation" aimed at establishing agreements, understandings and conventions with all the organisations, bodies and/or agencies providing adult-education initiatives, in order to favour their local affirmation. Under Article 5 of the Order, the activities of the Adult Education Centres are aimed not only at courses for the attainment of educational qualifications, but also for the reception, listening and guidance, as well as the primary, functional and adult literacy, the learning of language skills, the development and consolidation of basic skills and know-how, the recovery and development of cultural and relational skills both suited to the activity of participation in social life, and to the return to training of persons in conditions of marginalization.

The CTP are the places where the courses of Italian as second language are located, for adults and young (over 16) of foreign origin. Also the courses for attain the secondary school – first degree certificate are usually located here, addressed both to the foreign origin and autochthonous citizens. As shown in the 4.4 paragraph, also in the Florence area these centers are the most frequented by foreign origin students, in order to realign their curricula with the Italian formal educational system.

Quality assurance

One of the most important ways to assure the quality CVET provision in Italy is the accreditation system for providers. All providers whether public or private must be accredited to deliver publicly-funded training and guidance (as legislated in Law 59/97). All regional and local authorities must follow the national criteria outlined in the legislation. In 2002, the legislation was extended to cover minimum standards for vocational qualifications as well as training structures. Accreditation is necessary for providers wanting to deliver the continuing training of workers employed and unemployed. To receive accreditation, the operational facilities of public or private providers must have: management and logistical capacities; teachers with appropriate vocational skills; proven record of effectiveness and efficiency; links with local groups and enterprises.

The "Agreement for the definition of the minimum standards of the new accreditation system of the VET institutions for the quality of services", signed on 20th March 2008 by the State-Regions Conference is the most recent measure adopted in this field and it aims at guaranteeing a homogeneous qualitative level of the training offer the entire national territory, also following the recommendation proposals on the EQARF. In the Agreement a clear distinction is maintained between the function of control of the process and the role of the actuator institution. Regarding the application of operational tools for the evaluation and self evaluation of the training offer, it has been realized and widespread the Italian guide for the self evaluation of schools and training institutions and of the Peer Review methodology, complementary to the self evaluation, that has find an application both at single training institutions and School network vocational training centres.

Admission criteria

Adults that have any previous background in VET, can undertake the IFTS system, (Higher Technical Education and Training system introduced in Italy by Law 144/1999); based on "pathways" aimed at allowing youth and employed/unemployed adults to achieve a high cultural level, together with an extensive and deep technical and vocational training.

Distance learning

Till the present moment, it does not exist an integrated system for distance learning programmes; training offers is provided by private institutions and universities consortia – with also the participation of enterprises – that try to meet training needs emerged at territorial and/or sectoral level. From the analysis of the distance learning programmes available, it emerges a wide availability for Office-automation courses, Quality, Operating System, Company Certification (ISO 9000-ISO 14000), Health and Safety at work, e-commerce.

Measures and instruments to foster access to CVET

Moreover, recent measures adopted by the Government to face the crisis (please, refer also to 2.3), extend the training possibilities of Joint interprofessional funds for Continuing Training *(Fondi Paritetici Interprofessionali per la Formazione Continua)*, that can be used to finance special training plans. In fact, besides the different activities for supporting income foreseen for workers suspended or excluded from the labour market, there is also the obligatory participation to short and medium-length training initiatives, addressed to the recovery of transversal and basic competencies (also linguistic and information technology competencies).

Non-formal education

General background (administrative structure and financing)

With regard to the segment of the adult population, we should distinguish between continuing training, in which technical, vocational and transversal skills are acquired on the job and adult education or learning, where the basic skills and the skills that in general refer to the active population, are acquired in formal (at Adult education centres and schools-evening courses) or informal off-the-job contexts. Implementation of non formal education and training is an attempt to respond to the need to introduce flexibility, transparency and skills and many efforts are being promoted at national level to promote a more harmonized approach in the process.

Vocational training in Italy mainly takes place in formalized contexts aimed at obtaining qualifications rather than competences. More specifically, the enormous formal and juridical value of educational qualifications linked to formal education paths and the fact that there is little or no tradition of brief or adult training, have created a situation in which it is difficult to make visible the social and cultural value of training in itself and of their related certification.

The legal framework14 regulating formal learning – and, under some points of view, informal and non-formal learning, considering the overarching strategy undertaken by theCountry (since the 1990's) in dealing with Education, VET and Labor market as strictly linked issues – is set by two main acts: Law 53/03 (Moratti Reform), reforming the education and training system, and the Law 30/03 (Biagi Reform), on the labor market and employment system, which are strictly connected.

The Reform Law 53 of 2003 established various general principles on the validation of learning; among these principles, it is particularly relevant the exploitation need of the qualifications obtained at the end of experimental vocational education and training paths and the exploitation extension to those who have reached 18 years of age; this principle aims at allowing the highest number of people to obtain higher educational levels (the agreement includes certification models). In particular, section 9 of the agreement refers to subjects who have to accomplish compulsory education or who have reached 18 years of age, who can be admitted to vocational training paths according to their knowledge and skills acquired in formal, non formal and informal contexts, against recognition of the formative credits through transparent procedures established by the Regions and Autonomous provinces.

Major characteristics of non-formal CVET

With regard to the adult education, in recent years, non-formal training has also observed a substantial growth, being provided by a number of public and private actors and by third-sector associations, obviously linked with the increase in the training-course demand from some sectors of the adult world. It is worth mentioning that mostly classroom or distance-learning courses are provided (in particular in major cities, but in also increasingly in smaller towns) by:

- popular universities;
- third-age universities;
- civic networks for cultural promotion (civic schools for adult education, municipal libraries, museums, etc.);

- agencies, bodies and social volunteer associations, often in agreement with the Regional or Local Authorities or project managers, and are financed with ESF resources.

In many cases, the training opportunities are similar in contents and methods to those offered by the Adult Education Centers, and to those linked to 'continuing training on individual demand' (for example, courses in English and other foreign languages, Italian courses for foreigners, computer and multimedia courses). However, for the purposes of lifelong learning, the aim of these courses is above all to provide opportunities absolutely different from traditional school/training schemes and thus more "reassuring" and "free" for individuals who are diffident towards training. It may often occur that these pathways contribute to rebuild an interest and motivation for learning.

In Italy a formalised or institutionalised national validation system is still lacking, but the establishment of a validation system for non-formal and informal learning has become a strong and widely shared priority in the last ten years in Italy. An important step has been the Agreement of February 2000 between State and Regions, and subsequent Decree No. 174/2001 issued by the ML, providing:

- focus on skills and competences certification and enhancement of individual experiences as training credits;
- start-up of a definition process of minimum skill-certification standards;
- definition of various certification tools (e.g. the Citizen Training Booklet, *Libretto formativo del cittadino*, see box below*),* in order to facilitate the recognition of formal, non-formal and informal learning as well as to standardise the validation procedures.

Over the last few years, the question of learning validation has been put among the issues dealt in the context of the most recent reforms (L. 30/03 and L.53/03) concerning education, vocational training and labour, trying to focus on knowledge and competences wherever acquired.

Example of project aiming at paving the way to the accreditation of non-formal and informal learning: The "Citizen's Training Booklet".

Objectives:
The Training Booklet is a logbook created to collect, summarise and document the various learning experiences of the working-citizen, as well as the competences and skills acquired – at school, in training, at work, in daily life.

Background:
The creation of a "Training Booklet" has already been envisaged in various national provisions (e.g., Agreement signed on 18 February 2000 between State and Regions and Ministerial Decree

---

DM 174/2001 on skill certification). Later, D.Lgs. no. 276/2003, implementing the 'Biagi' Law (Article 2.1.i), confirmed and integrated the provisions of previous measures by launching the process towards a social and institutional definition and sharing of the "Training Booklet". The process leading to the approval of the "Booklet" ended with an agreement on its format (approved by Interministerial Decree of 10 October 2005) and with the shared decision to begin experimenting on the "Booklet". This experimentation was managed autonomously by each Region under national supervision, and with support and monitoring provided by Isfol. The experimental phase effectively began in the second half of 2006, using proposed candidates from 13 Regions and Autonomous Provinces, involving activities conducted according to the different application methods adopted in each Region.

Key actors involved:
The "Training Booklet" is issued by the Regional and Autonomous Provincial Authorities, who can nevertheless delegate this task to other actors. As holder of the "Booklet", it is the **working-citizen's** responsibility to update it. The "Booklet" is divided into two sections: the first containing personal details, information about educational background, professional experiences, educational and vocational qualifications, as well as training experiences; the second section describes the specific skills acquired during various learning pathways.

"Training Booklets" provide personal information on individuals, together with their formal and non-formal learning curriculum for the purposes of job-seeking, occupational mobility and transition from one training system to another. For the labour market and **business world**, the "Training Booklet" facilitates the recognition of individual skills and competences within the context of work placement and occupational mobility, and further describes the worker's training pathway and career progress.

Outcomes:
The "Training Booklet" was effectively experimented in 9 Regions and Autonomous Provinces between 2006 and 2007, where it was issued within employment centres and training bodies. The "Training Booklet" proved above all to be useful to apprentices, workers undergoing continuing training activities, and disadvantaged individuals. On the basis of the results of the experimentation conducted in 2006-2007, ISFOL – that has also provided technical support and managed the monitoring process – is now collecting the results in order to provide the conditions for an effective implementation of the Booklet, thus individuating priority context. At the moment (2009) a first implementation of the tool could concern apprenticeship, continuous training and disadvantaged workers.

More recently (2006) a Technical Table for the national standards system has been established with particular reference to competences held and acquired in formal, non-formal and informal learning contexts. The Table, aimed at defining and implementing a "National Qualifications System" is composed by MLPS, Ministry of Education, Regions and Social Partners. This political issue will allow to integrate the different standards at each level and to relate in a common frame the typology of qualifications with the titles, qualifications and diploma delivered by the Ministry of Education, MLPS, Regions and Universities. In this context, it is worth mentioning the role of the Italian universities: the Ministry for Universities and Research that has set up a working group to draw up Guidelines for the accreditation of previous learning, enabling universities to use quality-based methodologies for the recognition of non-formal and informal learning in university courses.

The only really implemented national and institutional practice so far seems to be the IFTS; within this channel, in fact, it has been possible to recognize and certify learning and competences through a specific set of minimum standard which is structured in *"capitalisable units"*. Credit recognition occurs:

1. through the recognition of "incoming credits";
2. during the training;
3. outside the training, so facilitating the total or partial recognition of competences acquired.

Another good example is the National Civil Service: the national regulation (Law No. 64/2001) states that competences acquired through the social service can be recognized as credits towards vocational training pathways or valuable access requirements to regulated professions.

Moreover, some regional administrations (Basilicata, Emilia Romagna, Piemonte, Provincia Autonoma di Trento, Veneto, Valle d'Aosta) are directly defining and implementing policies and operational strategies towards the validation of non formal and informal learning and for the recognition of training credits within specific formal lifelong learning pathways or for the acquisition of titles and official certificates.

Target groups and modes of delivery

Concerning groups with special needs, some districts (Province) have undertaken specific interventions in order to support the integration and the achievement of training pathways of second-generation immigrated pupils, through the non curricular courses of Italian language. Furthermore, actions aimed to support learning processes and motivate immigrant youngsters through individual counselling have been launched. Specific projects have been undertaken for guidance of immigrant women, in order to reduce gender gap.

Decision makers, researchers and guidance professionals agree on a new idea of curriculum related to a new system of Guidance, beyond any system of pre-set models. The life cycle (considered as evolution to adult age) requires continuous updating under the deep recent social and cultural transformations. Modern Guidance relates to several kinds of beneficiaries and from activities manly focused on youngster or students, nowadays a relevant number of adults participate (women, foreigners, unemployed or job seekers, temporary contracted, socially marginalized groups).

Therefore, differences in personal and social experiences or planning and satisfaction criteria, are crucial factors in defining the wide span of needs and demands for the Guidance system. In fact, different categories of beneficiaries embed more and more segmented clusters of needs that very often are not met by the present. Guidance system must be analysed in order to get satisfying reply. Within the three years pathways experimentations, most of Regions will have established public services including welcoming, information aimed to guidance, training pathways aimed to guidance, guidance counseling, competence balance, job insertion. All these interventions are aimed to help people to make choices, to strengthen individual professional identity, to put in value the individual specific resources, in order to define a personal and professional project and to prevent early school leaving.

Due to the rise of compulsory education to 16 years, the VET system is aware of the importance of realizing integrated guidance actions, connecting VET systems (school, vocational training and labour market) and institutions at different level.

The reform of the employment agencies (Legislative Decree n. 181/2000) highlighted the liability of all subjects involved: workers, job services, VET agencies. For this reason, job services have to fix up personal and professional data application forms for job search, the subscription of an engagement to be immediately available for a job. The reform established the following standard steps:

- Enrolment, registration of personal data and statement of immediate availability to work;
- First-level guidance and fulfilment of a "professional form";
- Second-level guidance (needs diagnosis, individualized action plan).

The approach adopted by the employment agencies is personalized and based on the creation of an individual relationship between guidance professionals and users.

The need to guarantee guidance services based on innovation and quality, has been stated by the regulations concerning the accreditation of training and guidance structures (based on Ministerial Decree n. 166/2001). Regions are responsible for accreditation procedures and must set up a regional model for accreditation. Every year, Regions are commissioned to verify the maintenance of accreditation requirements.

In this framework are placed the manuals, realized by Isfol on 2004, aimed to offer a technical support both for Regional and Provincial administrations and for training and guidance agencies and operators.

The competences and the training of guidance and counselling personnel in Italy have been subject of an animated debate. The legislative framework doesn't consider the relationship among the actors and the structures in which they operate, both at national and local level; this has led to the multiplication of initiatives and actions involving, often in a confuse way, human resources with different competences and qualifications.

At the current moment, guidance and counselling personnel have different competences and qualifications. The Italian regulation has not yet established neither specific training pathways or minimum requirements for functioning as guidance professional. Following the reform of Employment services (1999) most of guidance activities take place within the Centres for Employment (CPI) or the Agencies for job search (Law n. 30/2003). Guidance activities take place also within schools, universities, vocational training centres, voluntary associations' counselling offices (e.g. *Informagiovani*).

In addition, human resources managers, school and university teachers, communication experts. Usually, the minimum required qualification is an high school degree, but empirical evidence are also qualified for providing guidance services. Professionals have, in most cases, an university degree and/or a master's degree.

The Ministerial Decree n. 166/2001 (Accreditation of subjects providing guidance services) regulates the accreditation of training and guidance structures and states (art. 10) the establishment of minimum standards of professional competencies of guidance professionals. The Decree identifies two subjects dealing with guidance:

- The guidance operator, charged with doing needs diagnosis, planning individual and group guidance interventions, managing welcoming initiatives and screening users needs;
- The tutor of job insertion, charged with analysing local Labour market, planning the assistance intervention for job insertion, counselling, tutoring, managing relations with local stakeholders, supporting users in making their own curriculum and applications.

The State-Regions agreement of 2nd August 2002, defined the credentials of guidance professionals, at Regional level. Subsequently, the description system and the certification of competencies would be harmonized at National level. In 2007 only 8 Regions and Autonomous Provinces established criteria concerning guidance professionals' profiles. In 2008 has been set up – by Isfol and the Ministry of Labour – a School for Guidance Professionals (Scuola per Professionisti dell'Orientamento). The School represents a reference point for the set up of an integrated system for training, updating and competence development of guidance professionals and offers a wide range of high-qualified training courses, seminars and workshops. Many courses and masters are offered also by public and private universities.

Opportunities for young refugees, asylum seekers in the local VET System

No specific courses or programmes are organized and or foreseen for the target of refugees, either in Florence or elsewhere in Italy on a systematic base. Occasionally, local associations accredited as training agencies or other institution of the VET system organize specific courses for immigrants (or rarely for refugees), but usually also these courses are not linked with the real labour market.

During the year 2008, the Toscana Regional Authorities, in the frame of a FSE project, trained trainers in order to have a first group of evaluators able to check and certificate the informally developed competences and skills in the LLL (D.D. 21/11/2007 n.5636). Until now, the opportunity represented by this kind of certification is not yet used for refugees and asylum seekers, who would benefit more doing the fact they often do not have the documents with them (also regarding their formal studies).

4.1 Training and working biographies

Farida tells us that she never went to school and she is illiterate. She speaks Somali, but she cannot read or write. She knows only some words in English, in Norwegian, in Italian. In Somalia she always worked in the countryside, pasturing sheep. When she was in Libya and in Norway she worked as cleaner. In Italy she never managed to work. She declares that she could not find work or a training course because she is alone with a baby to care for.

On the contrary, **Maisa and Zahra** (the other two women), have both attended the school in Somalia. **Zahra** from the age of 7 years old to 15 studied in a school for midwives, and at the end of it she received a diploma. She tells us that, when in 1991 Siad Barre was deposed and the Somali school system was not free anymore, she had to stop her studies, because she had not the financial possibility to go ahead. In Somalia she worked for 14 year in her mother's food shop. From 1997 to 2002 she lived in Saudi Arabia and then in Kuwait and she worked as a carer. Also in 2009, for about 7 months, she worked with a regular contract as a carer near Lecce in Italy.

Amir obtains the Secondary school certificate in 2001 in Somalia (4 years) and he starts to attend the first 2 years of High school (instead of 4). In the meantime, he does many works: he manages the family's oil mill, he works as a cashier in a food shop and he works as a welder. After his arrival in Italy, besides working for some seasonal black labor, he attends for 5 months some evening training classes at a secondary school in order to obtain the diploma.

Hassan tells us that he , left from Somalia with the Elementary school certificate and a baggage of working experience as those of guardian at his father garage, assistant mechanic, baker/pastry chef, bricklayer, cashier in a bazaar, he worked for 2 years as a steel industrial worker and he attended two training courses, the first one for the maintenance of public green spaces (8 months) and an informatics course (72 hours).

Bassam has a different story. He tells us that when he was three years old, he was put in a military college, where there were circa 600 people (children and young minors). In 1991 the war burst out. He remained in this college until 1996, helped by the Red Cross and by another Irish organization. He attended primary and secondary schools at the college, but he was not able to go ahead in his studies, because it was necessary to pay teachers furtively and he had not the possibility to do that. In total, he studied 11 years. He learned English at school and Arabic, reading the Koran and during his stay in Egypt. He worked in Italy with many jobs, as that of farmhand, bricklayer and cleaning work.

Educational and employment biography – Bassam

Where	When	How long	Employment
Palermo	2004	20 days	Farmhand (black labour), 8 hours each day for 15 euros. He ate and slept at the farm.
Bologna	2005	15 days	Bricklayer (black labour)
Firenze	May 2005-July 2007		Industrial work (short term contract)
Firenze	2005	1 month	Farmhand (short term contract)
Firenze	December 2005-April 2006		Bricklayer (black labour)
Firenze	May 2006-July2006		Industrial work (short term contract)
Firenze	September 2006-November 2006		Cleaning work (short term contract)
Firenze	November-December 2006		Farmhand (short term contract)
Firenze	January 2007-May 2007		Cleaning work (short term contract)
Poland	2007-2009		Bricklayer (short term contract)
Firenze	2009-2011		Cleaning work and bricklayer

Educational and employment biography – Zahra

Where	When	How long	Employment
Somalia	1987-1995	8 years	Midwife School and traineeship
Somalia	1986- 1997/ 2003-2007	14 years	job in mother's food shop
Saudi Arabia/Kuwait	1997-2002	5 years	carer
Lecce (Trepuzzi)	2009	7 months	carer

Educational and employment biography – Maisa

Where	When	How long	Employment	Reasons for unemployment
Catania (Sicily)	2007	1 month	Carer	The person died
Aprilia (Roma)	2010	20 days	Carer	The person died
Firenze	2011	2 months	Carer	The person died

Educational and employment biography – Amir

Where	When	Employment
Somalia	2001	Secondary school certificate (4 years)
Somalia	2003	2 years of High school (instead of 4)
Somalia	1998-2006	Managed the family's oil mill, work for the production of *MAKIINAB* (Somali bread), work as a cashier in a food shop, work as a welder
Italia	2008-2011	Seasonal black labor: pruning, olive and grape picking
Italia	2010	Attending for 5 months some evening training classes at a secondary school in order to obtain the diploma

Educational and employment biography – Hassan

Where	When	Employment
Somalia	1996	Elementary school certificate
Somalia	1997-2007	Guardian at his father garage, assistant mechanic, baker/pastry chef, bricklayer, cashier in a bazaar
Italia(Terni)	2008-2010	Steel industrial worker
Italia (Terni)	2008-2010	Intensive course for the maintenance of public green spaces (8 months)
Italia (Terni)	2008-2010	Informatics course (72 hours)

4.2 Italian courses

Farida and Zahra had never the possibility to attend Italian courses. **Farida** does not speak and she does not understand the Italian language, on the contrary **Zahra** has a basic knowledge of it, learnt during the years passed in Italy. Moreover **Zahra** has a basic knowledge of English, and a good knowledge of Arabic, learnt at school in Somalia and when she lived in Saudi Arabia and Kuwait.

Bassam and Amir tells that they attended an Italian course, **Bassam** at the "Villa Pieragnoli" in Florence, **Amir** at the "CARA" in Comiso, but in both cases, for different reasons, the course has not been finished.

Italian courses – Amir

Country	Course duration	Typology of the course
CARA in Comiso	3 months	Circa 40 participants
Association of mutual help *Kulanka*, Firenze	8 months	Circa 15 participants

4.3 Obstacles related to VET system and employment

Amir tells us that he would like to attend a mechanic training course, but the training agencies said always that these kind of courses were not available at the moment. After his arrival in Italy, he went to several employment agencies and he enrolled at the employment center, but they never called him for work.

It is interesting finally to describe the experience of **Hassan**. He tells that at the end of the course for the maintenance of green space which he did in Terni, he did not manage to obtain the certificate of participation and, when he arrived in Florence, he lost a lot of time and energy to obtain it. He would like to become an electrician. He obtained information for training courses but they were too expensive.

4.4 The VET system in the Province of Florence

As already highlighted, the Florence VET system has not specific vocational trainings for refugees or people under International Protection.

The local formal VET system is similar to the national system. The Florence Province Administration manage the VET offer related with the labour market.

The local principal centres are:

1. The **Centro di Formazione Professionale** – CFP of via Capo di Mondo, 66 – directly managed by the Florence Province Administration. Most of the vocational training activities of public and of private agencies are supervised by the CFP. Many of the activities below are directly organized and / or supervised by the CFP:

2. The Adult Education Centres (**Centri Territoriali Permanenti** – **CTP**), instituted by the Ministry of Education, which offer courses for adults and young over 16, namely for attain the primary and secondary schools degrees. Moreover, the CTPs offer courses on Italian as second language, English Language, ITC, etc.

   In the territory of the Florence Municipality, there are 2 CTPs, one inside the "School-Town Pestalozzi" (via delle Casine, 9 in the District N° 1 – Florence City Center) and one inside the middle school "Beato Angelico" (via Leoncavallo, 12, in the Florence District N° 5 – where the higher number of families with non Italian citizenship live).

   In the rest of the Provincial area, there are other 7 CTP:

   Bagno a Ripoli Antella-Grassina, Via Belmonte, 40 – 50012 – Bagno a Ripoli (FI);

   Inside the secondary school "Giovanni della Casa", Via Don Minzoni, 19 (Borgo S. Lorenzo), 50032 – Borgo San Lorenzo (FI);

   Inside the secondary school "Matteucci", Via Buozzi, 65, 50013 – Campi Bisenzio (FI);

   Inside the secondary school "Bacci-Ridolfi", Viale di Vittorio, 31, 50051 – Castelfiorentino (FI);

   Inside the secondary school "Busoni – Vanghetti", Via Liguria, 1, 50053 – Empoli (FI);

   Inside the secondary school "Lastra a Signa", Via Gramsci, 139, 50055 – Lastra a Signa (FI);

   Inside the secondary school "Maria Maltoni", Via Rosano, 16/A, 50065 – Pontassieve (FI).

3. **Corsi serali Comunali** – CSC (Municipality Evening Courses), which offer the possibility for the adults to graduate in the secondary schools of 2nd degree. All the courses are 3 years long and have a duration of 3 year and they permit the access to the University. According to the data of the school year 2010/2011, the students with foreign citizenship, attending the evening courses in Florence were 70: 15 from Perù, 8 from Albania and Romania, 4 from Ucraina, 3 from Brasile, Marocco, Costa d'Avorio, Cina, Russia e Somalia, 1 o 2 from other countries. In total 6 minors, 19 aged 19 – 23 years, 15

over 40. In total 50 women and 22 men. The only control made by the CSC regards the residence permit, necessary to participate in State exams.

Recently, due to the cut in public spending, the Firenze Administration, decided to close the evening courses since next school year. At the same time, the Municipality activated a new educative service for young people, drop out from the 1st or 2nd year of high schools.

4. The **Scuola Professionale Edile di Firenze** – SPEF, is a private school jointly founded by Confindustria Firenze and trade unions Organisations in order to qualify the personnel employed in the building sector.

5. The on line LLL programme **TRIO**, managed by Toscana Region (and co-founded by Italian Ministry of Labour and FSE), namely the "Progetto Stranieri" (Foreigners Project), http://www.progettotrio.it/trio/progetto-stranieri. html , which aim is to "facilitate the foreign citizens integration with the local community through the language literacy, the knowledge of the territory from the cultural and institutional point of view, the labour market rights, duties and principal regulations".

No courses explicitly addressed to refugees and asylum seekers are available in Florence, but the association Arci collects the enrollments by the refugees living in Villa Pieragnoli and Paci for the vocational courses organized by the above described CFP of Florence Province. The courses are organized if it is reached a minimum number of enrolled students. The courses expenses are paid by the Province Administration.

During the interview we made, Arci referents reported that the main difficulties are: the lack of visibility and the lack of informations on vocational courses. In some cases the candidates are not able to provide their educational qualifications documents, often requested for attending the courses. Arci itself organized some courses, i.e.: course for metal-workers (once a year, duration of 3 months); course for kitchen help; course "Perla" for women and disadvantaged people.

Vocational courses and training promoted in Florence by Arci in 2011

Course	Duration	Number of participants	Gender and status	Age	Citizemship	Results of the first 6 months of 2011
Proiect "Perla" 1 leather, 2 catering 1 drop out	40 hours (theoretical)300 hours stage choosed by participants	4	2 M 2 F – 1 asylum seeker 3 refugees	26, 35, 23, 23	1 Azerbajiani 2 Somali 1 Eritrean	1 Drop out 3 Course completed (no job placement)

Course	Duration	Number of participants	Gender and status	Age	Citizemship	Results of the first 6 months of 2011
Prototyping (leather)	250 hours (classroom hours: 170 stage hours: 80)	1	M 1 refugee	24	Somali	Course completed with Certificate of attendance (no job placement)
POP – Percorsi per l'Occupabilità e il Placement – constructions of masonry	760 hours (classroom hours: 120 stage hours: 640)	4	4 M – 1 asylum seeker 3 refugees	28, 23, 31, 31	3 Somali, 1 Turkish	1 Drop out 3 Degrees of professional qualification (1 job placement)
Tourism sector: housekeeping and hotel reception	210 hours (of wich 60 for stage)	2	2 M – 2 asylum seekers asilo	20, 21	1 Albanian, 1 Kosovarian	2 Course completed with Certificate of attendance (no job placement)
Addetto assistenza di base	800 hours	1	M – 1 refugee	22	1 Somali	Certificate of attendance
Cooking course for adults political refugees	226 hours	5	4 M 1 F – 4 asylum seekers 1 refugee	21, 30, 26, 30 23	1 Kosovarian, 2 Turkish, 1 Pakistani 1 Eritrean	4 course completed with Certificate of attendance
Demetra	160 ore + stage	3	2 M 1F – 3 sub-sidiarian protection	36, 26, 21	3 Somali	3 course completed with Certificate of attendance (no job placement)

Vocational courses and training promoted in Florence by Arci in 2010

Course	Duration	Number of participants	Gender and status	Age	Citizemship	Results
Course for welder (Institute Don Facibeni of Firenze)	120 hours	1	1 M _ subsidiary protection	31	1 Somali	1 course completed (no job placement)
Hotel reception (Apifinser of Firenze)	300 hours	4	3M 1F _ 1 asylum seeker, 3 sub-sidiary protec-tion	30	3 Somali, 1 Ivorian	3 course completed with Certificate of attendance. (2 job placement)
Course for electicians (Institute Don Facibeni of Firenze)	120 hours	1	1 M _ subsidiary protection	22	1 Somali	1 course completed (no job placement)
Course Inail on safety inthe work place	210 hours (of wich 60 of stage)	16	3F 13 M _ 2 umanitarian, 6 subsidiary protection, 4 refugees, 4 asylum seekers	20, 21	1 Kurdish, 4 Pakistani, 2 Eritrean, 1 Afgan, 1 Rep. Dem, Congo, 1 Ivorian, 6 Somali	2 course completed with Certificate of attendance (no job placehment)
Domestic care	220 hours + 80 of stage	1	1F asylum seeker	30	1 Ivorian	Certificate of attendance
Welding course (Ipros – Circondario Empolese Valdelsa	600 hours + stage	3	3M _ 1 asylum seeker, 2 umanitarian protection	20, 21, 22	1 Senegalese, 2 Somali	EU Qualification (2 job placements)
Course for metalworkers, only for asylum seekers and political refugees (at Vocational School of Firenze Munici-pality)	250 hours + stage	8	8 M _ 1umanitarian protection,1 refugee, 6 subsidiary protection	18, 30, 30, 36, 24, 23, 25, 36	6 Somali, 1 Afghan, 1 Eritrean	8 Certificate of attendance. (3 job placements)

Chapter 5: Good practices: "Villaggio La Brocchi"

1. STATE/CITY
Italy, Florence

2. Project/organization
Project: Project "Villaggio La Brocchi" **Contacts:** Email: accoglienza@progettoaccoglienza.org Telephone and fax: +39 055 8459800 **Address:** Loc. Cannicce 7/1-2-3, 50032 Borgo San Lorenzo, Firenze **Project manager:** Associazione Progetto Accoglienza **Managing and promoting body:** Associazione Progetto Accoglienza

3. Description of the actions carried out

The "Associazione Progetto Accoglienza" manages:
- the "Casa di Accglienza "Verso Sud"" (is working from October 2004) until 31st December 2011 received 26 families with a total of 93 people from 15 different countries whereof 29 women, 19 men, 42 childreen;
- the "Casa Madre dei Semplici" is working for 19 years and it received 71 families (261 people) coming from 21 different countries;
- The "Casa di Pietro" is an apartment fot long staying and it received 12 families from 3 countries.

The project realizes not only the reception for immigrant families with minors, but it carries out also an accompaniment, training, introduction to work and responsabilization for a real integration. The diversity of the contributions to this center is reflected in the several activities organized, from the reception of the migrant families with minors to the cultural and training manifestations, from the services offered by the Intercultural and Peace Education Documentation Center to the screening of movies and musical evenings, from the hospitality of the house for holidays "La Tinaia" to the multiethnic catering service "Ethnos".

At the same time to the arrival in the center, the health, social, scholastic, literacy, support and integration, training for adults and minors accompaniment starts. These services are offered both internally and through the City social service, the Asl health service, the projects done in collaboration with "Società della Salute" and "Comunità Montana", the public scholastic services and those realized in collaboration with a network more and more crowded of other associations, organized groups and parishes. This center carries out also several training workshops that can be connected to the different competences of the person for adults living in the center. Moreover it carries out art therapy, frame, photography, multiethnic cuisine and arabic workshop. It organizes training courses and internships in some companies. Together with the "Cooperativa Archimede" some gardening courses. In collaboration with "Medici Contro la Tortura" and "Amnesty International", a center operator writes the personal memory of the migrants together with him/her, in order to present it to the Commission for the recognition of the refugee status. The center is working for an additional support project entitled "Far from violence" financed by the European Fund for Refugees (EFR) in a network with other Italian realities that receive vulnerable migrants and in collaboration with

"Società della Salute" and "Comune di Borgo San Lorenzo". With "Istituto degli Innocenti" some workshop for children are organized, with the future project to broaden the participation to the childreen of the territory in order to create some sharing moments, to make the center more dynamic and to estabilish new ties and relationships. Besides the projects carries out in the center, this structure has organized some activities in the schools of "Unione dei Comuni Del Mugello" since ten years ago with literacy courses, intercultural workshops and study groups.

4. Points of force
The atmosphere is welcoming, there is the possibility of use several instruments, a group of close operators, a network of volunteers and voluntary associations. Good relations with the local authorities, with Progetto Nordafrica", with "Centro di Documentazione Interculturale e di Educazione alla Pace". Another point of force is that in the center there is not an high number of people.

5. Criticities and obstacles
The people who arrive in tha last period are more and more psychologically weak for overlapping frailties due to a second forced migration and to the high complexity of the Libyan situation. Many people who migrated in Libya, mainly from Central Africa, were forced to escape again to more precarious situations. In order to give a response to this new situation it would be necessary to carry out reinforced paths and to reduce the waiting times for the legal recognition (all of this with the realization that to 59,9% is denied the refugee status and very probably these people will remain in our territory).
In order to face these more and more complex frailties, we feel the need to constatnly bring ourself up to date and to work in network to share knowledges and experiences.

6. Partner network
"Associazione Progetto Accoglienza" collaborates with "Istituto degli Innocenti" (that is the holder of the structures), "Provincia di Firenze", "Comunità Montana Mugello", "Comune di Borgo San Lorenzo" and "Comune di Firenze", "Prefettura di Firenze", "Regione Toscana".

Chapter 6: Integration problems in Italy for people under international protection

Year by year, critical situations emerge in Italy concerning the effective integration of people under international protection, due both to the deficiency of support instruments to the socio-economic integration of refugees and to the black, informal labour market, independently of the present context of economic crisis and the general level of unemployment in Italy. When refugees exit from the governmental reception centres and/or from the SPRAR system, they remain without any reference points or services. The services provided for by the Local Authorities, where the refugee lives, are often the only support system they have. Even if serious obstacles to the use of these services still remain, as the difficulty or impossibility to obtain the registry enrolment without a stable residence. The consequent failed residence recognition makes the local public services actually inaccessible, in particular social assistance and health care.

A particularly emblematic situation is the one we find in the territory of Florence, if one considers the living and working conditions of the Somali refugees[12].

Access to Regional Health Services and taking residence in Tuscany for those who are entitled to international protection

From the statistics concerning the social-sanitary conditions of those entitled to International Protection, compiled by MEDU (Physicians for Human Rights) inside the occupied building „Kulanka"[13], show that more than 40% of the Somalis that live in this building do not have a National Health card. The impossibility to obtain civic registration does not, indeed, allow them to register with the regional[14]

---

12 " Italy has always been, right from the beginning, one of the Somali refugees' first destinations – because of its colonial history. The statistics concerning Somalis who have asked for political asylum during the past 20 years clearly show that the number of arrivals mirror exactly the political events and the degree of insecurity in Somalia. In 1991 the fall of Siad Barre and the resulting armed uproars that followed caused ca. 1700 Somalis to ask for asylum in Italy. The attempts at pacification that were enacted in the second half of the nineties and during the first years of 2000 reduced the arrivals significantly – they came down to insignificant numbers – whereas in 2003 they rose to 1700, and in 2008, after the continuation of war action and the intervention of the Ethiopian army, the civil war caused, as far as Italy was concerned, the arrival of 4800 asylum seekers. [...] Throughout the nineties, Italy proved to be utterly unprepared to deal with the arrival of Somali refugees showing strong shortcomings in legislation and administrative matters as well as reception structures and integration as concerned. These numbers were always handled from an emergency perspective that has tried to depict „the Somali issue" as a sudden and transitory phenomenon that could be resolved by using ad hoc measures, even though it has in the last 19 years been a lasting phenomenon. In particular, diverse mechanisms in order to protect Somali refugees have been adopted, but never on a wider normative level and always reacting a *posteriori* when situations of uneasiness and difficulties had already come into being. [...] The condition of the Somali refugees was resolved only in 2007, when Italy enacting a European Community norm introduced Sussidiary Protection that was granted to all those who had fled their own country because of armed conflicts – a condition that holds true in the case of Somalia. In the course of the last 18 years, together with the normative shortcomings of the Italian system, a defect in the reception structures and the total lack of a sound strategy of integration, all of which have resulted in an unbearable living condition of Somalis and which, as will be seen, have led to their departure. Particularly the missing residence permit and the ensuing impossibility of taking up any form of work together with the shortcomings of the reception structures have led to Somali refugees' very poor living conditions as well as a situation in which they are denied fair economic resources and housing." C. Fringuello, *L'esodo dei somali in Italia*, in *Rifugiati. Vent'anni di storia del diritto d'asilo in Italia*, C. Hein (a cura di), Donzelli, Roma, 2010.
13 See Chapter 1, 1.3.4., "Occupied buildings in the City and Province of Florence"
14 Article 29 of the Directive 2004/83/CE of the Council (April 29, 2004) which defines the minimal norms for the nations of the European Union concerning the importance of international

Health Service as well as making it impossible to access the Local Authority Housing programme that is part of the social services. In Tuscany, in order to enter an ASL (Local Health Centre) you must show your residence permit and civic registration or a certificate declaring you are actually living in that city and district. To this purpose we would like to quote a study undertaken by MEDU:

> [...] it is always impossible to fulfil this basic requirement or at least very difficult for these refugees due to the fact that the Local Authority has systematically denied up to now civic registration for those who live in occupied buildings. Whereas, according to existing norms, the civic registration – which is a fundamental prerogative to social rights – should be guaranteed as a personal right of a human being for Italian citizens as well as to foreigners who habitually live in Italy – without taking into account the nature of their housing or on whether housing is available or not (2). Even in the case of the number of people who are regularly registered, however, only 54 % has a Health Service card. The remaining refugees, even tough having the right are not registered with the National Health Service because of the bureaucratic difficulties described above.

The main illnesses are affections of the nervous system (28%, mostly headaches) and affections of the respiratory system of different importance (21 %). Gastro-intestinal disturbances, blood-diseases and contagious diseases or parasites represent 14 % of the cases. As, many of these conditions can be resolved at the out-patient departments, refugees must apply for outsource hospital services – paying much. The impossible registration with the Regional Health Care, denies, indeed, the access to physicians of the general health care system which is the normal access to prevention, diagnosis and treatment of the principal problems concerning health, and which guarantees a therapeutic effect[15].

Chapter 7: Excurse: Living on the margins of the City

The City-world

The contemporary city, in each latitude, is subject to the pressure of the migration of populations who move from the suburbs to urban agglomerates.

According to the World Population Prospects, in the period 2000-2010 world migration towards developed countries can be quantified in 2.600.00 people

---

protection. This Directive declares that each member state, country of asylum, must guarantee that persons entitled to international protection have access to health care in the same measure as it is granted to its citizens, with particular mention of people who show signs of special needs (pregnant women, disabled persons, victims of torture etc.)

15   Rule of the Home Office nr. 8 (May 29, 1995). MEDU (Pysicians for Human Rigths), *Citta' senza dimora, Indagine sulle strade dell'esclusione*, Infinito edizioni, 2012, pp. 94-96

every year coming from Asia (50%), Latin American and the Caribbean (30%) and Africa.

According to this data, current migration cannot be compared to the past. The increasing flows towards the cities, urban and peri-urban agglomerates, is representative of the movement of people and families towards better chances in work and life: due to an exponential growth of poverty and inequalities, it is a huge movement restoring the balance of opportunities among a poor and a rich world, a phenomenon which was defined as "urbanizing the poverty" and summarizes different dynamics: the urbanization of the poor or even very poor masses within the countries or, above all, through national borders and the production from the inside of the metropolis of an increasing number of groups who live in conditions of social and urban marginality.

The international organisations that deal with the migration of refugees and asylum seekers (OECD, UN, MIP, UNHCR) and the institution concerned with statistics (for instance, Eurostat) agree in recording some significant changes in the flows towards all European countries, where the most recent migration presents a heterogeneous composition more than the initial phases:

– the increase of the women component, due both to family reunification with men who migrated first, and to women migration *per se*. For example, it is worth to mention the women's flows from the Philippines, Dominican Republic and from Ukraine;
– the growth of the legal "temporary" immigration, which is the basis of seasonal programmes to satisfy the job applications in the sectors that are mostly disqualified and abandoned by autochthones;
– the growth of humanitarian immigration. The movements caused by droughts, conflicts, political repression etc. have increased the number of refugees and asylum seekers. The OECD stated that the proportion of these groups on the total amount of immigrants consists of 10% of the long term immigration;
– finally, the growth of not authorized immigration; some estimates state that immigrants without legal permits represent the 1-2% of the total resident population in the European Union, notwithstanding that this data may vary according to the State taken into consideration.

The European cities are nowadays border-territories that have the increasing responsibility to research new integration policies and this responsibility grows according to the general reduction of the welfare.

The territory, the physical space of the city, due to the fact that it incorporates the signals of relations and integrations, has a decisive role in including and marginalizing the immigrants.

That is why nowadays in the territory, in the urban and living integration lies the challenge of immigration and the territorial and living factors, more than ever, determine the decisions on policies to be adopted and the results of the fulfilled ones.

How does the city – space and the social system, activities and changes in relations – work in the framework of the integration of immigrants? How does it contribute to include and exclude? How can the planning and the programmed action contribute to make a "plural city"?

The difficult living

Immigration is a structural and dynamic phenomenon that has always influenced, continuously and deeply, the urban fabric and the shape of the city. The plural city is a theme linked to the big intercultural tradition of the cosmopolitan city in which the presence and the relation with the Other represents for the "host of hosted" population an enrichment and a chance to renovation.

Under each latitude, immigration is the urban pattern: in the countries of origin it is a process of rural exodus towards the cities, which determines the explosion of the old social and urban fabric; this kind of movement goes from the city of the country of origin to the cities of the host country and then towards territories which are mostly permeable to the settlements of new people.

After twenty years from the first significant arrivals of migrants in Italy and Tuscany, this urban dimension of immigration has been subjected to the "social matter" through which it was declined. A "social" build up on assistance and control: reception and marginalization.

This double face of the policies and public discourses on immigration is particularly visible in the living context. The living integration is the most critical about the integration conditions of immigrants. The arrival of new components of immigration, the different components of new arrivals, the increase of the families, the stabilization on the territory, as well as the main presence of immigrants living under severe discomfort, living in conditions of exclusion, have developed and at the same time polarized the living demand of immigrants.

We can state that, on the basis of research works made by various research centres (Censis, Cnel, Ismu, Nomisma, Scenari Immobiliari, Sunia), there has been no improvement in the field of living opportunities and the quality of solutions in correspondence to a relevant increase of immigrants in job, income, social access to all services.

This living vulnerability is not necessarily linked to a particular condition of socio-economic discomfort: it seems to be even present at whatever level of integration immigrant families may be. Other than an evident over-representation of immigrants in the severe discomfort level, a lot of immigrants, who are not poor, live in bad conditions, while those who are poor are often homeless; sometimes these precarious conditions concern easily the immigrants who have a job and an income.

With the aspirations and expectations of the immigrants, what emerges from various research reports (Censis, Cnel, Ismu, Nomisma, Scenari immobiliari, Sunia, Uil and some documents from Michelucci Foundations) is a situation of structural and continuous disadvantage of the immigrants in the access to housing compared to Italian people, with the same economic and working conditions and whatever their social integration is. This could be summarised in some final considerations.

1. The first and important consideration is that the immigrants are particularly affected by discomfort and by the living exclusion and they have risk profiles which diverse – because specific – from the rest of the population. They are negatively influenced by the general difficult framework of the housing market and of the procedures of accessing to housing, and by other disadvantages. From a policy planning point of view, it means that we must understand what the immigrants' living discomfort is about and what, instead, overlaps the other form of discomfort concerning the population. On the one side there are groups of immigrants who suffer from problems of ordinary living discomfort: these are difficulties similar to the ones we can observe in a lot of segments of the population with low income; on the other side there are situations that face conventional policies because close to marginality. For both kinds of situations the signals of discomfort are shown in a specific form in the immigrant population (Tosi, 1994).

2. The disadvantages of the immigrants have both a direct feature (it means that they are intentionally directed against specific categories: in our case the rules that limit the immigrants' access to the opportunities offered by public housing or the discrimination in the access to rent) and an indirect feature (it concerns the difficulties that aside from a discriminatory intention are caused by an unfavourable context for the underprivileged, for example the socio-economic profile, the working conditions, the insufficiency of the living welfare policies).

3. The research data show that, in the migration universe, the conditions tend to polarize and to differentiate, tracing the articulation and segmentation of the majority society. The boom in the buying of houses by immigrants in 2004-2007 and the majority condition of autonomous rent of their families are index of progression under the living profile; however, this positive index goes together with a growth of the discomfort and living exclusion situations, in a superior proportion compared to the ones of the rest of population (although the phenomena of living poverty grows even among Italians).

103

4. The over-representation of immigration in poverty and living exclusion situations aim at neglecting the problems that affect also the immigrants who have an autonomous rent or a shared one: overcrowding, inadequate housing, an excessive rent burden even under standard situations.

What we are illustrating is a picture with light and shadows which paints a contradictory map of the living integration situation that takes place on a large scale in the free rent market (and recently even in the buying market).

The public policies have not influenced a lot, they have only postponed the general measures (the immigrants must have the same opportunities to access housing and the same assistance or support as the Italians) without taking into consideration that the laws and norms (national and local) maintain or increase the disadvantage conditions that affect immigration. The examples are numerous: the permit to stay, at least for two years, to access the opportunity to public housing, the verification of the habitability for family reunification, the difficulty in obtaining/maintaining the permit to stay, the discrimination on the private market, the worse difficulties in access to credit. The few specific conditions (such as the one of the "Centri di Prima Accoglienza" – "First Reception Centres") are not linked to the latest opportunities anymore, which are living and autonomous.

The question moves towards the terrain of policies and conditions that determines hierarchies and priorities.

Precarious living

The most critical aspect is the one concerning the presence of many immigrants living in precarious and informal living conditions. According to the report published by UN-HABITAT, the UN agency for the living settlement, the big movements towards urban areas determine the creation of "slums", which is a word used to define a complex variety of situations that in other languages are indicated with specific local names and often with more than one for the same language.

The new shantytowns constitute one of the "city-world" scenarios: according to the definition by the anthropologist Marc Augé (2007)

"[…] urbanisation has two contradictions but at the same time indivisible aspects. On one side, the world becomes […] a big city where you can find everywhere the same big economic and financial firms, the same products […]. On the other side, the city, the big city, represents one world. […] The differences within the world, the difference between rich and poor, the ethnic differences, the cultural difference, the difference of origin and conditions: in the big city everything is mixed up. […] in the city-world exists violence, exclusion, ghettos, young and less young, different generations, immigrants, clandestine: in one word, everything complex and unequal that exists in the world".

Although the word slum is applied to a large variety of typologies of urban settlement, what they have in common is the fact that they are areas characterized by social and economic isolation, property or irregular property entitlement and health and environmental conditions under the standard living conditions.

In the case of Tuscany Region and in particular in the case of the metropolitan area of Florence immigration is mostly present in precarious living conditions. Marginal and transitional situations of improvised living, concerning groups of immigrants in the first phase of their social and working integration process or in problematic phases of migration flows, in the context of the search of a minimum possibility of ordinary survival.

Together with an interesting majority, of people and families of immigrants who have integrated in the local society positively, there is an increasing minority of groups who live under discomfort conditions and who are in informal and precarious living solutions, even though they do not face any particular condition of poverty and marginality.

The extension of this phenomenon coincides with the processes of transformation of the urban panorama. In the suburban areas of the cities (even in some parts of the historical centres), in a chaotic dynamic of urban transformation, we find marginal spaces, abandoned urban empty spaces or others waiting for a new destination, where evictees, immigrants, people and a population of diminished and precarious situation find a housing possibility.

The geography of poverty

The map of precarious living in the metropolitan area of Florence illustrates the strategies of people and families who find themselves obliged to live in slums: together with situations (usually of a small and medium consistency) to be found in the abandoned spaces of the city centre in an apparent casual order in the suburban places. There are not, at a first glance, any readable dynamics, however the informal settlement map illustrates the uncertain process of transformation of the economic, territorial and infrastructural systems in their dialectic with the centres and government instruments. A process that implies asynchronies, incoherencies of time and space where informal living finds that transitory permeability that the city of the historical centres and the consolidated suburban areas do not permit, almost never. There is a gap, a break in the city and its contrary and it is not easy to recompose it at a first glance. However, the two cities – the official and invisible ones – mix up not only in the space but also from the point of diachronic view.

People in the slums

More than giving purely quantitative data, the interest of our researchers was to comprehend and deepen the genesis of different situations, their evolution or the reason why they become chronic.

Forms of precarious living have always concerned immigration, above all in the first phases following the arrival, or in situations where a short term migration project brought some groups to accept precarious living solutions in order to concentrate economic resources in remittances or in savings to return home. The characteristic of these situations was their being transitional and reversible within the integration processes which concerned also the living situation, even if with a bigger effort compared to the working dimensions.

The observation of the phenomenon we are dealing with, beyond the strong variability of places and the settlement consistency, maintained a quite stable dimension through the years and it dealt with the same families and groups. It is a sign of a specific weakness of some of the most recent components of immigration.

In this new scenario where significant components of immigrants are involved in phenomena of marginalization and social exclusion, what emerges is a specific risk that particularly concerns the new arrivals.

Other than the immigrants recently arrived, there are people who belong to minorities such as Roma people from Romania, or the emigration of refugees or displaced persons.

The data of our study show the absolute prevalence of citizens coming from Romania (44% on the total); the second nationality until nowadays, as it was in 2007 and 2008, is Morocco (20% on the total); Somalis represent 17%, and mostly they are asylum seekers or immigrants with the status of a "humanitarian permit".

Towards a plural city

The phenomena of exclusion and marginalization of the population in the urban territories depends on the old functioning system of local political-administrative institutions.

Today these phenomena, which are new for our countries, imply a dislocation of the social policies: including the assignment of new functions to urban and living policies (such as the functions of the prevention of social exclusion, the ones of possible conflicts and the ones to balance the management of living together).

A house is not only an object, a pure and simple shelter. Vice versa it is a complex good, a group of goods, material and symbolic. The rootedness and the belonging to the city begin from the house and receive an impulse from the systematization in a dignified building.

Even when one manages to "survive" (such as a precarious job, some kind of income or a minimum basis of survival), the instability and the inferiority of living conditions causes who suffers this the denial of full recognition of the right to citizenship and condemns them to an exclusion zone, and to a diminished existence. (Paba, 2001).

A new idea of an urban citizenship is strictly linked to a decisive action against all forms of segregation and subordination of the populations who live in the city. A plural city, hospitable, permeable, is the propaedeutic space for a new local democracy.

In an open world, the forced destiny of the cities will consist in making a plural and fragmented multitude to live together. Pointing at exclusion, the reduction of the rights of immigrants as a great danger which will make more difficult and risky the challenge that everyone must face.

Generally speaking, the challenge is to change the way we think about and govern the city. In the new institutional framework the planning of new and more efficient social policies is essentially the capability of the regional governments and the municipalities to innovate. All of the changes that have occurred – and all of the most significant laws in recent years – give important competences to the Regions and to the Municipalities.

A fundamental point to put in practice these objectives, is the awareness that the immigrants are not the "problem" of the city, but they are an important part in the solution of these problems, in the renewal of its identity.

Immigration is not only a source of labour force for a continent that needs it. It is not only a demographic resource for the reproduction of the European societies, to face the ageing of the societies and to finance the pensions' system.

Above all, immigration is a human resource which renews the social capital of these societies. It allows cultural diversity which is necessary to secure the complexity of a social system and its ability to adapt to its evolution.

More than integration of the immigrants in the city, we should talk about the movement of co-production of the city, something like "doing-together" with a reciprocal adaptation of who hosts and who is hosted. A process which is often in conflict and always violent for who emigrates because departure is always a terrible uprooting, something that causes insecurity for oneself and for one's relatives. And on this insecurity of the departure further suffered in the hosting countries and for which we blame the immigrants.

If politics is the art to govern these different questions in the public space and to invent new and essential compromises among contradictory interests, then immigration must be put in place as a political question, in the real sense of the word, because it needs, if not genius (nobody can do the impossible), at least a bit of courage.

Chapter 8: Recommendations

As a general premise, it is necessary to evidence that the general problem in Italy for refugees and asylum seekers is that up to now there is no specific law protecting their status. This fact influences the insertion of refugees and asylum seekers not only in the VET system, but also in the labour market, in housing, etc. It is fundamental the approval by Italian Government of a comprehensive law on the protection of asylum seekers and refugees, which must be in line with both international instruments and legal standards on the subject and with the national legislation on immigration.

Our specific recommendations take into account the concrete situation of the city of Florence, structural deficiencies, individual problems, etc. As regards statistics, at local level (as at Italian national level) we have difficulties to have official disaggregated data, which would be of considerable help when organizing the VET system for asylum seekers and refugees on the basis of their specific needs.

Even the school teachers, as the trainers of the local VET system, do not know, and therefore are not able to face, the specific needs, expectations and hopes or problems of this specific target group.

So the first recommendation is:

Monitoring the life situations of refugees, asylum seekers, unaccompanied minors and their educational needs.

In keeping with the specifications currently applicable in Florence, monitoring of integration policy measures and the social and educational reporting puts until now the focus on migrant groups or in a generically defined "foreign origin" group. It does not take account of asylum seekers or persons having the legal title to stay as refugees: in facts the local authorities, schools teachers and professional centres trainers even do not know that this target group exist. It is essential to involve teachers and trainers in the process of checking, analyzing and monitoring the situation and of identifying problems and possible solutions, aimed to eliminate inequality and disadvantages of these groups. Particularly with respect to educational planning, it is important to collect data regularly on the educational participation of refugees in the various districts schools and VET agencies/centres, and to use the data for evaluation of implemented activities. The goal should be to prepare a qualitative, problem-related educational report, giving indications for the policy makers in education and vocational training in Florence.

The second recommendation is:

Creating a network among unaccompanied minors host communities and the local entities concerned with schooling, VET, labour insertion, in order to let unaccompanied minors to be defended from labour exploitation and from the risk to become illegal when 18 years old.

The situation of youngster is even more worse: namely when they arrive in Italy, without parents and often without documents, usually aged around 16 or 17, according to the law, they must be inserted in a host community for minors. In some days 60% of them move away (from some place the rate arise 100 %), in particular when they are inserted (unlawfully) in centers for adults, as often happens. In order to try to shorter the long times of the procedures for asylum, many other minors declare to be over 18.

It is difficult to know how many among them join relatives or friends and how many enter in the circuit of children labour exploitation. Sometimes, they are put unlawfully into the Immigrants Detention Centers (Centri di Identificazione e Espulsione – CIE) or in the Centres for asylum seekers (Centri di Accoglienza per Richiedenti Asilo – CARA) together with adults. The only legal way in fact is their insertion in community-houses for children or in foster families, but also in Florence, as evidenced by the interviews, many of them live in occupied building, without relatives. Also for those who are regularly in communities, courses of Italian language are not frequently activated and only few of them attend school or VET.

For obtaining the residence permit, when they become adult, they must have regularly frequented at least 2 years of courses. The above mentioned precarious situation in facts compromises this possibility and the day of their 18 birthday often become the day in which they receive the expulsion order from Italy. Usually they don't leave Italy, but they became illegal.

In order to protect minors asylum seekers from the risk of children labour exploitation and from the other above described risks, it is necessary to insert them as soon as possible in the educational system, creating a network among host communities and the other local entities concerned with schooling, VET, labour insertion.

II.

A life in limbo: Barriers to VET and labour market integration for asylum-seekers waiting for the granting of Leave to Remain

Pamela Clayton, Paul McGill & Sarah-Jane Pretty

Introduction

After intensive research into the situation of refugees and asylum-seekers [in Glasgow] in terms of their integration into the educational and labour market, it was decided that the focus of the Glasgow city report would be specifically on asylum-seekers as the main target group. Without the decision for 'leave to remain', a refugee does not have 'refugee status' and is classified as an 'asylum-seeker'. The consequential barriers to educational and labour market integration of this particular group are focused on along with their stress, frustration and disengagement caused by the asylum process in the UK.

Section 1 gives a brief description of the history of settlement in Glasgow by both economic migrants and refugees fleeing from oppressive regimes and wars. Section 2 details the statistic profiles of both recognized refugees and asylum-seekers. Section 3 maps formal and non-formal vocational education and training structures that can be accessed by migrants and analyses how accessible some of these are for asylum-seekers. Section 4 describes the biographies of seven refugees and explores the barriers and protective factors (external and internal) in relation to integration. Section 5 explains the 2002 Nationality and Immigration Act and its impact on asylum-seekers in terms of access to employment, in particular – an exclusive policy that goes against the grain of the inclusive ethos of the Scottish Government and formal and non-formal support networks in Glasgow. Section 6 is a case study on an example of 'Good Practice' and Section 7 details some recommendations from the findings of the city report.

Acknowledgement and thanks are owed to Maggie Lennon from the Bridges Programmes; Gareth Mulvey from the Scottish Refugee Council, and Rose Filippi and Remzije Sherifi from the Maryhill Integration Network who have all kindly taken time out of their busy schedules to review and give valuable feedback during the writing of the report. Acknowledgement and thanks are also owed to Paul McGill for his contribution by writing much of the report, and to Rose Filippi for arranging and interviewing refugees/asylum-seekers for the biographies – due to the sudden and terminal illness of Pamela Clayton who, sadly, could no longer continue with this work.

1. A short history: Glasgow and the Scottish context

From the seventeenth century onwards, Glasgow has been settled by several groups of migrants. The first main group consisted of economic migrants from Ireland. In the early nineteenth century thousands of displaced Highlanders, evicted by their landlords, made their homes in Glasgow and later in the century European Jews established communities which still exist in the south of the city. After the Second World War, Indians and Pakistanis arrived and by 1971 there were about 12,000 living in Glasgow. Other newcomers included Italians, Poles and Chinese. By the 2001 census 5.5 per cent of Glasgow's residents described themselves as other than "white", of which the biggest group was of Pakistani ethnic origin. Glasgow's current population is around 578,000.

Scotland has a population of around 5.3 million. Statistics from the National Records Office Scotland indicate that the number of people living in Scotland who were born abroad has grown further recently. There was an increase in 2004 from 204,000 to 326,000 in 2010. The five most common overseas countries of birth were Poland (53,000), India (26,000), Republic of Ireland (22,000), Germany (20,000) and Pakistan (16,000). According to the Scottish Refugee Council, 18,000 asylum-seekers have been dispersed to Glasgow since 2001 and Glasgow City Council's estimated in October 2010 that there were 2,800 refugees and 3,500 asylum-seekers living in the city.

The first recognized refugees arrived in Glasgow in the late twentieth century, fleeing from oppressive regimes and wars, notably coming from Uganda, Vietnam and the Balkans. In 1999 and 2000 Glasgow participated in a short-term reception programme for refugees from Kosovo – organized by NGOs (non-governmental organizations). The 1999 Immigration and Asylum Act was enacted in order to disperse asylum-seekers from London and the South-East to other regions of the United Kingdom which had more housing available. A new agency was established, NASS (the National Asylum Support Service), which made contracts with local councils that would provide support and accommodation. In 2006 NASS ceased to exist and its functions were taken over by the UKBA (United Kingdom Border Agency). Glasgow City agreed to accept asylum-seekers in 1999 and in 2000 signed a contract with NASS to provide 6,000 accommodation units. Glasgow was to become the destination of the largest number of dispersed asylum-seekers of any single local authority in the United Kingdom[1].

---

1   Source: www.icar.org.uk/?lid=9982.

2. Statistic of the target group

It must be clarified at the outset that the term 'asylum-seeker' refers to those (aged 18+) who have newly arrived in the country and are waiting for the decision as to whether or not they may be allowed to stay in the UK on the grounds that it would be dangerous for them to be deported. As will be shown later, the term 'newly' is misleading, as asylum-seekers can wait for a long time before a decision is made. The term 'refugee' refers to those who have been granted leave to remain in the UK and are now recognized as bona fide 'refugees'. It is important to differentiate between the two groups [as their situations are not the same] and therefore, their statistical profile is presented by this report in the following two sub-sections.

2.1 Statistical profile of Glasgow's refugees & others given Leave to remain

Refugees are entitled to the same rights as any United Kingdom citizen, including full access to education, housing, employment and the health service.

It is much harder to find information on refugees given permission to stay, and since individuals awarded ELR (Exceptional Leave to remain)[2]; HP (Humanitarian Protection) or DL (Discretionary Leave) are not tracked by the Home Office, it is difficult to know how many there are in Glasgow[3]. Although many do stay in Glasgow and some refugees from other cities join fellow-nationals living in close proximity in various parts of the city, for the same reason some Glasgow asylum-seekers go to other major cities once allowed so to do. The DWP reported that 2,080 refugees in Glasgow were registered job-seekers in 2005 and in 2006 there were 500 refugee children in school. Job-seekers faced considerable difficulties, despite a DWP nationwide survey showing that before arriving in the United Kingdom, nearly all refugees had formal education, over half were qualified and nearly a quarter had a degree, over 40 per cent had been employed and 17 per cent spoke English well. After arrival, 60 per cent spoke English well, largely due no doubt to their participation in ESOL classes, 15 per cent were in education (3 per cent studying for a degree) and 4 per cent were in training; but fewer than one-third were in employment, concentrated in low paid employment, with some earning below the NMW (National Minimum Wage). This was despite a hunger to work and contribute, and despite often holding

---

2   ELR status no longer exists per se.
3   Source: www.icar.org.uk/?lid=9982.

highly skilled employment in their countries of origin. Many of those in employment had fixed term employment, employment via agencies and in some cases zero hours contracts. Nearly one third had undertaken voluntary work in the United Kingdom. Proficiency in English was the single most important factor in finding a job and at a decent level[4]. This latter assertion has been questioned, however, due to later research (detailed in the next paragraph), that employment outcome figures were not any higher in the sample of migrants from English speaking countries.

More up-to-date, but similar figures for Scotland – not Glasgow exclusively – have been produced by the Scottish Refugee Council's findings in 2010 of 262 questionnaire responses (as part of its ongoing longitudinal study of refugee integration). The sample includes people who arrived in 1998 through to 2010, with higher numbers responding who arrived in 2007 – 2009. Interestingly, there is a higher representation of women in the sample than of men. With regards to issues around employment, it was found that of the 262 respondents only 32 were in some form of paid employment. Large numbers were unemployed or in education: 59 were unemployed, 64 were in education and 49 were not allowed to work. Those in work tended to be in low paid, low status jobs; many worked casually with restricted hours. Ten respondents worked full-time – that is, over 30 hours per week – but only 2 people earned over £15,000 per annum and 3 people were paid under £10,000 per annum, thereby not achieving the national minimum wage. About 71% of the respondents had worked in their country of origin; the contrast between the occupations that they had had and the jobs they were doing now highlighted that underemployment was high. For example, one woman working as a cleaner used to be a teaching assistant; a few care assistants used to be teachers; a postal worker used to be a silk screen printer[5].

The new government Work Programme (launched across the UK in June 2011) for those registered unemployed (and are therefore on Job-Seekers Allowance) for more than twelve months has not helped those refugees attending the programme who need specialist support away from this mainstream provision and who are now denied access to those parts of the Bridges Programmes'[6] training opportunities which are funded by the European Social Fund (ESF)[7]. The Scottish Refugee Council also has a service for refugees funded by ESF and so the same restrictions apply to them. The Work Programme is a serious barrier to

---

4   Source: www.asylumscotland.org.uk/asylumstatistics.php.

5   Source: Mulvey (2011).

6   See Best Practice, Section 6 of this report for information on the Bridges Programmes.

7   This is because the ESF funding cannot be used to help people who are on other funded schemes, such as the Work Programme.

specialist intervention support despite the fact specialist interventions are the ones that work. The consequences are that refugees are more likely to be left with low-skilled, low-paid jobs.[8]

Since educational institutions do not normally collect information about the status of their students in terms of whether they are refugees or not, it is not possible to know how many have entered vocational training in the formal sector. Finance (e.g. for travel costs and learning materials) and childcare have been identified by the Scottish Refugee Council as the major barriers to entry into full-time education.

2.2 Statistical profile of Glasgow's asylum-seekers

Although there are barriers to integration into VET and the labour market for people with refugee status in Glasgow (as aforementioned), the focus of this report is on the difficulties faced in particular by asylum-seekers due to a legal framework that denies them access to employment and full-time vocational training and education; thereby making integration into Glaswegian society a lot more difficult.

Surveys of asylum-seekers were carried out in 2006 and 2008. The 2006 survey was carried out by COSLA (Convention of Scottish Local Authorities) and data is also included from a DWP (Department of Work and Pensions) survey and a Scottish Refugee Council report. The 2008 survey was reported by ICAR (Information Centre about Asylum-Seekers and Refugees). Over 5,000 asylum-seekers were living in Scotland in August 2006, of which all but 82, who were living with friends or relatives elsewhere, were in Glasgow, whose total population was 578,800. According to Home Office figures, almost half came from six countries: Iran, Pakistan, the Democratic Republic of Congo, Somalia, Turkey and Iraq. Other notable countries of origin included Afghanistan, Albania, Algeria, China, Nigeria, Sri Lanka, Sudan and Zimbabwe. Just under a quarter came from a mixture of other countries. There were over 1,500 children attending school in Glasgow, of whom two-thirds were in primary school. Until 2006 all dispersed asylum-seekers lived in Glasgow City Council property, but this was changed in that year. Fourth-fifths were living in GHA (Glasgow Housing Association) property under contract to Glasgow City Council property while the rest were housed by the YMCA (now known as Ypeople), Glasgow and the Angel Group. Although scattered around the city, the majority lived in a relatively

---

8   Sources: Maggie Lennon (Director of Bridges Programmes) and http://www.bridgesprogram mes.org.uk.

small number of neighbourhoods. Despite NASS support for those whose claims were under consideration, there were at least 154 destitute asylum-seekers and refugees, including dependent children, recorded by the Scottish Refugee Council[9].

In 2008 Glasgow was still the city with the largest number of dispersed asylum-seekers in the United Kingdom and although the national composition was similar there appears to have been greater geographical concentration. The majority now lived in Sighthill, in the north of the city. In January 2008 there were 3,913 asylum-seekers receiving accommodation and support; 606 failed applicants receiving support; and 55 receiving subsistence only. The numbers in all categories had fallen since 2005. The biggest national group receiving full support was now from Turkey[10]. In November 2010 the UKBA cancelled its contract with Glasgow City Council on the grounds of cost and stated its intention to give accommodation contracts to the private and voluntary sectors. However, in November 2011 the housing contract was given to the private company Serco Limited (Serco Civil Government) for Scotland and Northern Ireland (and they are not obliged to provide housing for failed asylum-seekers).

Asylum-seekers do not have the right to take up paid employment opportunities or full-time vocational education or training (16+ hours per week) that leads towards formal qualifications. The main options therefore are ESOL learning and voluntary work. While these can be helpful routes towards future employment should they be granted leave to remain, many asylum-seekers find it difficult to secure suitable voluntary work, and some may even find difficulties finding suitable ESOL provision, as was found in the research interviews with a sample of asylum-seekers (see the biographies). Additionally, demand for ESOL classes far outstrips provision, with a current waiting list of 900-1,000 across the city, according to Maggie Lennon, director of the Bridges Programmes[11], who stated that the impact of this means that asylum-seekers whose English level is low cannot access vocational programmes (for health and safety reasons). Furthermore, many ESOL classes take place in the afternoon and this is not suitable for those with children. To exacerbate the situation even further, there is more uncertainty about ESOL provision (along with other learning provision) as colleges in Glasgow are facing cuts and having to look at merging together – as is the case for Anniesland, Cardonald, and Langside Colleges. There are also cuts in community-based ESOL provision. Often the voluntary work that asylum-seekers are able to take up is based with projects aimed at helping asylum-seekers in Glasgow. Therefore, opportunities to integrate with the wider community are restricted.

---

9   Source: www.asylumscotland.org.uk/asylumstatistics.php.
10   Source: www.icar.org.uk/?lid=9982.
11   See Best Practice, section 6 of this report for more information on the Bridges Programmes.

The process of seeking asylum and refugee status can be time-consuming and stressful, as confirmed in interviews with asylum-seekers and refugees in Glasgow. Asylum-seekers have reported frustration at long delays for the Home Office to come to a decision about granting indefinite Leave to Remain and subsequent appeal delays. The UKBA often appeal against their initial decision being over-turned in the courts. Policies were introduced to counter the length of time it took to make decisions. The Case Resolution Directorate was established in 2006 to clear the backlog of 450,000 asylum cases still outstanding after several years, with the plan for them all to be resolved by July 2011. The consequence of Case Resolution was that 90% of asylum-seekers in Glasgow who met the criteria to be assessed in this way were granted Leave to Remain. The 2007 National Asylum Model (NAM), which also took over any outstanding Case Resolution cases, aimed to ensure that cases were dealt with promptly in order for rapid removal or integration to take place. These policies were welcomed in part by such organizations as the Refugee Council and the Equality and Human Rights Commission, but they raised concerns over certain issues, such as Case Resolution decisions giving people Leave to Remain outside 'refugee status' which effectively denied them full refugee rights, and lack of time for cases to be properly prepared under NAM[12]. Paradoxically, the quickness of decisions where Leave to Remain is granted can cause problems for asylum-seekers who find themselves with refu-gee status and may no longer have access to support given to asylum-seekers. One problem is that although they may now be entitled to full integration into the labour market, their level of English may prevent them from accessing employ-ment. Despite the speeding up of decision-making processes under NAM however, there are – albeit far fewer than before, according to Maggie Lennon – still those who slip through the net, in particular where it comes to appeal processes.

Those asylum-seekers whose applications fail can find themselves destitute, with no entitlement to housing, public funds or employment. According to an article in the Inside Housing website in June 2012, a survey conducted by Glasgow Caledonian University [and commissioned by the charities Refugee Survival Trust, the British Red Cross and Scottish Refugee Council] found that out of 364 asylum-seekers presenting to 13 support agencies across Glasgow during a period of one week in March 2012, eighty-eight were destitute as they had been refused asy-lum and their appeal rights were exhausted. The average time of destitution was one-and-a-half years. (One survey participant had been destitute for six-and-a-half years.) Twenty-nine countries were represented in the group of destitute

---

12   For full details, see: http://www.refugeecouncil.org.uk/policy/briefings/2009/caseresolutionsupdate and www.equalityhumanrights.com/uploaded_files/research/refugees_and_asylum_seekers_re search_ report.pdf.

asylum-seekers; the most common being Iran, Iraq, Sudan and Zimbabwe. Gary Christie, head of policy at the Scottish Refugee Council, is quoted in the article: *'Destitution is not a policy failure by the Home Office, it is a policy outcome. [...]'*[13]

3. Vet provision in Glasgow and legal framework for access

3.1 Formal VET system

In Scotland formal VET takes place in colleges and in the workplace environments. Vocational training is mainly targeted at young people aged 16-18 years. There are Skillseekers and Modern Apprenticeships programmes where the young person spends most of their time on placement with an employer, and a smaller proportion of their time within a learning environment – in most cases a college, often on a day-release basis, where they work towards nationally recognised qualifications awarded by the Scottish Qualifications Authority (SQA). Asylum-seekers are legally prevented from participating in such programmes because they are full-time training opportunities for which the Scottish Government provides funding. Whilst there are other vocational training programmes aimed at older workers, these are often driven largely by labour market needs and are subject to short-term funding to meet any gaps in the labour market. There are from time to time government-funded programmes aimed at specific groups facing barriers and disadvantages in the labour market in general, or in specific sectors, for example initiatives that target men into care work, or older workers into semi-skilled manual employment.

The college sector in Scotland has traditionally provided a wide range of vocational educational programmes, although in more recent years colleges have offered academic programmes such as Higher National Certificates and Diplomas that articulate directly with degree programmes at universities. Vocational programmes do continue to be offered by colleges through both part-time and full-time modes of study, although the vast majority of the provision is full-time. Again, programmes lead to nationally recognized qualifications and attract government funding, so asylum-seekers would not be able to access these opportunities. Once refugee status has been granted, however, there would be the possibility of access, although other barriers may be presented, such as finance, travel costs, child care, and lack of suitable entrance qualifications and insufficient level of skill in

---

13   Source: http://www.insidehousing.co.uk/care/one-in-four-glasgow-asylum-seekers-are-destitute/ 6522282.article.

English language. Colleges in Glasgow have supported asylum-seekers in other ways, such as provision of ESOL and other non-formal programmes (see below). Some of the ESOL provision in Glasgow has had a vocational element, for example ESOL for the construction sector or social care sector.

In the higher education (university) sector the most likely barrier to accessing full-time study to any recent arrival in the UK would be funding, given that there is a three-year residence requirement in order to qualify for financial support for fees, student loan and means-tested bursaries. Those not ordinarily domiciled in Scotland would be liable for paying substantial overseas fees for studying. Children from asylum-seekers families can enroll at school immediately upon arrival and there are EAL (English as an Additional Language) teachers in school with high numbers of overseas pupils. The Scottish Government set out in 2007 that young people from asylum-seeker families who had lived in Scotland for three years could be granted the same funding status as those ordinarily resident. In Scotland there is a part-time fee waiver scheme, which means that part-time study at higher education is free to those in receipt of state benefits and on low incomes. As asylum-seekers are supported by the National Asylum Support Service (NASS)[14] and, being outside the state benefit system, are not counted as being on a 'low income', they cannot access part-time study at higher education level through the fee waiver scheme.

Before the 1st July 2012, those who did not qualify for the fee waiver scheme, and those in further or higher education may have been eligible for an Individual Learning Account (ILA), which is an annual award that people could register for who earned below the national average income (set currently at £22,000). Learning had to be provided by a recognized institution and lead towards a qualification[15]. Asylum-seekers were never entitled to ILA anyway, but the changes in eligibility criteria since the 1st July 2012 have had a serious impact on refugees already studying in ESOL programmes. This is because only people who are not in education, do not have a degree or above and are not taking part in a National Training Programme (Modern Apprenticeship, Get Ready for Work or Training for Work) can apply for ILA[16]. In a nutshell, nobody who is in further or higher education can now access ILA. This therefore includes refugees attending ESOL programmes who now cannot access ILA funding support for vocational training.

Although, technically, asylum-seekers are not entitled access to full-time further education courses, colleges do have the discretion to waive fees and provide

---

14 For information on NASS please see website: http://en.wikipedia.org/wiki/National_Asylum _Support_Service.

15 Source: http://www.ilascotland.org.uk/ILA+Homepage.htm.

16 Source: http://www.ilascotland.org.uk/News+and+Events/News+and+Events.htm.

bursaries and many asylum-seekers, according to Maggie Lennon, have actually been able to access full-time vocational training, including HNC's (Higher National Certificates) and HND's (Higher National Diplomas). What has changed is that the rise in numbers of migrants from Eastern Europe soaking up fee waivers and bursaries detrimentally affects asylum-seekers' access.

The other main means by which people gain qualifications and develop their careers is through combining studying for qualifications with paid employment. Many professions have a requirement that members undertake a certain amount of continuing professional development annually in order to maintain a good level of knowledge and skills within the field, or to progress in a hierarchical manner within the profession. However, many employed people study for vocational qualifications for their own development and career prospects. Often formal and informal communication within the workplace raises the awareness of such opportunities. Asylum-seekers would not be able to access these communication networks as they would not be in paid employment, although in cases where there have a work shadowing opportunity or work experience this would provide them with the opportunity to become aware of possibilities that would potentially be open to them should they gain refugee status.

A gulf in legal status and associated rights exists between asylum-seekers on the one hand and refugees on the other, who have gained the right to remain. Asylum-seekers are extremely restricted in relation to formal structures and have to rely on accessing non-formal systems in order to access information, advice and learning. These non-formal systems may be of considerable value in signposting and supporting asylum-seekers, but given the legal restrictions, they stop well short of providing a fast-track route to enhanced career prospects and integration and equal status with the those of working age in the wider population, the vast majority of whom are economically active or engaged in vocational training or learning opportunities.

Skills Development Scotland (formerly Careers Scotland, along with other organizations) is the national provider of vocational guidance. This is an all age service and provides free and impartial guidance to young people in schools as well as to adults in their contact centres across Glasgow. However, in January 2012 funding cuts led to the loss of the two dedicated careers advisers for asylum-seekers and refugees. This service was now 'mainstreamed'. Asylum-seekers are able to access vocational guidance from Skills Development Scotland and from local economic development companies and voluntary sector organsations around the city, but immediate options are limited, given their distinctive legal status from refugees.

3.2 Non-formal VET system

In Glasgow there are several organizations and projects that make up the profile of the non-formal VET system. This ranges from statutory involvement by the Scottish Government and Glasgow City Council, to the college sector and voluntary organizations. Some of the funding for this provision has come from the Scottish Government's Race, Religion and Refugee Integration Funding Stream, while other sources are European Social Fund, Glasgow City Council, Big Lottery and the Comic Relief charity. There has always been an emphasis on partnership working where providing for Glasgow's dispersed asylum-seekers is concerned and that was why the government set up the Scottish Refugee Integration Forum in 2002.

The ATLAS Development Partnership, part-funded through the Equal Programme of the European Union, was led by Glasgow City Council and work began in 2002. It was a partnership of statutory and non-statutory organizations, and one of its aims was to support the social and vocational integration of asylum-seekers in Glasgow. The initial focus was "Action for Training and Learning for Asylum-seekers". Transnational partners were from Denmark, Portugal and Finland. It began with research, which discovered that there was a paucity of information on asylum-seekers; that organisations needed to be better prepared for their arrival under the dispersal policy, and that asylum-seekers were keen to access training and work. As a result a number of projects ran from 2005 to 2007 in four areas: orientation, information, advice and guidance; promotion of community cohesion; ESOL (English for Speakers of Other Languages); and pre-vocational support[17].

Unfortunately the 2002 Nationality, Asylum and Immigration Act[18] resulted in new asylum-seekers being banned from taking up paid work or full-time vocational education and training, which created difficulties for the Equal programme in the United Kingdom generally. This fact explains the limited focus of the projects developed. The projects most relevant for this study are summarised here, under the headings: Advice and guidance, ESOL, APEL and Non-ESOL learning opportunities. The list is by no means exhaustive[19].

---

17 Source: www.glasgow.gov.uk/en/YourCouncil/Atlas
18 See Section 5 of this report for further information on the 2002 Act.
19 The main source: www.equal-works.com

3.2.1 Advice and guidance

- Capacity-Building for Careers Advisors – this was action research carried out by Glasgow North Ltd and the Scottish Enterprise Glasgow Social Justice Transition Team in order to improve the provision of guidance to highly-skilled and professional asylum-seekers and refugees. It was carried out in conjunction with employers and asylum-seekers as well as with careers advisers.
- Education and Employment Worker – the Scottish Refugee Council employed a worker to give asylum-seekers information about the labour market and training opportunities so that they would be ready in the event that their claims were successful.
- Glasgow Asylum-Seekers Support Project – an Information and Advice Worker was employed to give specialist information and support in community-based settings throughout Glasgow and to carry out capacity-building in local centres so that they could improve their levels of support. A multilingual web site was developed, carrying information and details of relevant agencies.
- Glasgow Guide and Orientation Service – the central call centre of the City Council provided bilingual workers at specific times to take calls from asylum-seekers or their representatives and a printed orientation guide to Glasgow was produced. This was aimed mainly at social integration and signposting of services as opposed to addressing vocational guidance.
- Pilot Orientation and Integration Project – Integrating Toryglen Community developed a comprehensive integration and orientation programme to give local asylum-seekers the information and advice they needed.
- Re-Focus – Anniesland College worked with Glasgow City Council Social Work Department, Greater Glasgow Health Board, Drumchapel Opportunities, Careers Scotland (now one part of Skills Development Scotland) and Dumbarton Road Corridor Community Forum to develop a network, with support materials and workshops, to create easy pathways for people from disadvantaged groups (including asylum-seekers) to move towards mainstream employment.
- The Red Cross has been working with asylum-seekers offering a life skills programme called the Chrysalis Project to help asylum-seekers to develop their cultural awareness and awareness of services and systems that can assist them and their families with integration and learning opportunities.
- The Scottish Refugee Council has offered support to professional asylum-seekers; signposting to specialist services and a wide range of direct services including counselling and information. The Scottish Refugee Council also

had the contract for RIES (Refugee Integration and Employment Service), which provided support and advice about housing as well as education and employment. Although the funding ended in September 2011, the Scottish Refugee Council still perform the function – albeit to a lesser extent.

- RITeS (Refugees Into Teaching in Scotland) was a project supported by the Scottish Government in association with the University of Strathclyde and a number of partner organizations: the Scottish Refugee Council; Glasgow City Council; The Bridges Programmes; the Universities of Glasgow; the West of Scotland and Strathclyde; the West Forum and Anniesland College. The project assisted and supported refugees and asylum-seekers who had teaching qualifications. Funding for the project ceased at the end of March 2011.

3.2.2 ESOL

- ESOL Framework Project – thirteen ESOL units were developed at levels from Beginners up to Upper Intermediate level, with additional student materials, teachers' guides, activity packs and audio materials; thirteen National Assessment Bank sets of material were produced; all materials were tested and revised; and over one thousand candidates obtained the new ESOL qualifications while 157 practitioners received training.
- There are various providers of ESOL throughout Glasgow, including all the colleges and within other community-based settings such as Healthy Living Centres and Glasgow Culture & Sport venues.
- Literacy Project – Rosemount Lifelong Learning developed new ESOL and literacy support materials for non-literate ESOL learners. It provided teaching in small groups or one-to-one, with on-site free childcare. The Workers' Educational Association (WEA) provided similar opportunities through Scottish Government adult literacy funding for Glasgow.
- Volunteer Tutor Project – Glasgow ESOL Forum provided a handbook and support materials for volunteer ESOL tutors, who offered regular classes in community-based organisations such as Rosemount Lifelong Learning, Maryhill Citizens Advice Bureau (CAB) and Oasis Women's Group.

3.2.3 APEL

- Accreditation and Employment Skills – an APEL (Accreditation of Prior Education and Learning) model was developed and piloted by Anniesland College for asylum-seekers with work experience as motor mechanics. The aim was to match their work, education and skills with those expected in Scotland and to build a portfolio that would enable them to find work in this field.

123

- National Academic Recognition Information Centre (NARIC) Qualifications Comparability Orientation – teacher credential evaluation training was delivered to six careers guidance workers and teachers working on refugee teacher accreditation issues so that refugee teachers could more easily access accreditation and re-qualification in order to obtain teaching posts.

3.2.4 Non-ESOL learning opportunities

- Peer Advocacy Pilot Project – training was offered to refugees and asylum-seekers to become advocates on a voluntary basis. This was offered through the Citizen's Advice Bureau in Glasgow.
- Street Level – through Ypeople (formerly YMCA Scotland), asylum-seekers, refugees and others developed a multimedia arts community website.
- Yin2Work Service (offered by Ypeople) – this project is aimed at supporting black and minority ethnic groups into employment within the care sector, where they are underrepresented. It targets refugees who have a sufficient level of English language skills. Work placements are offered and there is the opportunity to work towards a nationally recognised qualification – Scottish Vocational Qualification (SVQ) Level 2 in Social Care.
- The Bridges Programmes – this project provides asylum-seekers and refugees the opportunity to have work shadowing and work experience placements. This gives asylum-seekers a highly valuable opportunity to get first hand experience of working environments whilst waiting for a decision to be made about their application for asylum. The initiative aims to help asylum-seekers to integrate with the wider community and break down any barriers that exist. Bridges also offers refugees a 15-week Employment Support course offering confidence-building, work placements and help with CVs, interviews and applications.
- Glasgow Chamber of Commerce set up a New Glaswegians Project for asylum-seekers and refugees to improve their language skills and update their professional skills
- Anniesland College established an 'English for Doctors' programme as part of its proactive approach in providing specialist vocational language training.

Most of the activities consisted of work to prepare professionals to work with asylum-seekers. Little direct vocational education or training, apart from ESOL, was provided for asylum-seekers as a result of the aforementioned 2002 Act.

4. Biographies: Experiences of life as an asylum-seeker in Glasgow

Interviews were conducted with individuals who are or were recently asylum-seekers in Glasgow. Countries represented in the sample were as follows: Algeria, Pakistan, Mauritania, Kuwait and Zimbabwe. The sample included both women and men. The purpose of the interviews was to find out about the background of the individuals prior to leaving their countries of origin and to determine both the challenges and supports in relation to their settling process within the UK, specifically in relation to their experience of engagement in vocational education and training. The interviewees varied in terms of their knowledge and experience of the UK and in relation to their English language skills. These challenges and supports have been framed below as barriers and protective factors. For purposes of confidentiality, their names have been changed.

4.1 Barriers

4.1.1 The initial barriers that all asylum-seekers are likely to face concern their lack of community and cultural preparation, along with the considerable stress of the asylum-seeking process. This process tended to be lengthy, frustrating and disempowering.

The length of time that Amina from Algeria and her family had to wait to get confirmation of refugee status was a big factor that had impacted upon her life since arriving in the UK. It took seven years for the Home Office to grant Amina leave to remain. During this process, Amina felt she had 'no security', was 'powerless' and also 'very frustrated'; this had a very negative influence on her and her family's mental health. Instances such as dawn raids, sudden deportations and the general unfairness of Home Office policy and procedures left a mentality of fear and uncertainty for many asylum-seekers in the same situation as Amina. It was a hugely hindering factor to her integration, feelings of self-worth and her ability to contribute positively to the local community.

Mudikani fled to Glasgow in 2006 by plane as a student from Zimbabwe and after a year claimed asylum due to the events still unfolding there and the effect it was now having on her family. She had her application for asylum rejected, despite having clear evidence about what had happened to her family. She tried to launch an appeal, but this right was denied, and a fresh application had to be made which eventually led to refugee status being granted for the statutory five years.

Due to her poor English when she arrived in the UK, Rabab from Pakistan, who arrived in Glasgow in 2008 lacked confidence and suffered from poor mental health. The trauma she experienced in Pakistan was compounded by the stressfulness of the asylum process, which she feels was the largest barrier for her to be able to develop her confidence to begin to take on voluntary roles and improve her English. Rabab has been waiting for over four years now for this decision and has found it stressful to have been in this situation for so long.

As a Bedoun (sometimes known as Bedoon, Bidūn, Bidoun), Faran is a stateless person in the eyes of his country, Kuwait. This status meant that he did not have access to education or any form of state support, was discriminated against and had no rights. He has now found himself in a similar situation as a 'destitute asylum-seeker' due to his claim for asylum being rejected and the decision on his appeal pending. As a destitute asylum-seeker, he is unable to receive any benefits or attend any college courses even though he had previously been attending a city centre college. Faran is waiting to hear news about his appeal and is currently relying on friends and organizations that support destitute asylum-seekers for support and accommodation. This status is particularly stressful mentally for Faran and his health is suffering.

Karim fled from Palestine in 2006, travelling through Syria, Turkey, Italy and France before reaching UK shores in 2007 when he was dispersed to Glasgow. He is not married, has no children and his family remain in Palestine. Karim's biggest barrier has been the length of time he has been waiting for his leave to remain in the UK. Without these papers he is unable to progress in life; for Karim, they are the key to moving on in education and employment. At one point Karim was offered a position as a coach in a third division football team in Scotland, but because he doesn't have his papers he was unable to take the offer. This was very frustrating for him, as, before arriving in the UK, he had worked as a Football Coach for children between the ages of 12 and 13 years. He had been very successful and his occupation was also his passion in life. Karim feels that his skills are being weakened by the length of time he has had to wait for his papers. He also adds that receiving his leave to remain is the only way the Home Office actually begins to view you as a human being. Karim is generally a very optimistic and active person, but lately he has been feeling discouraged by his situation. This has affected his mental and physical health by making him depressed, and also he has started smoking. He has been waiting for a decision for four years.

4.1.2 Restricted access to achieving recognized vocational qualifications apart from ESOL can be a barrier to career progression. Najmah from Pakistan – who was married and is now separated – moved to Glasgow in 2008 with her three children due to safety issues and instability in her country. She has been attending ESOL classes and is now at Upper Intermediate level at Clydebank College.

Alongside her ESOL classes, Najmah is also taking a course in customer services. However, although this course is run by the college, it is not a recognized SQA (Scottish Qualifications Authority) qualification because due to her status as an asylum-seeker, she is not officially allowed to take any full-time courses apart from ESOL. However, if colleges had the resources available and enough demand, it would be possible to run a 2-year part-time course in a SQA course [thereby making it accessible to asylum-seekers]. This therefore depends on the individual educational institutes rather than any regulations set by the SQA.[20] Najmah's dream job would be to work in a bank or be an accountant, but as she is still awaiting the decision of the Home Office and cannot access part-time, recognized qualifications in this field, her career plans cannot proceed.

In the same way, Rabab had aspirations to train as a beauty therapist, but has had to wait until a decision is made by the Home Office with regards to her status, before being in a position to start upon this career path. Faran, as a destitute asylum-seeker has no access to vocational training programmes of any type. Before his claim was rejected, he was able to complete courses in digital camera techniques, customer services and consumer complaints. Faran enjoyed these courses and is disappointed he cannot continue to attend college due to his status. Karim is interested in attending a formal coaching course in Glasgow to advance his skills in this field, but he does not have access to this due to his asylum-seeker status.

4.1.3 Poor access to formal English language tuition (ESOL) can be a barrier. The six further education colleges in Glasgow are struggling to meet demand and may have to operate waiting lists, meaning a significant delay for the asylum-seeker hopeful of breaking down the language barrier. This was the experience of Saidou from Mauritania, who arrived in Cardiff by boat from Spain in 2007, leaving behind his four children aged between 17 and 24 along with his ex-wife. Although he attended an ESOL course at Central College in 2009, he was not able to attend in 2011 due to the long waiting lists. He was placed on waiting lists by several city colleges that offered ESOL. In his case, he was then advised that there was community-based provision being offered. However the venue for this was a Christian church and being a practising Muslim, Saidou declined this offer.

4.1.4 Pathways to integration and support can be difficult to find. Interviewees reported finding this difficult initially at least, with one interviewee reporting real barriers. Saidou reported experiencing racism, discrimination and fear that

---

20 Najmah's situation highlights the structural imbalances within the further and higher education establishment where some colleges can waive fees and offer bursaries to asylum-seekers whilst others do not or cannot offer this support to asylum-seekers. See Section 3 of this report.

he was a terrorist. He expressed considerable dissatisfaction with how he was treated by UK security officials. He reported a sense of people thinking that asylum-seekers are either terrorists or are uneducated and abusing the system, as opposed to the reality that they are seeking to have their human rights met and social justice. He has become disillusioned with the UK, and as an asylum-seeker in a major city with high numbers of asylum-seekers, had not even been able to access English language tuition in a suitable venue, far less any voluntary employment or other education or training. His goal was now to settle in another country.

4.1.5 Some asylum-seekers arrive with few or no educational qualifications from their country of origin. This was the case for Najmah, who had received basic education in Pakistan up to the age of fourteen, but was unable to take on any further education or work as her father died. She was needed to stay at home and help her mother. This was also the case for Rabab, who had been brought up in a very traditional religious family in which it was considered inappropriate for women to pursue educational qualifications beyond school or to seek paid employment. These difficulties, coupled with the language barrier, made it particularly difficult for Rabab to participate in ESOL classes in Glasgow. Faran did not receive any kind of formal schooling or training in Kuwait due to his Bedoun background. Before 1984, the Bedoun lived peacefully in Kuwait, but then the authorities in Kuwait began to restrict Bedoun children's access to education and their families' rights to state support. Education was provided by volunteers for some Bedoun children in the local Mosques; Faran was able to access this for a while.

Even when asylum-seekers enter the UK with higher-level qualifications they often face structural barriers in transferring their skills. In many ways Rabab, Najmah and Faran are not typical; as most asylum-seekers have gained qualifications and worked in their countries of origin, as the Scottish Refugee Council's survey in 2011 found. Despite a lack of formal education, however, Faran picked up many skills, practical abilities and experiences, such as carpentry, floor laying, hairdressing and cooking. Before coming to the UK he worked as a fisherman in a boat and then started to export goods between Bahrain and Iran. He also worked for seven years in Saudi Arabia as a barber.

4.1.6 A highly significant barrier is the lack of recognition of qualifications that asylum-seekers arrive with. This includes degree level qualifications that are simply not recognized as such in the UK. The implication of this is that any aspiration that the individual may have to enter the profession for which they were qualified is not a realistic prospect in either the short or medium term. Law and teaching were amongst the professions represented in the interviewees. Amina had studied law and administration to degree standard and worked in the family law firm in Algeria before having to flee the country with her husband and son. In Mauritania, Saidou had been educated to Baccalaureate (equivalent of France's national secondary-school diploma) level and then had gone on to specialize in teaching. After attending an institution for teacher training (1986-88) he worked as a history teacher until 1992. Before leaving Palestine, Karim completed a degree in Commerce and also took a Diploma in Football Coaching. Mudikani had finished her A Levels in Zimbabwe and was two months into a degree in music and musicology before having to flee to Harare.

4.1.7 Financial barriers were found to be significant as well as lack of recognition of qualifications. Funding arrangements for full-time study are different for anyone who has been in the UK for less than three years, after which time – unless they are asylum-seekers – they have parity with the wider population, as they are considered to be ordinarily resident, and no longer liable for the overseas fees. The Scottish government rule about asylum-seekers being treated as home students for University entrance applies only to children who have been at school in the UK for a minimum of three years and who have the necessary higher passes. No asylum-seeker can be treated as a home student unless they meet these criteria. A further financial barrier is that asylum-seekers cannot access part-time higher education through the fee waiver scheme for those on low income and social security benefits[21].

4.1.8 For some asylum-seekers a barrier is their emotional response to the negative experiences that they have been through in their country of origin. If there is unresolved trauma, this can be damaging, especially when it is combined with so many other transitions in life that require adjustment, such as a new cultural environment and climate. When Rabab arrived in Glasgow from Pakistan she found it very difficult to adjust to the way of life. Traumatic experiences in her home country, isolation, the cold weather, and her inability to speak English were factors that began to affect Rabab's mental health, resulting in depression, paranoia, panic attacks and high blood pressure. For almost one year Rabab was reluctant to leave her home. It wasn't until she met some women at a local community centre who advised her to attend community ESOL classes that she began to find pathways to friendship, support and services that would assist her integration into life in Glasgow.

4.1.9 A barrier for some asylum-seekers with children is the extent to which their family can access opportunities on the same basis as their peers in the wider

---

21   See section 3.1 of this report.

population. Najmah mentioned in her interview that her children found it difficult to accept why they seemed to be treated differently, for example when their school mates were going on an educational trip overseas and they were not allowed to join in.

4.1.10 When asylum-seekers are eventually granted permission to remain in the UK, almost certainly they will not have been in paid employment for many years. It is therefore difficult for them to secure employment, and reliance on state benefits – Job Seekers Allowance may be the only option. According to Gareth Mulvey, this cannot be dismissed as being due to the economic downturn, as many of the respondents in their survey (2011) struggled to access work prior to that downturn. For those who are successful in securing paid employment, this may be part-time, low paid and very different from the level and type of employment that they had expected. This was the case for Mudikani, who was working as a part-time care assistant via an agency, whilst studying for a Social Sciences degree.

4.2 Protective factors

4.2.1 Protective factors amongst the interviewees varied. Where there was the opportunity to utilize experience from their home country, this made a significant contribution to their success. For example, Amina was able to make good use of her education and training in a law firm in Algeria to become actively involved in assisting asylum-seekers and refugees with accessing services, support and advice. Amina was one of the first groups of asylum-seekers in Glasgow in 2001 and initially it was very difficult to access appropriate information, advice, support and language classes. However, services emerged and began to respond proactively to the needs of the newly arrived asylum-seekers and Amina was able to access ESOL classes at a local college and undertake voluntary work with the Scottish Refugee Council and Maryhill Integration Network.

4.2.2 The interviewees were generally very positive about their experience of volunteering in Glasgow. This helped with developing English language skills, increasing social opportunities for the family and establishing support networks. A common theme seemed to be a desire to help others in similar situations to themselves. It seems that many asylum-seekers wish to draw on difficult experiences in life and put these to effective use in a helping role. Not only was there a desire to help others by working with them directly in a voluntary capacity, but also active commitment to campaigning for human rights. There seems to be a positive cycle activated once the asylum-seeker becomes actively involved in voluntary work, in that this improves their English language skills; helps them to become more integrated, confident and settled in their new community with realigned career ambitions appropriate to their new context.

4.2.3 Engagement with locally based voluntary sector organizations was a very significant protective factor for the interviewees. These included Ypeople (formerly the YMCA), Scottish Refugee Council and the local integration networks. Rabab made good use of the Maryhill Integration Network and this built up her confidence and was a contributing factor to her improved level of mental health and well-being. Amina accessed the Scottish Refugee Council and the Y. A key project was the Dialogue Group facilitated by the local Integration Network, which allowed her to have a say in the delivery of services to asylum-seekers and refugees. Saidou reported finding support in local community groups that promote integration whilst 'living in a gap' waiting for paper to grant him refugee status.

4.2.4 The character strengths of the interviewees served as protective factors. What came through in the interview with Amina, for example was that she was an extremely able, well-educated and strong-willed individual with a keen sense of social justice and a vision for the future of her family. Likewise, Mudikani had a strong desire to better herself, coupled with a determination to help others in vulnerable situations. She also had a vision for the future, and whilst ultimately her dream would be to be able to settle happily in her homeland again, she was building plans for a more likely stay in the UK, having secured refugee status. Najmah developed greater confidence once engaged in ESOL classes and linked in with other asylum-seekers at the Maryhill Integration Network.

4.2.5 For asylum-seekers with children, simply having dependents in itself may have been a protective factor, bringing a focus and a purpose in life, but as well as that experience of schools and nurseries in Glasgow were positive and an important source of support. Local children were found to be supportive of their peers from different backgrounds. Help was available for selecting a suitable school and becoming enrolled.

4.2.6 One of the interviewees reported that she had found a new life in the UK that provided her with rights, protection, stability and opportunities – all the key things that she lacked in her former life in her home country. Whilst there was general frustration at the limitations regarding vocational opportunities, interviewees were gradually able to build networks of support and have realistic plans for their futures.

4.3 Concluding remarks

The interviews conducted with asylum-seekers and refugees in Glasgow for the present report showed that a lack of cultural and social capital were significant barriers to progression. Institutional barriers such as governmental bureaucracy were present as well as an element of racism and discrimination. Interview data showed that, for asylum-seekers and refugees, securing desired learning opportunities; training or even voluntary employment can be highly problematic. In a competitive labour market and severe financial constraints amongst providers there were also challenges in securing suitable opportunities, including ESOL tuition and voluntary work experience. Often the options are limited and vocational goals have to be delayed considerably or abandoned while less desirable opportunities are settled for. There is a clear link between asylum-seekers being prevented from working and their over-representation in low paid employment once they have been granted leave to remain and refugee status. Asylum-seekers lose ground as compared with their peers in the wider population who may be able to sustain low paid employment and aspire to progress from there. For many of the asylum-seekers interviewed, their cases took several years to be considered and this can often happen at a stage in life when they would be expecting to be building their careers. Many regard this frustrating period as being held 'in limbo'.

5. An ethos of inclusion against a policy of exclusion

The question could be posed as to whether the principles of integration in Glasgow really are different from the reality of barriers to integration faced by asylum-seekers in the present political climate? Gareth Mulvey implies that they may not be:

> "The integration of refugees into their new countries has long been an issue of concern and interest for governments, civil society and academics alike. Governments at all levels, be it the European Union, the British Government, the Scottish Government or local authorities have key roles to play in facilitating integration. However, many in the voluntary sector and numerous academics have expressed concerns that policy and practice is not supporting integration, and indeed may be operating against it."[22]

Gareth Mulvey, has however, stated that the Scottish Government embraces the ethos of inclusion and integration from day one. According to the Scottish Government website:

> "Scotland has a long history of welcoming refugees and asylum-seekers. A total of £5.6 million from 2008-2011 was issued through the Scottish Government Race, Religion and Refugee

---

22   Source: Mulvey, 2011.

Integration Fund. This funding stream was designed to assist the Scottish Government to improve the lives of minority ethnic and faith communities in Scotland, including asylum-seekers and refugees, by tackling the inequalities that currently exist, increasing race and faith equality and promoting good relations between different racial and faith groups as well as by reducing the incidence of racism, discrimination, and religious intolerance in all their forms. Since 2001, over £12.5 million has been invested to aid the integration of refugees and asylum-seekers in Scotland. This funding has not been purely for the benefit of refugees but also for the benefit of local people in the communities they live in.

Helping refugees to integrate helps vulnerable people create new lives and contribute to their new communities."[23]

In the Scottish Refugee Council website's latest news report, Gary Christie, Head of Policy and Communications at the Scottish Refugee Council is quoted:

"Glasgow City Council for over 10 years, with the support of all political parties, has provided a welcome and humane response to the arrival of people seeking asylum. The Council, statutory agencies, voluntary, community and faith organisations have all played a role in helping refugees to rebuild their lives in safety and contribute to Glasgow's economic, cultural and social life."(July 2012)[24]

The Scottish Government is responsible for devolved issues relating to asylum-seekers, which include integration initiatives, such as English language classes and translation assistance, and services such as health care, education and legal advice. However, as Scotland is not presently an independent country, it comes under the jurisdiction of the government at Westminster and its policies of exclusion that go against the ethos of integration stated by the Scottish Government. Two such policies are highlighted below.

The aforementioned article refers to the motion passed overwhelmingly at Glasgow City Council on the 28th June 2012 condemning the UKBA's policy of forcing people seeking asylum into destitution[25]. They called on the UK Government to provide asylum-seekers with financial support to avoid abject poverty. Councillor Susan Aitken moved that the:

"Council condemns the United Kingdom Border Agency (UKBA) policy of destitution and the eviction of refused asylum seekers that is increasing the strain on the charities and communities supporting their most basic needs. Council believes that the number of destitute asylum seekers now living on the streets of Glasgow represents a humanitarian crisis that requires an urgent response. [...]"[26]

Susan Aitken endorsed the Scottish Refugee Policy Forum conference report recommending that all asylum-seekers should be provided with UKBA cash

---

23 Source: http://www.scotland.gov.uk/Topics/People/Equality/Refugees-asylum.
24 Source: http://www.scottishrefugeecouncil.org.uk/news_and_events/latest_news/1751_glasgow _city_council_stands_up_for_destitute_asylum_seekers#site_layout.
25 See page 10 regarding destitute asylum-seekers.
26 Source: Ibid.

support and demanded that the UK Government change existing rules severely restricting local authorities in support they can provide to failed asylum-seekers.

The main thrust of the Nationality, Immigration & Asylum Act of 2002 was to extend powers of detention, hence the 'dawn raids' that took place in Glasgow and elsewhere. It aimed to allow the UK to take a much tougher stand on 'unjustified claims'. Asylum-seekers would be expected to make their claim for asylum as soon as they arrived, or they would not be supported. Detention could happen at any point, not just close to the point of removal. It made clear the definition of an asylum-seeker in the UK as *'someone who is at least 18 years old, is in the UK and who has made a claim under the Refugee Convention or under article 3 ECHR, at a place designated by the Secretary of State, which has been recorded by the Secretary of State but which has not yet been determined [...]'*[27].

Certain Articles of the Act have, by their implementation, created an environment of exclusion for asylum-seekers, in particular where it comes to access to vocational and educational training (VET), and the labour market. The consequence of the fundamental change brought about by the Act regarding the right to work in the UK has meant that since the 23rd July 2001 applicants for asylum are no longer able to work until they are given a positive decision – irrespective of how long the process takes. (This measure does not affect asylum applicants who were allowed to work before 23 July 2002, or those who applied for their work restriction to be lifted before 23 July 2002.) The government at Westminster justified this new policy on the basis that most asylum decisions would be made in less than six months and based on its view that employment acts as a 'pull-factor'.

Evidence from the biographies appears to negate the former justification. However, in recent times the decision-making process has shortened, with cases being brought to a decision earlier – taking around 6-9 months as opposed to several years in some cases. However, very recently, for some cases the time taken for a decision to be made is lengthening again to 18 months, for example. There is no legislation in place to ensure a decision is made within a set period of time.

The Refugee Council, in response to the latter justification that access to employment encourages more asylum-seekers to come to the UK states:

"There is no evidence that giving asylum-seekers who are awaiting the decision for permission to work encourages more asylum applications. In fact, research commissioned by the Home Office (Home Office Research Study 243: Understanding the decision-making of asylum-seekers, July 2002) demonstrates that this is not a reason why people apply for asylum in the UK."[28]

---

27   Article 73, Section 18 of the Act.
28   Source: http://www.refugeecouncil.org.uk/Resources/Refugee%20Council/downloads/briefings/ nia_act_02/ed_1_dec02.pdf.

The Refugee Council states that the policy to end the work concession for asylum applicants was pushed through *"in haste and without consultation."* They present several arguments opposing the denial of access to employment on several grounds: The public feel that asylum-seekers should pay their way; there will be significant extra costs in supporting asylum-seekers; UK employers will be denied access to a pool of skills and resources that are needed to deal with current skills shortages. Asylum-seekers who have to wait more than 6 months for a decision, and particularly those with specialist occupations, such as health professionals, who need to keep their skills up to date, will be adversely affected.[29]

Article 11(2) of the European Reception Directive (2003/9/EC) made provision for asylum-seekers to be granted permission to work if they applied for this permission after waiting a year for an initial decision on their asylum claim. In July 2010, the UK Supreme Court gave a judgment that Article 11 (2) should apply equally to a situation where an asylum-seeker has been waiting for a year for a decision on their first asylum claim and to a situation where an asylum-seeker has been waiting for a year for an initial decision on their 'fresh' claim for asylum. This means that if an asylum-seeker is refused asylum and they make a fresh claim, they are to have the status of 'asylum-seeker' again and be covered under the protection of the European Reception Directive that provides provision for an adequate standard of living and access to healthcare, as well as the rights stated above to apply for permission to work.

Despite the ethos of integration of the European Directive and UK Supreme Court in this matter, the response of the UK government and UKBA has been to undermine integration of asylum-seekers into the labour market by the implementation of barriers to access through policy. This issue has been highlighted by the Immigration Law Practitioners' Association (ILPA) in their information sheets: Permission to Work Judgment 2, dated 4th August 2010 and Permission to Work Judgment 3, dated 24 August 2010. Part of the problem was that the government could refer both to Article 11(2) of the European Directive which permits conditions on access to the job market to be imposed, and to Article 11(4) which permits priority access to the job market to be granted to others before asylum-seekers. The consequence has been that, effective from the 9 September 2010, asylum-seekers with permission to work cannot be self-employed; cannot set up in business, and can only take a job of a type listed on the UKBA's shortage occupation list that is very restrictive. This is due to the fact that the positions are skilled, and very often highly skilled, although not all skilled or highly skilled work is included. Engineers, teachers, medical practitioners, social workers and care assistants are included in the list, but most jobs within these areas

---

29   Source: Ibid.

are not included. For instance, in the case of teacher positions, asylum-seekers can only access teaching jobs in schools for children with special educational needs or teaching maths, physics, chemistry or biology in secondary schools. According to ILPA:

> "[...]the restrictions may well mean that an asylum-seeker, who is entitled to permission to work, gets no benefit from this at all because most asylum-seekers will likely not have the skills or experience to take none of the listed jobs."[30]

According to Melanie Gower in her article: Asylum seekers and the right to work – Commons Library Standard Note, dated 7 November 2011, the government has decided not to opt in to the amended reception conditions directive by the European Commission due to its proposal to shorten the length of wait necessary before applying for permission to work from 12 months to six months.[31]

6. Good Practice

In view of the time and space constraints of this city report, only one organization will be presented as an example of 'Good Practice'[32]. The Bridges Programmes has been chosen as one of the successful support agencies for this case study, as the focus of the report is on barriers to the integration of asylum-seekers into VET and the labour market.

6.1 An overview of the organization

The Bridges Programmes is an agency dedicated to providing employability and empowerment support to refugees, asylum-seekers, third country nationals (referred to as clients) and anyone living in Glasgow whose first language is not English as well as campaigning for the rights of refugees, asylum-seekers and third country nationals. They operate from Govan in the South West of Glasgow, but do not work alone. They have they established 4 main groups of partners who are funders, host employers, delivery partners, European and UK partners.

---

30   Source: www.ilpa.org.uk/infoservice.html
31   Source: http://www.parliament.uk/briefing-papers/SN01908
32   The following information is sourced from the Bridges Programmes' website, unless otherwise stated.

6.1.1 Funders

In the last financial year, funding was obtained by Big Lottery, European Social Fund (ESF Priority 1), European Refugee Fund (administered by UKBA), Comic Relief, Glasgow City Council and the Scottish Government (Race Religion and Refugee Fund), which has recently awarded Bridges Programmes another 12 months funding.

6.1.2 Host employers

Bridges has worked with over 150 employers from the public, not for profit and private sectors in the last 5 years and they are the most important stakeholders because they make possible Bridges' delivery of integration into the workplace. Some recent host employers are presented in their different sectors below: –

Public: Glasgow City Council; South Lanarkshire Council; Scottish Court Service; Greater Glasgow NHS; Govanhill Health Centre; Maryhill Health Centre; National Museum of Scotland; Burrell Museum; Dalry Nursery and over 17 schools across Glasgow.

Academic: Glasgow University; Strathclyde University; Glasgow Caledonian University; West of Scotland University; Anniesland College; The Open University of Scotland.

Private: Laing O'Rourke Scotland; Cruden's Construction; Sir Robert McAlpine; BUPA, Tesco's, Hamilton Burns Solicitors; BBC Scotland; Scott House Management; Blythswood Square Hotel; Hilton International; Enterprise; Laura Ashley; Ashgill Court Care Home.

Not for Profit: Second Opportunities; Spruce Carpets; Glasgow Dyslexia Support Services; Artists in Exile; Scottish Business in the Community; Christian Aid; Sense Scotland; Waverley Trust; Ethnic Minority Law Centre.

6.1.3 Delivery partners

Bridges works in collaboration with partner organizations to deliver their support services, some of which are detailed below: -

Rangers and Celtic Football Clubs (through the Old Firm Alliance and funded by Comic Relief): Bridges has delivered Life Skills support and placements and the clubs have delivered a range of sporting activities such as coaching skills and healthy living lessons to a mixed age group of clients aged 18 to 50.

Anniesland College: As part of the college's 16 plus ESOL curriculum, Bridges has delivered six 13-week Life Skills classes to young clients over the last 3 years.

City of Glasgow College: Since 2008 the former Metropolitan College that is now part of the City of Glasgow College has been delivering a series of vocational ESOL support in Social Care, Customer Service, Education, Construction and Finance devised by Bridges and in partnership with some of the host employers.

British Red Cross: Refugee journalists with employment skills are training to be community journalists through the Red Cross' New Voices community newspaper with the support of Bridges.

Scottish Court Service: As well as providing placement opportunities as a host employer, the Scottish Court Service partner with Bridges to deliver short employability support to clients on a yearly basis.

The Open University in Scotland: In promoting access to Higher Education, Bridges has worked in collaboration with the university since 2006 and in 2008 Openings for the Future was launched at Bridges, which included hosting a careers and guidance advisor from the university to help clients access a range of courses from Openings courses to full degrees.

GRAMNET (Glasgow Refugee and Asylum network): Bridges is an active member of the network that brings together academics, researchers, practitioners and clients for mutual benefit.

6.1.4 European and UK Partners

Bridges engages in shared learning and transfer of good practice with partners in other parts of the UK and across Europe, and occasionally hosts visits from similar programmes from countries outside Europe, such as Australia and New Zealand. In the UK Bridges works in association with many organizations and has presented its practice at many conferences. It works very closely with Employment Forum based in London, and they are at present working together on a project to support Finance professionals. In addition to its transnational work funded by the European Commission, Bridges is regularly asked to share its practice with European and world partners and has presented its work at conferences and seminars in Greece, Sweden, Berlin, Poland and England. It has hosted projects from Norway, Finland, Denmark, France, Australia and New Zealand. The Bridges Best Practice guide has been disseminated widely across Europe. Bridges is currently aiming to develop a new European partnership under the call for Community Actions in the European Integration Fund in order to promote faster integration to the workplace through employer engagement and vocational training for the target group.

(Partners will be from Scotland, England, Flanders, Reunion Islands, Poland and Germany.) Other European partnerships include: –

E-EPSOL (Education and Employment Pathways for Speakers of Other Languages): This is a two-year project that ends in 2013 knowledge exchange partnership whereby European partners will be piloting and adapting key methodologies and training materials developed by Bridges and Anniesland College[33].

IMPART (Improving Participation of Migrants in the Workplace): This partnership focuses on accreditation of qualifications and experience for migrant workers and refugees and fostering anti-discrimination practices in the workplace. The Commission for Integration and Migration of the Berlin senate heads the partnership and Maggie Lennon spent 5 weeks on secondment to the Commission in order to support the partnership and draft their plans to mainstream their work.

6.2 Bridge's work placement programmes

Various opportunities are available to practise skills and past experience in the Scottish labour market. Depending on background and immigration status, job tasting sessions, work shadowing, work experience and volunteering opportunities are offered. Although the placements are unpaid, travel is paid for and Bridges can arrange and pay for childcare if required. The placements are intended to provide valuable experience of working with an employer in Scotland which could enhance job prospects as the experience could be included in CVs (Curriculum Vitae) and application forms; furthermore references could be obtained from the host employer involved. Although there is no obligation for the employer to offer the client a job at the end of the placement, many people do secure employment after being on one of the programmes and a few have actually been employed by host employers at the end of the work placement. With certain work placements, where there may be contact with the public or where there may be health and safety issues, English has to be at Intermediate level 1 in ESOL. A typical placement is for 12 days (either one day a week for 12 weeks, or two days a week for 6 weeks).

Bridges can also help asylum-seekers who are not allowed to work, by placing them on work shadowing placements or offering a chance to volunteer with voluntary organizations. With regard to work shadowing, this involves the client working alongside someone who is doing a similar job to what the client used to have. It gives them a chance to improve their vocational English and to see how the job is done in Glasgow, as well as refreshing and/or developing skills.

---

33   Source: www.e-epsol.eu.

6.3 Employability Support

For those who have permission to work in the UK, Bridges offers various ways to help them become job ready. Bridges runs courses for 4 weeks covering communication skills; CV workshops; application support; mock interviews with employers; visits to employers; information interviews with employers; personal action planning and skills recognition. These courses are called 'Equipped for the Future'. There are also individual workshops on many of these subjects and individual support can be provided to a client when he or she is offered an interview. Support does not end there because once a job is offered to a client, Bridges will arrange in work financial calculations in order to smooth the transition from being on benefits to paid employment. Bridges can go through staff contracts and calculate what the salary will be. Furthermore, additional support with English language linked to the workplace can be given.

6.4 Women's Empowerment

Specialist services are offered by Bridges to women with any kind of immigration status who are isolated in the city and face barriers to integration into VET and the labour market due to lack of child care; poor English; no previous work experience or training. Short 6 day courses over 3 weeks are provided to bring women together from across the city and to help them form friendships and networks. Moreover, the women will be supported to identify their skills and understand how past experiences can be valuable in building a new life. Bridges will help with the development of a Personal Action Plan for short, medium and long-term goals. Childcare is provided and paid for by Bridges, and travel expenses are also paid.

The impact of this specialist support has been that clients have gone college to study English; gone into volunteering or work placements; attended night classes; found work; are studying for HNCs and HNDs at college, and one or two clients have applied to go to university.

6.5 Mentoring Service

For vulnerable women and young people under the age of 25 that are already clients of Bridges (and who may be isolated or lacking in confidence perhaps due to financial hardships, poor English or no social network), a mentoring service is provided by the programme. The mentors (who have been trained how to work with people from different countries and understand the asylum system and difficulties faced by clients) use their own life and experiences to help clients integrate into life in the UK and identify their goals.

Mentors telephone their clients once a week and meet them clients every two to three weeks for about 2 hours to talk about any concerns or worries or how they (the clients) are getting along. Mentors can help clients get to know the city if they have just arrived or if they do not feel confident enough to go out by themselves. Mentors help clients achieve small steps towards a bigger goal; understand what opportunities there are; help identify solutions to problems and have fun.

6.6 Conclusions drawn

The Bridges Programmes is a dynamic and forward thinking establishment that realizes the importance of networking and strengthening the different forms of cooperation between refugee organizations, employers and the VET sector, not only in the UK but abroad, in order to integrate refugees and asylum-seekers into educational and labour markets. They support the target group by not only offering work placements and work shadowing opportunities but by addressing specific internal and external challenges related to being an asylum-seeker or refugee in order to help empower the target group to fulfill their potential in education, training and employment.

> "Bridges has been working with the asylum and refugee community in Glasgow since 2002 and is recognized as an innovative and influential organization, dedicated to partnership working and the full integration of asylum-seekers and refugees in the city."[34]

7. Recommendations

In view of the data gathered and research in the field of access into VET and employment of refugees, the following recommendations could be made, which not only take into account the specific situation in Glasgow but also at a national level.

1. Employment – Asylum-seekers are not allowed to do paid work due to the changes in the 2002 Act regarding the right to work in the UK. Asylum-seekers want to work and denying access to employment is a barrier to career progression as well as jeopardizing future labour market integration. Asylum-seekers should be allowed access to the labour market in order to give them: the possibil-

---

34   Source: http://www.equalworks.co.uk/resources/contentfiles/3540.pdf.

ity of contributing their skills and resources to society as well as through taxation; the possibility to be financially independent; the opportunity to develop their full potential and engage in work life.

Furthermore, asylum-seekers should not be subject to exclusive policies [that arguably go against the European Reception Directive (2003/9/EC)] implemented by the government and UKBA such as: the delay in making decisions on applications for permission to work after a asylum-seekers have been waiting a year for an initial decision to be made on their first asylum or fresh asylum claim and restricting the types of work accessible, that by their nature, exclude many asylum-seekers from being able to take on these jobs.

2. ESOL Provision – There needs to be more ESOL provision available to meet the high demand for it. Learning the language of the host country is vital for integration at all levels from social and cultural to academic, professional and political. Limited access to ESOL is a barrier to integration into further vocational and educational qualifications and the labour market. Moreover, the provision should be made to include people who may have special needs and mental health issues due to their situations. For example, more ESOL classes in the morning would suit people with young children at school, so they can attend when children are there and do not have to worry about extra childcare. Another recommendation would be the provision of ESOL classes with crèche facilities available for people with babies or pre-school children.

3. Vocational training and education – Asylum-seekers are only allowed to attend courses that are under 16 hours per week, which means that many people are denied the opportunity to enroll in full-time courses that could enhance their career prospects. The 2002 Act was endorsed by the government with the justification that most asylum applications would be dealt with within six months from the initial application. It was not until 2007 that the New Asylum Model was introduced, which aimed to give an initial decision very quickly. Subsequently the days of hundreds of cases waiting for over five years to be resolved are over. Many decisions are made within 6 months, but as stated beforehand, timescales are lengthening again in some cases and, as can be seen from the biographies, people are still waiting. Therefore, there should be a ruling that even if the initial decision has not been made within the time period of 6 months, full access should be granted to asylum-seekers who have the ability to undertake vocational training and education.

III.
Vocational integration of refugees and Asylum-seekers in Hamburg – roundabout routes from model to structure

Maren Gag

Introduction

A policy of extreme segregation towards refugees and asylum seekers had become established in Germany for several decades. Slogans such as "the boat is full" were used in the past to 'translate' discriminatory conditions in legislation for foreigners into a populist language for the general public, creating a climate of fear about influx of large numbers of foreigners. That was not altered by the reduction in flows of migrants to Germany, with considerably fewer people coming than in the 1990s. Due to European refugee policy (Dublin Convention) and the geographical situation of Germany, hardly any refugees arrived any more, or else on arrival they were sent back to the European countries in which they first set foot on European soil. Germany has just under 200,000 refugees who are engaged in the asylum application process, or whose applications have been rejected.[1] Many of those who come to Germany are not granted asylum. About one third of applications were officially recognised by final legal decision in 2009.[2] Without recognition, refugees are required to leave the country again. Many of them get *'tolerated'* status (limited leave to stay, subject to review), because deportation is not possible on humanitarian grounds. But this *'Duldung' [toleration]* does not give them a right to residence, it is only a time-limited suspension of the deportation of a person who cannot leave the country. For many years, refugees and asylum seekers had no access to education and training or to the labour market. The focus here is on the sub-group of persons who are not officially recognised as refugees, but rather as asylum seekers, tolerated persons, and persons having a right of stay for humanitarian reasons.

The first European initiatives and funding programmes, and the German Government's new regulations on leave to stay have created a turnaround – tolerated refugees are increasingly included in integration policy programmes.

---

1   Central Registerof Foreigners, 2010. They have temporary residence permits under international law, humanitarian or political reasons.
2   Federal Office for Migration and Refugees, 2009.

Political thinking has begun to change. Some major legislative barriers have been removed with the amendment to the Immigration Act and implementation of right to stay regulations. And the shortage of skilled manpower in Germany is also an important factor. Strategies for recruiting more skilled labour give priority to programmes for activation and development of potentials already in the country. Thus the "Nationalen Aktionsplan zur Weiterentwicklung des Nationalen Integrationsplans der Bundesregierung" [National Action Plan for Further Development of the National Integration Plan of the Federal Government] [3] refers to the labour market potentials of the persons with right of stay and refugees already present in the domestic market (Bundesministerium für Arbeit und Soziales 2011).

The implementation of innovative promotion instruments is generating major impulses for practice and policy. One important development had been set in motion by the European Community initiative EQUAL – for the first time in Germany, it set up a range of education and employment policy tools for school and vocational support for refugees, asylum seekers and tolerated persons (2002-2007). Important pioneering work was done in Hamburg by the initiation and installation of large networks (development partnerships) (Schroeder & Seukwa 2007). The Hamburg Senate has provided exemplary support for these activities since 2002, by contributing public funds to funding these networks and by providing constructive strategic cooperation.[4] Since then, the SAFE HAVEN Hamburg network has operated as a cooperation association with a number of organisers of practical work in further vocational training and in support to refugees, together with strategic partners from the authorities, the labour administrations, and business companies. It functions as a subsystem at the interface between formal and non-formal programmes of the regular system of vocational education, and supports vocational integration of refugees and asylum seekers in Hamburg.

The networks are important counterpoints in a discriminatory everyday reality for refugees in Hamburg. Even though the experimental implementation of schemes such as the network projects conducted in Hamburg are subject to political controversy, these activities are particularly important in the context of mainstreaming. Cooperation of various different players with the involvement of

---

3   The National Integration Plan (NIP) published in 2007 was the first overall concept for integration policy. Its implementation involved the Federal Government, Laender and local authorities, and also the representatives of migrants of many NGOs. The NIP was launched by the Federal Chancellor and is kept up to date to reflect progress. That is why the National Action Plan is now being launched.

4   Under the leadership of passage gGmbH, a number of network projects were implemented in Hamburg – Qualification initiative for asylum seekers and refugees (2002-2005); SAFE HAVEN Hamburg – vocational integration for refugees (2005-2007); SAFE HAVEN Hamburg Plus (2008-2010), and since 2010 SAFE HAVEN Hamburg Plus II. See www.fluchtort-hamburg.de.

decision makers from Hamburg's government, administration and business companies means that the network forms a platform for conduct of the debate, with the goal of eliminating obstacles and advocating equality of opportunity. That is the principle applied in the efforts to influence integration policy in Hamburg in favour of long-term inclusion of refugees and asylum seekers.

On the basis of this practice, the present case study considers what factors and concepts improve or impair refugee-sensitive vocational integration work. It also considers whether factors can be identified that show consideration of this target group in local Hamburg VET and integration policy, and it discusses resistance on the part of policy makers and administration. It uses biographical case studies on the educational and employment careers of young refugees and asylum seekers, showing numerous career interruptions and individual survival strategies. It also reflects exclusion and inclusion mechanisms of formal and non-formal educational programmes in Hamburg.

Good practice examples are shown in selected approaches, illustrating the concept and its implementation, and discussing the challenges and obstacles. That also permits conclusions on the cooperation relationships between numerous organisations and institutions in Hamburg. The final part of the report presents conclusions and recommendations. A matrix is presented to give an overview of the available programmes in the Hamburg VET system in the Annex.

Some of the sections (in Sections 1.1, 1.2, 4. and biographies) were prepared with the participation of network employees. I acknowledge with thanks the contributions by Lotfi Benbrahim, Franziska Gottschalk, Katerina Hibbe, Edith Kleinekathöfer and by Ilka Tietje and Franziska Wolfrum.

1. Hamburg – a safe haven?

Hamburg is one of the most important industrial centres in Germany. The Port of Hamburg is Germany's largest seaport, playing a key role in trade, services and transport far beyond the limits of Hamburg itself. That is associated with a long tradition of trading relations, which has linked Hamburg with the world for many centuries. Since 2002, the city has been pursuing the aim of expanding business activities and increasing the population, with the political concept "Hamburg – A Growing City". Hamburg is a city state, and one of the 16 Laender (federal states) of Germany.

According to the 2007 micro-census, 463,000 people living in Hamburg have a migration background, that is 26.3% of the total population of 1.76 million.[5]

---

5   Migration background is defined as follows: 1) the person does not have German nationality; 2) the place of birth is outside the current borders of the Federal Republic of Germany and immigration into

This percentage is substantially above the national average (18.7%); Hamburg takes a midfield position compared with other large German cities (Stuttgart: 40.1%, Frankfurt/Main 39.5%).

Historically, there are interesting examples which show that the city of Hamburg has always attracted migrants and refugees. In the mid 19th century, in the course of mass emigrations from Europe, Hamburg became an emigration port because so many people from Eastern Europe, Scandinavia and other countries went overseas via Hamburg – the "Gateway to the World", either to seek adventure or to escape poverty. The resulting flood of emigrants was causing headaches for the city authorities, which instructed the shipping line Hamburg-Amerikanische Packetfahrt-Actien-Gesellschaft (HAPAG) to set up vast accommodation facilities in the port for emigrants awaiting embarkation. The authorities wanted to ensure that the emigrants were concentrated outside the city centre, and to protect the local population from disease before the emigrants set off into a new future. Migration at that time was an "economic factor" in the city, with some 5 million migrants taking the route via Hamburg to America. Establishment of the emigrant district meant that the population of Hamburg was not directly in contact with the flood of migrants, which went directly to the port and provided with accommodation and food there until the ships set sail.[6]

Other documents from the past likewise show an awkward relationship with immigrants in Hamburg. In past centuries, the City of Hamburg had problems with issues of religious tolerance. For example, the Jewish refugees who fled to Hamburg from countries such as Portugal and Spain to escape religious persecution were then expelled from Hamburg and took refuge in Altona, which was then a neighbouring town (Beier 1993: 63).[7] No-one talks any more of the difficulties of certain groups of the population in living together, for example with the immigration of Polish farm workers, and railway workers' families in Hamburg-Wilhelmsburg around 1900, who came to Hamburg following the expansion of the Free Port of Hamburg and the industrialisation of this part of the city (Honigfabrik 1988). But there is greater awareness of the recruitment of "Guest Workers" from the 1950s onwards. Recruitment agreements were signed in various parts of Germany, including Hamburg, with various Southern European countries, to find workers to meet the demand for labour. For decades, the responsible politicians

---

the current territory of the Federal Republic of Germany was after 1949; or 3) place of birth of at least one parent is outside the current borders of the Federal Republic of Germany and immigration of said parent into the current territory of the Federal Republic of Germany was after 1949. Migration Background Study Ordinance of 29/09/2010, Federal Statistics Office.

6   www.ballinstadt.de Emigration Museum, Hamburg.

7   Altona was an independent town which previously belonged to the Kingdom of Denmark, and was not integrated into Hamburg until 1938.

and authorities maintained the view that the "Guest Workers" were just here on a temporary basis, and would soon return to their countries of origin.

The difficulties involved in the history of immigration, and its handling of the way immigrants and the local population live together, is also expressed in normative legislation – it was not until 2005 that legislation was passed in Germany to recognise at last that migrants and their children have for many decades been a part of the population of this country. On the other hand, the "Gesetz zur Steuerung und Begrenzung der Zuwanderung und zur Regelung des Aufenthalts und der Integration von Unionsbürgern und Ausländern (Zuwanderungsgesetz)" [Act for control and limitation of immigration and for regulation of residence and integration of EU citizens and foreigners (Immigration Act)] also refers to the fact that the decision makers in government and administration wanted to link the control of possible migration flows in particular to "demand for labour".

The limitation on immigration refers in particular to young migrants who came into the country as refugees. A whole range of laws and ordinances have been set up to ensure that refugees whose request for asylum has been rejected are excluded from integration policy measures. The "Asylbewerberleistungsgesetz" [Asylum Seeker Provision Act], adopted in 1993, sets standards for a certain group of the population (e.g. low level of benefits for living expenses, principle of benefits in kind, limited access to health provisions) and thus disadvantages them in a highly restrictive way. This has now been declared unconstitutional by the European Court of Justice.

1.1 The German asylum system – the situation in Hamburg

Reception and accommodation

The German "Asylverfahrensgesetz" [Asylum Procedure Act] provides for asylum seekers to be allocated to the Laender on the basis of specified criteria. Each Land has to take a certain quota in relation to its population ('Königstein quota'). The quota for Hamburg is 2.6%. The "Asylverfahrensgesetz" [Asylum Procedure Act] also stipulates that asylum seekers must be accommodated for up to 6 weeks, but not more than 3 months, at a reception facility responsible for them. If a person applies there with an asylum application, the first step is to determine which reception facility is responsible for him/her, and that is done with the "EASY" system[8]. Apart from the acceptance quotas mentioned above, allocation

---

8   An asylum seeker is allocated to a certain institution for initial reception. This allocation is effected on the basis of several criteria, and is determined by means of the "EASY" system. The EASY-system is an IT application for initial distribution of asylum-seekers in the Laender.

depends on current capacities of the individual reception facilities, and the country of origin of the person. The "Bundesamt für Migration und Flüchtlinge" [Federal Office for Migration and Refugees], which is responsible for conducting asylum proceedings, has 22 offices, with at least one in each of the Laender. Each of these offices is responsible for certain countries of origin.

Applicants for asylum in Hamburg are received at the contact point in Sportallee. That is where identification is conducted (determination of identity, taking of fingerprints), and the first hearing, and the details of the application are taken. If the asylum seeker is to be allocated to Hamburg, he/or she is given an extensive interview on the asylum application at the office of the Federal Office for Migration and Refugees in Sachsenstrasse and is then admitted shortly afterward to the "external accommodation site" Nostorf-Horst in the county of Ludwigslust-Parchim in Mecklenburg-Vorpommern (the neighbouring Land). The Nostorf-Horst facility has been used by the City of Hamburg since October 2006, on the basis of an agreement with the Land of Mecklenburg-Vorpommern. Hamburg has rented 30 places there on a continuous basis up to 2012, and additional places may be rented as needed. In total, up to 350 asylum seekers and 'tolerated persons' from Hamburg can be accommodated there. Refugee organisations have criticised the "outsourcing" of initial reception to Nostorf-Horst. The facility is about 7 km from the next town, that is Boizenburg, and is located in the middle of a forest. The refugees receive benefits in kind (meals are available in a community canteen) and EUR 40 per month pocket money. After a stay of up to 3 months there (the average is 20 days) these refugees return to Hamburg, where they are accommodated in the community accommodation facilities of the "Fördern und Wohnen" ("helping & housing") organisation, which are spread over the whole of the city. However, the government of Mecklenburg-Vorpommern recently served notice of termination of the agreement, because it needs the places itself to cope with the rising numbers of refugees. The City of Hamburg will in future have to accommodate newly arriving refugees within the territory of Hamburg, and is currently engaged in negotiating appropriate decentralised concepts with the districts.

Legal foundations of leave to stay

Refugees are granted a right of stay for the duration of the asylum proceedings.

On recognition of entitlement to asylum (Art. 16a GG, Basic Law) and on recognition of refugee status (S. 60 para. 1 AufentG, Residence Act), refugees receive a refugee passport, and as a rule leave to stay for a maximum of 3 years. 48,589 applications for asylum (first applications and follow-up applications) were submitted in Germany in 2010.[9]

---

9   Federal Office for Migration and Refugees, current asylum statistics, March 2011 issue.

In the same year, the recognition quota for asylum entitlement was 1.3%. In addition, refugee protection was granted pursuant to S. 60 para. 1 Residence Act in 14.7% of cases.[10] In 5.6% of cases, non-deportation was stipulated pursuant to S. 60 para. 2 -7 Residence Act (subsidiary protection). Where an asylum application has been rejected without right of contestation, the person concerned is required to leave the country. A notification of impending deportation is issued together with the rejection. If the deportation is to be suspended at the order of the supreme authorities of the Land, or for legal or factual reasons, a 'tolerated status' is granted. Although the status of *Duldung* [toleration] is intended to have a transitional or provisional character, the restrictive practice of the authorities responsible for foreigners leaves people in this status which lacks perspectives of integration for many years ('chain toleration'). It is only in recent years that the legal situation was relaxed in some respects. This situation has been constantly criticised by the churches and refugee organisations, but in principle nothing has changed in the regulation of existing cases (Decision by the Conference of Ministers of the Interior of 19/11/1999, and of 17/11/2006; ruling on longstanding cases of 28/08/2007) – on 30/11/2010 there were still 87,191 immigrants with tolerated status in Germany, over 60% of them having this status for more than 6 years.[11]

Access to education and training and to the employment market

Asylum seekers are permitted to reside only in the district or county in which the Foreigners Authority responsible for them is located (residence requirement). For persons with tolerated status, residence is restricted to the territory of the Land to which they are allocated.

In Germany, asylum seekers and persons with tolerated status receive basic benefits under the Benefits for Asylum Seekers Act. The regular monthly rate for a head of household is EUR 224.97. However, the law provides for the basic requirements in terms of food, accommodation, heating, health and body care to be covered by benefits in kind. Outside of the initial reception facilities, these needs may also be covered by payments in cash. Thus refugees in Hamburg who are no longer required to live in the initial reception facilities receive cash payments, but have no entitlement to their own flat. After one year of stay, asylum seekers and tolerated persons have subordinate access to the employment market (S. 10 BeschVerfV, Employment Procedure Ordinance).[12]

---

10 Federal Office for Migration and Refugees 2011.
11 Deutscher Bundestag, document 17/4310.
12 The Employment Procedure Ordinance stipulates that first it must be examined whether there is a priority candidate available for the job or training position; priority candidates are German nationals and EU nationals.

- After four years, provided that the Foreigners Authority has no indication that they have influenced their right of stay in an illegal manner, for example by evading deportation, they have a right to basic benefits at the same level as recipients of social benefits pursuant to Sozialgesetzbuch XII [Social Code XII], and have a housing entitlement.
- In the past, refugees and asylum seekers generally had no access to education and training or the employment market, but in recent years some enormous obstacles have been eliminated:
- After four years of stay with tolerated status, refugees receive unrestricted access to the labour market, provided that they are not themselves responsible for the reasons which prevent their deportation. Thus a major obstacle has been eliminated in the Employment Procedure Ordinance – previously this group was only entitled to "subordinate" access to employment and education, which meant de facto that they were excluded from these areas.
- The "Aktionsprogramm der Bundesregierung zum Beitrag der Arbeitsmigration zur Sicherung der Fachkräftebasis in Deutschland" [Action programme of the Federal Government for a contribution of employment migration to securing the skilled labour pool in Germany] gives young people easier access to education and training, where they have been in Germany with tolerated status for less than 4 years but for a minimum of 1 year.
- Young people with tolerated status are entitled after 4 years tolerated stay to benefits pursuant to the "Bundesausbildungsförderungsgesetz" [Federal Education Funding Act] and "Bundesausbildungsbeihilfen" [Federal Training Grants].
- The newly created S. 18a Residence Act gives people with tolerated status a residence permit if they have completed training here, and can demonstrate that they have a job in the vocational area for which they are qualified.
- S. 25 Residence Act created an opportunity for secure leave to stay for those refugees who have completed their regular school education in Germany.

1.2 Special situation of unaccompanied underage refugees in Hamburg

Unaccompanied underage refugees need provisions appropriate to their age and their psycho-social situation when seeking refuge in another country. However, the City of Hamburg applies a restrictive policy on refugees, and that also applies to unaccompanied underage refugees. These restrictions are particularly evident in the fact that young refugees always have to undergo age examination after their entry into Germany.

The procedures for unaccompanied underage refugees may be described as follows: when an unaccompanied underage refugee arrives in Hamburg, he/she reports either direct to the responsible Central Residence Office, or direct to a Youth Service.

The "Kinder- und Jugendhilfegesetz (KJHG)" [Youth Service is required pursuant to the Children and Young People Support Act] to take unaccompanied underage refugees into care (S. 42 KJHG). However, the age indication of the unaccompanied underage refugee is always checked by the responsible authority before taking into care, that is in Hamburg by the Children and Youth Emergency Service (KJND). The method used is not a scientifically based procedure, but simply face-to-face examination and personal assessment by the employee of the Youth Service. There are three possible results:

(a) The KJND employee concludes that the person is evidently underage (i.e. under 18 years old).

Consequence: the young person is taken into care

(b) The KJND employee concludes that the person could be over the age of 18.

Consequence: the KJND arranges for a medical age examination at the Institute of Forensic Medicine at Hamburg University Hospital Eppendorf.

Consequence: the young person remains in care until the result of the examination is obtained.

If the young person refuses to undergo examination, he/she is refused care on the grounds of lack of cooperation.

This circumstance is legally very much in dispute, and repeatedly leads to differences of opinion between the funding providers for refugee support and the Youth Service.

(c) The KJND employee concludes that the person is evidently over the age of 18.

Consequence: rejection of taking into care, with issue of a rejection notice. No medical examination of age is conducted. The refugee is then taken into the regular nationwide allocation system by the Foreigners Authority.

This decision is likewise legally disputed. The young refugee has no support or advocacy or legal advice in this procedure.

After a young person is taken into care, the Court for Family Matters is informed without delay, and the appointment of a legal guardian is proposed. The appointment of a legal guardian by the court normally takes between two and four weeks. In most cases, the Youth Service is appointed as legal guardian.

Residence in a care establishment should ideally be not longer than three months. Within this period the legal powers of representation are to be determined, health status is to be examined, school attendance organised, and an appropriate follow-up institution to be found in cooperation with the responsible Youth Service.

1.3 Delimitation between humanitarian aid for refugees and general integration policy

After adoption of the "Zuwanderungsgesetz" [Immigration Act] by the Federal Republic, the Hamburg Senate set new guidelines for Hamburg integration policy in 2006. They comprise the action fields of *Language, Education and training, Vocational integration, Living together in the city*, and *Migration-friendly Hamburg*. The "Action concept for integration of migrants, Hamburg" set out the following objective:

> "Development to become a growing, pulsating city with international flair depends very much on how far success is achieved in integration of immigrants and their families in economic, social and cultural life. Integration is related to the value standards of our society, the principles of equal rights and respect. Integration of all migrants living legally and long-term in Hamburg is an ongoing task, which is focused on and optimised to the main objectives in accordance with the existing Action Concept of the Hamburg Senate. Integration goals and their achievement are also to be made 'measurable'." Preamble, Hamburg Action Concept

The Action Concept makes it clear again, under the heading of 'Target Group', that it addresses those people with migration background who live here 'legally' and 'long-term', and to the host country population. It explicitly states that the situation of people without secured status of stay is not the subject of the Concept. Nevertheless, it concedes that offers are also made for this group of persons. The main emphasis there is less integration concerns than humanitarian concerns. The Hamburg Senate refers to the necessity to find a unified solution at Federal level, and restricts itself to the support it has given in implementation of a right of stay for tolerated refugees who have been living in Germany for a long time.

The funding programmes and priorities of the City are also set out in accordance with this integration policy approach, and likewise provide for a separation between different groups of immigrants, as can be seen from two illustrative examples:

(a) The main tool for promotion of social integration in Hamburg is the *Integration Centres*. They are located in districts which have a high proportion of people with migration background, and serve to support disadvantaged migrants. The first of these centres was opened by the City of Hamburg in the 1970s, and since then the programme has been expanded. The programme had to be reduced in recent years due to economies in the Hamburg budget, but despite this the work has been upgraded in the past few years, not least because the subject of integration has been given more attention nationwide, and has now been defined as a task with shared responsibility. In this context, the Federation has also restructured the language programmes, and Hamburg also benefits from that (see matrix in Annex).

(b) The Hamburg Senate has established a Central Office for Information and Advice for Refugees at the Hamburg Refugee Centre, to give counselling to tolerated refugees and asylum seekers. This Office also provides assistance for voluntary return, which was formulated as a goal of support work for many years by the Hamburg Senate. The mandate to prepare refugees for 'voluntary' and 'safe' return, e.g. to Afghanistan, is cynical in view of the constantly worsening security situation there and in view of the fact that structural obstacles in the German legislation on leave to stay permit no freedom of choice between stay and return (Schroeder/Seukwa 2007: 189). De facto, the Office is also concerned with legal and social counselling on problems associated with stay in Hamburg, covering a wide range of issues: right of stay and work permits, family and school, health, and housing.

In the context described here, the Hamburg institutions started their work on vocational integration of tolerated refugees and asylum seekers in 2002. It has proved necessary to take a long-term approach and sometimes to take difficult roundabout routes, to make use of the scope of freedom permitted within the law, and to support refugees in utilising their right to education, so that they can develop their potentials. The lines of differentiation described here between different groups of migrants characterise the integration policy paradoxes which the activities of the network had to face in the last ten years, and which often impaired their efforts to make Hamburg a safe haven for refugees.

2. Facts and figures on tolerated refugees and asylum seekers in Hamburg

As mentioned previously, this study puts the main focus on the life situations of those who are not legally recognised as refugees, but as asylum seekers, tolerated persons, and persons with leave to stay granted for humanitarian reasons, who are regarded as being required to leave the country again.

According to statistics from the Hamburg Central Residence Registry, the number of persons required to leave the country (*Duldung, toleration*) and asylum seekers has increased slightly, due to the rise in numbers of asylum seekers compared with the previous year.[13] At the end of 2010 there were a total of **5,931 persons registered in Hamburg as asylum seekers or persons required to leave the country**, compared with 5,719 persons in 2009.

---

13 Hamburg Ministry of the Interior and Sport: 2010 figures of Central Foreigners Authority, published 04/03/2011.

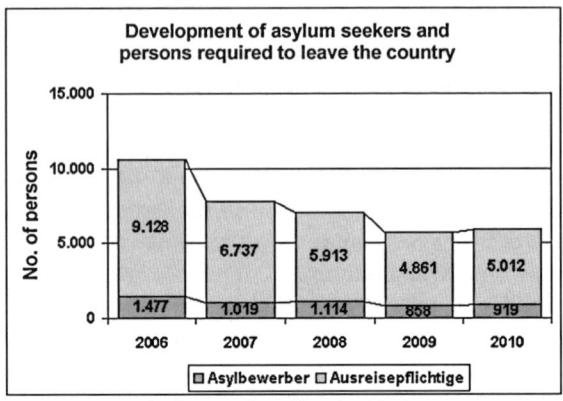

Asylum seekers Required to leave

Trends towards stabilisation of stay[14]

In the last ten years there have been considerable shifts in the number of cases, due to the application behaviour of specific groups of refugees and changes in the legislation for foreigners.

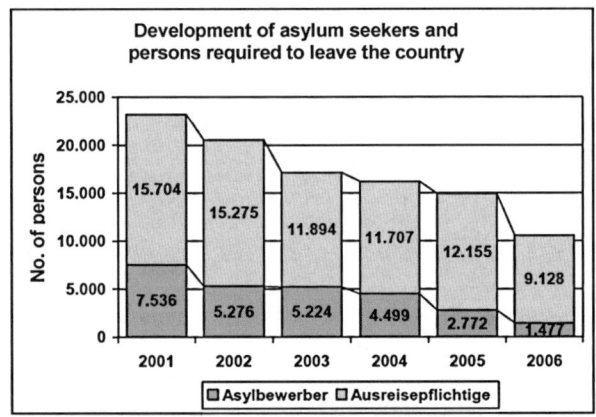

Asylum seekers Required to leave

In 2001 there were 2,783 foreign nationals actually remained in Hamburg as refugees. This group comprised asylum seekers and those who had decided not to apply for asylum. In 2000 the figure was a total of 4,692 persons, and in 1999

14   Variances in statistical data are caused in part by the fact that distribution of asylum seekers to other federal states has already been taken into account (Königstein quota), see also Section 1.1.

154

it was 5,572 persons. Context: a large number of people from Afghanistan, from the Federal Republic of Yugoslavia, and from a number of CIS countries entered Germany illegally during the 1990s, came to Hamburg, and declared that they wished to remain in Germany at present, for a wide variety of reasons. These persons deliberately decided not to apply for asylum, and repatriation did not come into consideration for various legal and factual reasons. Unlike the situation with asylum seekers, there was no legal basis for equal distribution to other Laender. It was not until considerably later, in some cases after several years of tolerated stay in Hamburg, that many of them (especially Afghan nationals) decided that they would apply for asylum after all.

In 2002 there were effectively 906 foreign nationals as asylum seekers or refugees in Hamburg. In 2003 there were effectively 706 foreign nationals as asylum seekers or refugees staying in Hamburg. The decline in 2004 was among other things due to accession of ten states to the European Union (including Poland and the Baltic States) on 01/05/2004.

On 01/01/2005 the Immigration Act came into force, giving the Foreigners Authority the possibility to issue residence permits to persons previously having tolerated status, and this was done in 1,300 cases. In 2006 and 2007, regulations on right to stay came into force (initially by decision of the Conference of Ministers of the Interior, later by legislation). The Residence Act which came into force in 2005 increased the legal possibilities for granting right of residence for humanitarian reasons.

The Conference of Ministers of the Interior had taken up the problem of people with longstanding tolerated status a number of times, most recently in December 2009, and decided to grant stay to certain foreign nationals required to leave the country. The regulation on longstanding cases which came into force in August 2007 gave persons with tolerated status who had been staying in Germany for eight years or more on 1 July 2007, or in the case of those living in a household with one or more underage children had been staying in Germany for six years or more, initially time-limited leave to stay (residence permit "on probation"). This was linked with access to the employment market on an equal basis, to enable them to earn their living by gainful employment, without claiming public social benefits.

This residence permit "on probation" would not have permitted extension under the legal provisions if the person had not secured a way of earning their living by then. The Ministers of the Interior at federal and Land level then decided in December 2009 to extend residence permits by two years if it could be assumed that the persons concerned would be able to earn their own living in this period. From 2010 onwards, the persons concerned received a letter from the Foreigners Department informing them of what conditions they had to fulfil and what documents were required for extension of their residence permits.

1,148 positive decisions on right of stay were made in 2010, based on various legal grounds. There were 1,587 positive decisions in the previous year. The drop in the number of residence permits granted is due to the large number of positive decisions in the years before that, with a reduction in the number of persons required to leave the country. The number of rejections is likewise down, from 652 in 2009 to 315 in 2010. Since 2005 a total of 10,087 residence permits have been granted, and 4,002 negative notifications issued.

It should be taken into account for interpretation of these data that it is not clear how far the refugees for whom positive decisions on right of stay have already been given are in fact able to secure employment and earn a living in the long term. That requires gainful employment which is sufficient to secure the family income. It can be observed again and again in the practical work of the network that people take up precarious employment when under pressure to secure their livelihood.

Asylum seekers

In 2010 the number of asylum applications nationwide was up on the previous year due to the increased number of asylum seekers from Afghanistan, Serbia, Iran, Macedonia, from 27,649 to 41,332. As asylum seekers are allocated to the individual Laender in accordance with fixed quotas, there is also an increase in the number of asylum seekers who remained in Hamburg.

Of the 3,574 asylum seekers in Hamburg in 2010, a total of 2,196 were allocated to other Laender, and **1,378 stayed in Hamburg** (in 2009 it was 770 persons).

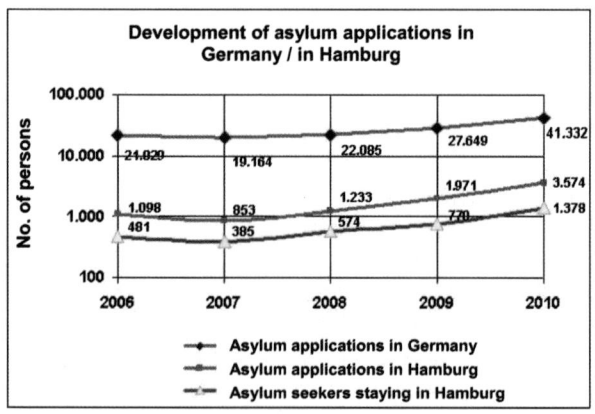

The 3,574 asylum seekers mainly come from the following countries:

Main countries of origin	No. of persons
Afghanistan	1,484
Macedonia	423
Serbia	328
Iran	296
Iraq	89

Tolerated persons (required to leave the country)

The number of people who decided not to submit an application for asylum, in order to get tolerated status, was 477 tolerated status applicants, mainly coming from the following countries of origin:[15]

Main countries of origin	No. of persons
Afghanistan	84
Turkey	62
Ghana	62
Serbia	34
Nigeria	23

The breakdown by sex was as follows:[16]
Asylum seekers: 63% male, 37% female
Tolerated persons: 64% male, 36% female.
The breakdown by age was as follows:
Asylum seekers: 45% underage, 55% adults
Tolerated persons: 29% underage, 71% adults.

Repatriation numbers have declined in the last ten years. Of the 451 deportations conducted in 2010, 238 were from deportation detention or prison (including 65 criminals). The main countries of origin were as follows:

Main countries of origin	No. of persons
Serbia	56
Macedonia	55
Turkey	45
Poland	23
Ghana	22

15   That means there is no redistribution to other states.
16   According to the statistics of the Central Foreigners Office of the Ministry of the Interior and Sport.

Gainful employment and employment availability of people
with migration background

There are no data available on employment and employment availability of refugees and asylum seekers. It is explained in a "Concept for vocational integration of people with migration background", published by the Hamburg Senate in 2010, that people with migration background living in Hamburg are severely affected by unemployment. The unemployment rate of foreign nationals in 2008 was 19.6%, that is more than twice as much as for the German population (8%). This tendency is also confirmed in the unemployment rate, which is more than twice as high (11.2%) for people with migration background than for the others. A striking aspect in the employment data is that employment of women with migration background is particularly low (49%), in other words less than one in two of women with migration background is in gainful employment.[17]

The Senate document also demonstrates that the indicated quotas of employment availability and employment of people with migration background by no means indicate secure integration in the employment market. They are often in precarious, badly paid employment. In relation to the proportion of foreign nationals among employees paying social security contributions (8.1%), the numbers in economic sectors providing low-skill services are particularly high: agriculture and forestry 27.9%, hotels and restaurants 27%, private households 18.8%, other services 16.2%, transport and warehousing 12.1%. Their numbers are exceptionally low in economic sectors with higher skill requirements: energy supply 1.7%, finance and insurance services 1.9%, and also public administration 3.3% and health and social services 5.6%.

The analyses of qualifications of people with migration background in Hamburg are likewise significant – the document notes that, according to the statistics of the Federal Employment Agency for 2009, 58.9% of unemployed persons registered in Hamburg had not completed any vocational training. Among people with foreign nationality, it was even more, at around 80.7%. There is also a high proportion among those that have no school leaving qualification: unemployed with no vocational training: one in three. Unemployed with foreign nationality: one in two (Doc. 19/5948).

The development of age structure is also important, showing that the percentage of people with migration background will increase in the future. In the age group of 55-65 year olds it is currently around 23.6%, but in the age group 0-5 years nearly one person in two living in Hamburg has a migration background, that is 47.3%.

---

17 Hamburg Parliament, Doc. 19/5948 of 20/04/2010.

3. Hidden treasures – limits and opportunities in vocational integration of refugees and asylum seekers in Hamburg

"At last I had the chance to make something of my life."
Arash[18]

This statement by an underage person who fled unaccompanied to Hamburg shows the paradoxical situation that for a long time refugees and asylum seekers in Germany lost decisive development years in their lives, having no chance for self-determination. The case study cited here is based on the analysis of the life worlds and the educational and employment biographies of six young refugees who found a safe haven in Hamburg in recent years. They are examples of refugee biographies typical of the many which we have seen in the course of Hamburg project work. The case studies are of four young men and two young women. They come from Afghanistan, Burkina Faso and Kosovo, and illustrate by way of example the kind of difficulties which they had to cope with (and still have to cope with) due to the legislation applicable here, and they also illustrate how they were able to achieve success in education and training despite these conditions. The examples recorded here give a range of insights into the functioning of innovative funding programmes which are sensitive to the needs of refugees, and into the limits of functionality of the Hamburg system of school and vocational education. Under these conditions, many refugees fail to acquire education on the basis of their individual circumstances, and are unable to gain access to the employment market. The examples given here are success stories, and most of them are now successfully engaged in educational progress or in active employment. The continuous network activities in Hamburg meant that the contact to these protagonists were maintained over a long period, and some of them were given support on repeated occasions, because it was necessary to eliminate obstacles in the course of their educational and employment career. That made it possible to obtain valuable insights into the social exclusion mechanisms, and the increasing inclusion mechanisms. These examples should encourage the players in government and administration in the European host countries to take the future wishes of refugees and asylum seekers seriously and to promote their potentials, taking special account of the extreme difficulties which they face in their life situation.

In the final publication of the scientific monitoring research on the Hamburg networks in the two funding periods of the European community initiative EQUAL, the educationalists Joachim Schroeder and Louis Henri Seukwa pointed out that the acquisition of education and progressing into further education and employment is dependent on the individual life situation in which refugees and

---

18   FLUCHTort Hamburg Plus, passage 2010.

asylum seekers find themselves. That covers a whole range of dimensions such as residence status, financial situation, stability of their social networks, housing situation and social links with other groups in society, their health condition – all of these things are decisive for success or failure in their education and training (Schroeder/ Seukwa 2007: 24). The authors follow the fundamental considerations of French sociologist Pierre Bourdieu and understand *"education as a product of individual access capabilities to and power to make use of various forms of economic, social and cultural capital"* (Schroeder/ Seukwa 2007: 25, Bourdieu 1983).

This theoretical perspective accompanying practice in Hamburg is used in the present case study, and serves as the 'golden thread' for analysis on the basis of the individual course of education and employment. Examination of the individual courses of education shows that there are certain significant characteristics and patterns which are representative of many refugee biographies – access to education and training is hindered or made impossible, they have no free choice of vocation when starting employment, and have to take whatever the system permits. The transition from school to work involves major risks, because the support systems for refugees and migrants are not compatible, and the funding programmes take no account of interruptions in biographies, and in particular do not promote cross-border connection capabilities as needed in the case of transnational educational careers. The case study also shows that increase in various 'types of capital' was possible in the further course of their careers. That made a major contribution to enabling the young refugees presented here to make better use of their opportunities and to create value added in their individual development, so that they could take on responsibility and shape the development of their lives themselves.

Looking at the situation in context, the refugee biographies show inclusion and exclusion mechanisms at various levels. The case study shows

- Systematic disadvantages in the educational biography of the *individuals*;
- *Institutional* characteristics of exclusion and inclusion mechanisms in the Hamburg vocational education and training scene;
- *Structural* relationships and changes in integration models, with the example of the City of Hamburg.

3.1 Structural obstacles undergoing change, and resource-based participation in training and lifelong learning

Enabling access

The biography of *Arash* gives a good impression of the barriers for access to education under the legislation applicable until 2005. The family had to leave Afghanistan due to the war situation there. *Arash* was "selected" by his family to migrate to the West. He left his family at the age of 14 years, and travelled to Germany alone, in the hope of finding better opportunities. The rest of the family fled to Kyrgyzstan. As an unaccompanied underage refugee, he was allocated to a youth flat on arrival in Hamburg, and was given supervision. His school career was marked by major interruptions. His school attendance had been irregular even in Afghanistan due to the war situation, and here he had to catch up with the material of three school years in a short period. In Hamburg he was allocated to the preparatory class of a grammar school ("Gymnasium"), but failed there. He then went to a comprehensive school, completing it with junior high school leaving certificate. On transition to further educational programmes, he failed due to the structural barriers of German legislation. He could not get a work permit, so had to take on occasional unskilled jobs to earn a living. Thanks to the special conditions of the Hamburg networks, he was able to work his way through qualifying programmes (modularised), because participation does not require a work permit. That enabled him to get acceptance for an internship in a building company. The company was willing to take *Arash* on as a trainee, but it took many months for him to get a work permit. In the end, it proved possible to get him a work permit thanks to an agreement between the network and the job centre, because this was an additional traineeship.[19]

> "The best moment of all was when I got my work permit at the beginning of the year, to work eight hours a day. That was the first time for ten years that I was allowed to do real work. I have kept that document.
> My dream was always to become an architect. But when I got the offer to take the training course in reinforced concrete construction, I said "Yes" straight away. The fact that EQUAL secured my right to stay gave me the security that I would not be deported for at least a year. At last a year of opportunity to show what I can do. Now I have the residence permit, and I want to complete my training. I want to make progress, to develop further. That's why I want to train as a foreman or technical building site manager. Then I can take on responsibility and make decisions myself." (Arash 2007)

---

19 The network had reached an agreement with the Hamburg Employment Agency that a work permit for a tolerated refugee/asylum seeker would be granted it the network prove that an additional training place had been created in a company (company has to prove its willingness to train one young person more than in the previous year).

Arash managed to achieve his dream via roundabout routes. After completing his education, he first worked in reinforced concrete. Then he had to change his vocational direction, for health reasons. After attending a college of construction engineering, he took up studies of construction engineering at the HafenCity University in Hamburg. The company had recognised his potential, and that opened up access for him to the real world of work, and helped greatly to stabilise his life situation. That is demonstrated by his very good results in the final exams at the Chamber of Trade for his professional qualification, earning distinctions in a number of subjects. *Arash* has now started a family and lives in his own flat. The network proved to be a reliable guide throughout his educational career, helping him to overcome the barriers and gain access to the next stages. The story of *Arash* shows that he was able to increase his vocational capital thanks to his motivation and perseverance, and that enabled him to live a life where he can continue his education and training on his own initiative, heading for progress and economic security, because he gained access to the funding instruments. He also makes use of his cultural capital by supporting other disadvantaged migrants by his activity as a mentor during their school education.[20]

The educational career of *Schoheib*, born in Afghanistan in 1985, was similar. He likewise had to struggle with major restrictions, after landing up in Hamburg with his family in 2002, following a one-year stay in Moscow. Having had 12 years of schooling in his country of origin without documentation, he succeeded in getting a junior high school leaving school certificate at a vocational preparation school here. Due to the restrictive legislative conditions, he was able to get a work permit only for low-paid sideline employment. He took work as a kitchen assistant, because he needed the money to support his family. The new scheme, which made it possible to acquire qualification in individual modules, enabled him to start gaining credits that would later count towards his educational qualification. *Schoheib* completed his training as a road builder successfully in 2009, getting a grade of "good" for theory and practice. The training and education period was a great challenge for him, because he was repeatedly faced with obstacles that blocked his way to "dual training". It was extremely difficult to avoid losing his motivation. The administrative work before he could get a work permit took so long that the training place was meanwhile taken by another young person. *Schoheib* got an employment contract without time limit in 2009, and has been working there ever since; he wants to continue his training for qualification to foreman or master level. He lives in a house on the outskirts of the city, together with his wife.

---

20 Arash does part-time work alongside his studies, in the project "Young Role Models", for mentors with migration background supporting other migrants at schools, in order to ensure their success at school. See www.verikom.de.

Under the current legislation, it is possible to place refugees in training after one year. If the waiting times for vocational preparation are used as early as possible after their arrival, for targeted basic support, it is possible to overcome the remaining legal obstacles. That also helps to prevent lack of perspectives and forced passivity leading to loss of motivation, which would then require great efforts to build up again later to generate the drive for education and training.

Recognition of qualifications

Another problem in access to the employment market is that foreign educational qualifications and vocational certificates are not recognised and/or those affected often do not have their documents because of the flight situation at the time of their migration. In addition, the vocational experience they have is devalued by lack of practical application in the years of waiting in Germany (Englmann 2007).

Mohamad fled to Germany to escape the Taliban regime in 2002, and has been living in Hamburg with his family since then. His asylum application was rejected, and he has tolerated status, but cannot be deported because the Hamburg Senate has stipulated that no families with children are to be deported to Afghanistan. *Mohamad* has training and professional experience as a doctor, acquired in his country of origin. His qualification is not recognised in Germany. He has been trying to obtain recognition via the official channels since 2009. That process has been quite an odyssey, giving various insights into the workings of the bureaucratic decision makers. The Central Office for Foreign Education (ZAB), Bonn[21], cast doubt on the authenticity of his documents after an examination period of nearly ten months, so the Hamburg Health Department sent his documents to the German Embassy in Kabul. There, after a period of two years, an examination report was issued indicating that proof of completion of a one-year hospital internship as a doctor was missing, and that for this reason it was not possible to grant him a licence for professional practice. But *Mohamad* is not able to complete an internship of one year in Germany because of his status of stay (toleration).

Reconstructing the process of examination of his documents, it is evident that processing took an unreasonable amount of time at various points because of lack of staffing, and because of excessive bureaucracy. In the course of this bureaucratic process, *Mohamad* was often desperate and depressed. He felt that the

---

21   The Central Foreigners Education Office (ZAB) is the central department which is responsible for evaluating foreign qualifications in Germany. The ZAB issues an individual certificate evaluation on application by the holder of a degree from a foreign university. It has information on educational systems worldwide. It is based at the "Permanent Conference of the Ministries of Culture of the States", which maintains an office for its coordination work.

responsible authority was discriminating against him, almost treating him as a criminal. In order to accelerate the proceedings, the advisers at the SAFE HAVEN network launched various initiatives to support *Mohamad*, had countless discussions with the Health Department, applied to the responsible Senator for support, submitted a complaint to the ZAB about the length of processing time, submitted a petition to the Petitions Committee of the Hamburg Parliament due to failure to act on the part of the authorities, and made a complaint to the Ministry of Foreign Affairs and the Integration and Refugees Adviser of the Federal Government. The lengthy bureaucratic process was explained by a need for special caution and care, in order to exclude the possibility of harm to patients in the event of mistakes in treatment which could occur in the course of his exercise of the profession.

There is a shortage of doctors in Germany. Many doctors are leaving Germany to practise abroad, because of the poor working conditions and earning opportunities here, especially in rural areas. *Mohamad* wants to work in his profession as a doctor. During the waiting time, he attended a training course for foreign students and medical staff. He was able to spend some time as an observer/assistant at a large hospital in Hamburg, giving him an opportunity to show his skills as a doctor, and received a very good report on his work there. This internship period meant close contact with German speaking colleagues and patients, giving a boost to his linguistic skills. He is highly motivated to make good any gaps in his knowledge. He is concerned that the long waiting periods could mean he loses the knowledge he has acquired in the adaptation training course. As a third-country national, he is currently not eligible for approval as a doctor (under the regulations of the Medical Council), but only for a restricted licence for exercise of the profession, limited in time and place (Englmann 2007).[22] It is still in dispute whether or not *Mohamad* completed the year of practical experience required in the course of his studies. According to information by a sworn translator, the differences in the documents were due to the notation used in conversion of solar years to the Christian calendar. However, this reason meant special challenges for the responsible authority, and the relationship between the applicant and the examining body was now characterised by considerable mistrust. But at least this meant that the documents could be resubmitted to ZAB with this explanation. In parallel to this, *Mohamad* travelled to Afghanistan to obtain the necessary document. The story came to a good conclusion – in August 2011 *Mohamad* received the notification from the Hamburg Health Department that he could continue his adaptation training. The Department wrote in this context:

---

22 Regulated in Germany by the Federal Medical Regulations (BÄO) in the version of the notification of 16 April 1987.

[..] Independently of this document, the ZAB corrected its previous statement by means of its letter of 08/08/2011, received here today, and stated that you have now proved successful completion of six-year studies of medicine at a recognised Afghan state university.

It is therefore now possible to grant you a licence for professional experience for preparation of the examination to be taken, in order to demonstrate equivalent knowledge. This period of professional experience is to replace the internship required in the medical training course. [..]

Letter to M from the City of Hamburg, Ministry of Health and Consumer Protection, of 16/08/2011

In November 2011 the Bundesrat (Upper Chamber of Federal Parliament) passed the "Recognition of Foreign Vocational Qualifications Facilitation Act", which enters into force on 01/03/2012. It is to give migrants a legal entitlement for their professional qualification to be examined within three months. The story of *Mohamad* shows that it may be difficult or even impossible, especially for refugees, to provide complete documentation of their education, because the documents are often lost in the course of war. A critical point in this Act is that the legal entitlement to follow-up education remains. It may be assumed that many migrants are dependent on adaptation of their qualifications due to the differences in organisation of the professional profiles and the contents in different countries, and due to the long waiting periods in which the migrants are unable to use their qualification. According to estimates by the Research Institute of the Federal Employment Agency (IAB), there are some 2.8 million migrants with foreign qualifications living in Germany, including 800,000 graduates. Many of them have to take employment below the level of their qualification. This legislation gives the chance to recruit more skilled people for entry into the employment market. But mostly this is only possible where appropriate funding can be provided for adaptation training. It is likely that there will still be major obstacles for access to education, qualification and the employment market for many of these people, especially migrants from third countries, and especially for those who are unable to submit documents.

3.2 Transitional phase between school and vocation

In Germany there are a large number of young people still subject to compulsory education requirements who do not get a placement in training or employment; a differentiated transitional system has been developed in the course of the last few decades to help disadvantaged young people to take the step into the world of work. Various training courses are provided in the different Laender of Germany, and are held at the vocational training schools (Schroeder, Thielen 2009).

Placement of lateral entrants in Hamburg's educational system depends on the age of the refugees. Child refugees (under 16 years old) are taken into remedial classes at the general education schools, with the goal of preparing them linguistically to that they can be integrated as soon as possible in the regular classes at primary school or secondary school. Young refugees aged 16 years or more often entered the country as unaccompanied underage refugees, and are still subject to compulsory vocational education – they are placed in special courses held at the vocational schools of the Hamburg Institute of Vocational Education (HIBB). The HIBB ran two programmes in 2002, with different curricula and pursuing different educational goals. One of these was the 'Vocational Preparation Year for Migrants' (BVJ-M), exclusively for young migrants from EU countries; the other was 'Preparation Year for Migrants' (VJ-M), for refugees and asylum seekers who do not have secured status of stay.[23] This programme, with allocation of only a small number of teaching hours and otherwise low level of resources, is mainly aimed at basic language teaching, and also provides practical training in workshops in various sectors, and teaching in a few general subjects (mathematics, English). This preparatory school gives opportunities for the students to catch up and obtain the junior high school leaving certificate. So far there has been no provision for placement in training, because that was not possible under the previous regulations.

Analysis of the educational careers of young refugees shows that in many cases the preparatory courses are not enough to compensate for the numerous disadvantages that young refugees have in transitioning from school to work.

Mental problems of traumatised refugees are mostly not detected

Many refugees are traumatised by exposure to violence in connection with war and expulsion from their countries of origin. A publication in the Deutsches Ärzteblatt (German Medical Journal) reports that about 40% of asylum seekers and refugees in Germany have suffered repeated traumatic experiences or torture in their country of origin.[24] There is little or no provision of therapy for this target group, and that has a negative influence on the course of their disease. Those affected often suffer from depression, disturbance, anxiety and progression of the condition.

The case of *Gyltene* is an example of that. She fled from Kosovo to Hamburg, together with her family, at the age of 17. Although she had attended a grammar school when in Kosovo, in Hamburg she was allocated to a VJ-M class at the trade school for construction engineering. Her exposure to war and flight led to a

---

23 Hamburg Ministry of Education and Sport (2002): Educational Plan for Vocational Preparation School (BVS), programme Vocational Preparation Year for Migrants (BVJ-M). Hamburg.
24 Deutsches Ärzteblatt (German Medical Journal) 2009; 106(49): A-2463/B-2115/C-2055.

post-traumatic disorder, which received therapy in Hamburg. After a three-year period in Hamburg, her parents returned to their country of origin, leaving *Gyltene* and her sister alone in Hamburg. For many years she was not able to go to Kosovo for a visit, because people with 'tolerated' status were not allowed to leave Hamburg. With the aid of the vocational preparation school and the SAFE HAVEN network, *Gyltene* was able to complete the preparatory qualification and numerous internships, she obtained her junior high school leaving certificate, and she did some unskilled jobs, so that in 2007 – having been granted a work permit – she was able to get a placement in training. She received careful supervision – from teachers, an adviser and a mentor – not least because her health problems caused her considerable difficulties. She completed her training as a medical assistant in 2010, but was initially not allowed to take the final examination because of absences due to illness. With the support of a lawyer, *Gyltene* managed to obtain the right to take the examination, and passed it with a good grade of 2. She was able to take up employment in the practice where she had done her training, and has set herself the target of continuing her training to become a medical practice manager.

Mastery of this life stage shows that *Gyltene* has a great deal of resilience, which she was able to mobilise despite major health problems. This capability is what Louis Henri Seukwa calls *"the habitus of the struggle for survival"*, which enables young people to overcome even very unfavourable circumstances to develop subjective strategies for coping and acquiring skills (Seukwa 2006).

It is tough without knowledge of German

Young refugees who get into contact with the German vocational school system for the first time due to their life experience following flight are normally unable to speak any German. They have accommodation in an initial reception facility, and are supervised by the Youth Service. So the question arises of how far it is possible for them to acquire a school leaving qualification in this period, as the examination is taken in accordance with regulations applicable for German native speakers. Their lack of knowledge of German reduces their chances of free choice of a vocational profile and of integration into the world of work. That is shown by the education and training careers of *Seydou* and *Semiera*.

Seydou war born in Burkina Faso in 1984, and fled to Hamburg in 2000 as an unaccompanied underage refugee. When still in Burkina Faso he was employed as an unskilled worker at a fuel station after leaving school. In Hamburg he completed the preparatory class at the trade school for construction engineering, then switched to the vocational training college and completed various internships in the craft trade sector. He also worked at a volunteer work experience camp to find out his vocational interests. *Seydou* then started training as a glass and building cleaner. Examination of the market in accordance with the priority rule showed that there were no other candidates for this training. So despite the regulations, he was able to get access to vocational training. But it was very hard for him, especially learning the written language in German. He was therefore only able to pass his Journeyman examination on the third attempt. That lengthened his training period by one year, which caused him great difficulties. Employment in his subsequent jobs was in each case terminated by his employer, for economic reasons. *Seydou* is now looking for a new job, and in the meantime he is preparing to take his driving test.

Another example is *Semiera*, who was born in Afghanistan in 1989, and fled from there to Hamburg with her family in 1999. She initially attended a remedial class at a Hamburg primary school, and then obtained her junior high school certificate at a primary/secondary school. Although she attended school in Germany for a number of years, and did a number of internships and a basic teaching qualification in the network, she found it very hard to overcome her language disadvantage as German is her second language. After three years training as a legal assistant, she failed the final examination. Thanks to individual catch-up teaching by the network project, she felt confident enough to take the examination again. However, she failed in one subject, so despite success in all the other subjects she had to take the whole examination a third time. That put her under enormous pressure, because a fourth attempt would not have been approved by the responsible Law Society. *Semiera* has now passed her examination, but for economic reasons she will unfortunately not be taken on by the law firm where she did her training.

These examples show that young refugees who come into the system as lateral entrants have great difficulty in following lessons at the vocational training school, and in passing the examinations. That is because the specialist teaching is often not linked with the language teaching, and the teaching staff are not trained to relate their subject teaching to teaching German as a second language. Neither the vocational school nor the companies provide individual support in the course of training.

3.3 From exclusion to inclusion?
Hamburger integration policy under review

The community initiative EQUAL made it possible for the first time to include tolerated refugees and asylum seekers in programmes and activities for vocational integration, under the regulations of a restrictive, exclusion-oriented refugee policy in Germany. As the successor to GI EQUAL, the Federal Ministry of Labour and Social Affairs launched the "ESF federal programme for employment market support for persons with leave to stay and refugees with access to the labour market" in 2008. The first funding round (2008-2010, with a programme volume of about EUR 34 million) gave considerable success. Of the 11,400 men and women involved, more than 50% of those contacted were placed in mainly regular employment, or in a dual training contract (Johann Daniel Lawaetz Stiftung 2011). Since November 2010, 28 networks (about 230 individual projects) have been launched in a second funding period, and provide advice, coaching, training, placement and public relations on a regional level. The programme volume of some EUR 50 million is to support refugees up to the end of 2013, helping them to increase and secure their chances of integration in the labour market.

For about ten years now, a very slow process of paradigm change has been proceeding in Hamburg for this group, helping them to overcome their disadvantages in education and the labour market. To promote the transfer of practical experience to policy making in Hamburg, results and recommendations are input as regularly as possible into current political debate. Although the Hamburg Senate has supported the activities in this field since 2002 in a manner which is exemplary for any administration in Germany, there is still a lot of work to be done to establish inclusion of this group on a long-term basis. The municipal and local authority integration concepts in Germany are still designed only for those immigrants who have secured status of stay.

In view of the political paradigm change, it is urgently necessary to give refugees not only humanitarian support and a chance to participate in special programmes, but also regular opportunities for integration. Modification of the integration policy models, as set out in the National Integration Plan, and as required by the EU regulations, would make it possible to overcome the artificial separation between different groups of immigrants.

Provision of education and training for refugees gives benefits for the public purse. However, fiscal arguments have so far been ignored by the politicians. In Germany there have been financial analyses available for many years, showing that increased integration would give a positive overall economic impact, considering the fiscal burdens and the fiscal relief it would provide.

> **Example:** The rural district council of Hersfeld-Rotenburg in Hesse has analysed the cost impact within the municipal administration, and calculated the saving of funds by integration of refugees in the labour market, using the example of "intercultural case management". Analysis of real cases of refugees and asylum seekers showed that out of 400 persons, about 200 were placed in training and employment, in a period of 25 months. These were persons who received advice and placement in the framework of intercultural case management. That enabled the municipality to save more than EUR 200,000 which would otherwise have been payable in regular benefits and pro-rata costs of housing provided by the municipality (Kreisausschuss des Landkreises Hersfeld-Rotenburg, 2010).

Cooperation with strategic partners, in particular the specialist ministries and the Employment Agency, and with numerous business companies, resulted in a range of initiatives being launched in Hamburg to raise awareness for inclusion of this target group. In keeping with the programme specification, this networking was associated with continuous "vertical mainstreaming" for transfer of good project results, with the involvement of the administration. That was accompanied by the goal of getting the administration to take up innovative developments and to initiate changes at the political level, which would then ensure that the innovative developments would become the regular case (mainstream) (EQUAL glossary). Numerous specialist conferences were held, giving a platform to refugees in the process of training, and to their employers. The networks repeatedly confronted Members of the Hamburg Parliament and of the Bundestag with project successes, and also with problems, and called for political support and statements. The dialogue between academics and representatives of practice, and networking at Federal level, also helped to put the spotlight on "Vocational integration of refugees" in Hamburg.

> "Thus networks are a specific form of 'governance', because networking of a range of players in civil society can produce potentially innovative, effective political results" (Schroeder, Seukwa 2007:220; Baumgarten/Lahusen 2006:178).

A start has been made – signs of inclusion of refugees

Even though Hamburg's integration policy is still based on a concept drawn up in 2006, the "Action Concept for Integration of Immigrants", which is not explicitly aimed at refugees, it is still possible to identify some indicators at the present time that show a change in the course of Hamburg practice, in the actions of government and administration:

- In Hamburg, up to 500 places per annum are funded for refugees in integration courses approved by the Federal Office for Migration and Refugees.
- The Hamburg programmes to support disadvantaged groups of young people in their training in Hamburg have also been opened for young refugees with tolerated status.
- The Hamburg ESF programme (European Social Fund) in the target area of "Regional competitiveness and employment" also implements the network project "Opportunities for refugees", which is co-financed by funds from the Hamburg budget.
- The "Jugend in Berufsbildung" programme [Youth in Vocational Education] funded by the City of Hamburg to cover any funding gaps for trainees (for example due to high costs of rent) is currently not available to refugees until they have been resident here for at least four years. Proposals for adaptation

170

of the programme are currently being examined by the Hamburg Ministry of Social Affairs, Family and Integration.

• The Ministry of Education and Vocational Training supports a coordinating office for "Networking of refugees and migration in Hamburg". Its role in the context of further education, vocational training, transition to work and work training is to provide an overview of qualification programmes for adults. Networking of the responsible offices at agencies and authorities, and regular dialogue with the institutions that put the policies into practice, ensures improved exchanges between experts and coordination of existing funding programmes.

The Hamburg Senate decided in its working programme to continue and re-focus the Action Concept for Immigrants of 2006.[25] The intention is to achieve intercultural opening of specialist policies, that is to introduce mainstreaming, putting the target group of people with migration background into focus in all concepts, programmes and activities. An "Integration" steering group was set up, chaired by a top representative of the Ministry of Labour, Social Affairs, Family and Integration. Participants in the coordination and advisory bodies were informed that, from now on, refugees were to be included in formulation of goals, measures for target achievement, and definition of success criteria in the individual areas. A document on this subject, to be presented to the Hamburg Parliament, has been announced for mid 2012.

4. Good practice experience

The effectiveness of individual integration measures for disadvantaged groups can be increased if conducted in a network. Carefully tailored, needs-oriented support encourage easy-access entry for participants – as demonstrated by the educational biographies presented here – and a flexible concept is also important. An arrangement with various sub-projects in a project group makes it possible to implement an integrated approach. Harmonisation of the individual programmes within the overall concept increases the chances of success of all the programmes, by setting up a broader range. Cooperation between 'refugee-oriented' establishments and 'company and labour market oriented' facilities with mutually related offers and contacts ensures access to the programmes, and provides a modular system of entry-level and skill building and placement offers at a high level of qualification.

---

25   October 2011.

There are two networks operating in Hamburg, that is SAFE HAVEN Hamburg and 'Opportunities for Refugees', both of them with many years of experience in vocational education and training. They have shown that well tailored measures provide good responses to the problem situations which many refugees and asylum seekers bring with them due to their biographies. The two networks, funded by different programmes (Federation and Laender) – work in close cooperation, and their programme concepts are well coordinated to one another. So there are offers of counselling, coaching, placement in employment and training, training preparation and supervision, qualification and application training, placement in internships, and continuing education for multipliers, to facilitate integration of refugees in the employment market. Some examples of practical approaches are presented below.

4.1 Individual support in transition to training and employment

The academic monitoring of network operations in Hamburg has shown that the success of education and training depends very much on whether the education and training organisations take account of the overall life situation of the refugees. There is a close relationship between the life situation of the refugees and their possibilities of seeking and acquiring education and training. They need not only an improvement in their legal status, but also financial security. Full social support should be made available, and housing conditions improved, and optimal medical care provided, so that they can successfully complete their education and training (Schroeder, Seukwa 2007: 265). The sub-project "Training supervision by mentors" is a model which implements this principle in concept and methods:

1. Country/City
Germany, HAMBURG
2. Project/organisation
Project: Educational support by mentors The Mentor project is a sub-project in the Safe Haven Hamburg project "FLUCHTort Hamburg Plus". **Contact** basis & woge e.V.; Steindamm 11; 20099 Hamburg; Phone: +49 (0)40-39 84 26 0 Responsible for project: edith.kleinekathoefer@basisundwoge.de Project assistant: ilka.tietje@basisundwoge.de **Organisation** basis & woge e.V. is a non-profit, state recognised organiser of social services in Hamburg. The main focus of the work is on the intercultural aspect and on working with particularly marginalised young people, regardless of their national roots. Alongside further education and advice for multipliers, in social work and consulting for people with a migration background, basis & woge e.V. has set up a wide ranging programme. It includes youth apartments, open offers, and health support, training projects for refugees and young adults with a migration background.

3. Illustration of practice

Situation

In the past years, the education, social and employment policy related to refugees was characterised by considerable restrictions. People in asylum processes and "tolerated" persons were excluded from many areas of society – young people did not have unrestricted access to general education or vocational training, they were not put in the same position in terms of benefits under the Children's and Young People's Support Act, most of them were unable to get a work permit, and approval for training was practically never given. They were not included in funding programmes relevant to the labour market. This meant that many young and adult asylum seekers and refugees were excluded from education and work for long periods. A change in policy has now started. Tremendous legislative barriers have been removed with the amendments to the Immigration Act and the implementation and extension of the right-to-stay regulations.

That is the context in which the "Educational support by mentors" project was set up, bringing refugees together with social work students. The pairs are chosen in such a way as to find a suitable mentor for each of the mentees. For example the mentor may have lived in the country of origin of the mentee for some months, or the mentor may have learned the same profession, or both of them are Moslems, or both had/have major problems with their parents. That promotes the exchange of experience and the giving of support. This is about all areas of life that need stabilisation, so that the mentee is enabled to continue and complete the training.

This form of support is described in educational science by the term "everyday support" (Prof. Dr. Louis Henri Seukwa). That makes it possible to get far reaching insights into the life situation of refugees, which is characterised by fear of deportation, poor housing and living conditions, lack of orientation, and discrimination. Mentoring makes it possible to get an overview of this life situation as a whole in the course of time, and thus permits an appropriate response. What then happens in mentoring may vary widely – it could be support at school, reflections on their own religion, accompanying them to a court hearing, going to a cinema together, or holding a joint discussion with the training instructor. This is about a contact which may but is not required to encompass all issues in life, and which does not impose anyone else's views. All the activities of the mentors vis-à-vis third parties are effected in consultation with the mentee, and there is a duty of confidentiality, in order to create a basis of trust. The mentees feel safe with this form of support, because they have someone to talk to about all their concerns, and do not have to go and seek out the right source of advice. This contact also gives them an insight into the life of a German, or of someone who was born here (many of the mentors have a migration background themselves), and in some cases this is their only contact with a "German" person. This intensive contact also gives them an insight into the life of a student, and may thus open up ideas for their own future.

The students enter into a voluntary commitment, and get continuous support by professional staff of the organising body after selection of the mentor. The tasks of the professional social worker include:

- Selection of the mentors
- Advising young refugees on training and qualification, and if appropriate transferring them to mentoring
- Advice to and training of mentors, for example on right to stay, on vocational training, on general equal rights legislation, etc.

The mentor project is designed not only to support the mentor/mentee couples, but also to advise young refugees in transition to training and qualification, and to place them appropriately. Where necessary, they transfer to mentoring.

The mentor project is accompanied by network structures which also enable the mentors to get further help and information on the possibilities from the network partners, and to get more insight into the diversity of practice.

To ensure factual training of the mentors, cooperation with the University of Applied Sciences, that is specifically with Prof. Dr. Louis Henri Seukwa, has been regulated in a Cooperation Agreement. Thus Prof. Seukwa organises meetings in the course of these studies to reflect with the mentors on the theoretical and practical issues associated with everyday support.

4. Most important milestones

The initiation of a project in which refugees and social work students are brought together as "mentor/mentee pairs". A "mentee" in this case is a young refugee undergoing vocational training or on the way to that, who has unsecured right of stay. A "mentor" for this project could theoretically be any student in the Social Work Faculty of the University of Applied Sciences. The mentors work on an honorary basis in this project, and receive only EUR 100 per month as reimbursement for their expenses (travel cost, costs of joint undertakings with the young person, telephone expenses, etc.). They normally finance their living expenses by a grant (BaföG[26]), and almost all of them have a job on the side

5. Most important hurdles:

The major hurdles which young refugees have to overcome before and during their training include paying the costs of training, their housing situation, and the resulting difficulties in the learning context, and also language barriers.

If the young person is doing a dual traineeship, he/she will receive a training salary, but this money is usually not enough to pay all the costs of living (rent, travel costs, food, learning and working materials for training, working clothes, etc.). He/she has to put in a whole range of applications to get supplementary benefits, and it is practically impossible to that effectively without support, because he/she does not know all the possibilities available, or the application procedures are complicated. If the young person is doing in-school training, the funding possibilities have to be examined and applied for.

The housing situation at the start of and during education often makes it difficult to achieve the required school performance to complete training successfully. Placement in accommodation is often characterised by the presence of a large number of unfamiliar people in a very small space, without any chance of withdrawing and without any private space. Often there is no calm workplace where the trainee can prepare or do follow-up work on the teaching at the vocational school. It is practically impossible for him/her to do any learning outside of the times at the vocational school/training company.

Dealing with language barriers, both in the spoken and written language, is dependent on support during training. The programme of support provided by the state (remedial teaching in small groups) has to be applied for, and often it is not enough, because that cannot provide the necessary individual learning support. Additional support through private-sector remedial teaching is needed for successful completion of the training. That means it is necessary to find suitable people to give this teaching, and to obtain the necessary funding. These additional hours require strength, energy and good organisational planning by the trainee to manage all this.

Although German is the second language for the trainees, they have to do the tests and take the examinations under the same conditions as the young people who grew up in Germany. They are not entitled to more time, and they are not allowed to use a bilingual dictionary to help them in doing the tasks set in the examinations and tests. They will lose marks for spelling errors when their work is assessed.

---

26 Bundesausbildungsförderungsgesetz (Federal Training Funding Act).

6. Networking partners (local, which types of organisation)
• Partner in the SAFE HAVEN Hamburg Network (FLUCHTort Hamburg)
• Jobs Agency (Agentur für Arbeit)
• team.arbeit.hamburg – Hamburger Arbeitsgemeinschaft SGBII
• Ministries of the City of Hamburg
• Hamburg Chamber of Crafts
• Hamburg University of Applied Science, Department of Intercultural Education
• Diakonisches Werk and Refugee Adviser of the North Elbe Church
• Institutions of Refugee and Migration Work
• Various Hamburg companies

Edith Kleinekathöfer, Ilka Tietje, basis & woge e.V.

This relationship with practice is also valuable for students at the Hamburg University of Applied Sciences (HAW), providing useful experience and preparation for subsequent exercise of their profession in social work. This contact gives them valuable insights into the life situations of refugees, relating this to reflection on their own life development and situation.

"I am Franziska W. I am 23 years old and a student of social sciences in my 6th semester at the Hamburg University of Applied Sciences. For the past nine months I have been working with Allieu (27 years old) in the framework of the project "Training support for refugees by mentors". Allieu is now doing his second year of training at a high-class restaurant located at Rödingsmarkt, for qualification as a chef. I was selected to support him due to my many years of experience in restaurants, and we were introduced to one another last autumn.

We set the goals of mentoring at our kick-off meeting. The focus of our cooperation was on support work at the vocational school and at the restaurant, in family matters and in his contacts with the authorities. Apart from improvements in his performance at vocational school, the primary goal of our mentor-mentee relationship is to keep his traineeship going. Allieu receives training grants for this purpose, and otherwise he has a great deal to do. I am not very flexible in terms of time, either, as I have three part-time jobs.

So after we have solved the weekly problem of finding a time to meet, we take an average of 90 minutes per week to discuss the current situation in his training restaurant and at his vocational training school, or talk about both the positive and the problematic sides of his private life. It is not unusual for me to get a phone call or text message in the evening, where Allieu reports the latest news or events. Depending on the situation at the time, we mostly arrange a meeting at short notice in a café, or I collect him from his training restaurant at the end of working time, or go with him to the authorities. Although Allieu is highly motivated, willing to make an effort, and very interested in training to become a chef, a lot of problems have come up in the training relationship in recent times. The main issue at present is therefore the risk of losing his training place, and how he should react to problem situations in restaurant operation. Allieu needs psychological support here, to motivate him and to work out alternative solutions with him. So at present we are looking for a new restaurant where he can complete his training with a positive outcome.

My task of providing everyday support to Allieu is enriching for me in many respects. It widens my pedagogical skills, particularly with respect to establishing a professional, trusting mentor-mentee relationship." Franziska W., Mentor in the project "Educational support by mentors"

175

4.2 Strengthening cooperation between school and out-of-school organisations

It is by no means self-evident in Germany to have institutionalised cooperation between vocational schools, working under the cultural authority of the Laender, and independent organisations, which fulfil state responsibilities in social work on behalf of local authorities, Laender or federal authorities. The funding system at the transition between school and employment in Hamburg is split into separate systems, and that often makes it hard for those affected to bridge the gap. In many cases the barriers are difficult for school students and trainees to overcome because of lack of transparency with regard to who is responsible for what, because of lack of information on the funding sources available, because of differences in working practices of the institutions involved, and because of their different knowledge of the life situation of the people seeking advice. That applies particularly to refugees and asylum seekers, who have considerable competitive disadvantages compared with other young people. This circumstance is to be compensated at least in part in the framework of the network activities of SAFE HAVEN Hamburg and "Opportunities for Refugees". The example given below shows that new forms of cooperation can be developed to improve the joint efforts for placement of young refugees in training or to open up further opportunities for them to continue their school education.

1. Country/City
Germany HAMBURG
2. Project/organisation
Project: Opportunities for refugees Opportunities for refugees is a network project by basis & woge e.V. and verikom – Verbund für interkulturelle Kommunikation und Bildung e.V. in cooperation with the Hamburg Institute of Vocational Training (HIBB). **Contact:** basis & woge e.V.; Steindamm 11; 20099 Hamburg; Phone: +49 (0)40-3984260 Project management: franziska.gottschalk@basisundwoge.de **Organisation:** basis & woge e.V. is a non-profit, state recognised organiser of social services in Hamburg. The main focus of the work is on the intercultural aspect and on working with particularly marginalised young people, regardless of their national roots. Alongside further education and advice for multipliers, in social work and consulting for people with a migration background, basis & woge e.V. has set up a wide ranging programme. It includes youth apartments, open offers, and health support, training projects for refugees and young adults with a migration background.
3. Illustration of practice
This sub-project by basis & woge e.V. is aimed at juvenile and young adult refugees who are interested in qualification, employment or training. The focus of the project is aimed at school students in the preparatory classes for migrants (VJM) at vocational training schools.

Basically there are three fields of action:

1. In-school educational and advisory modules for transitional management in the school leaving year:

School students in the preparatory classes for migrants (VJ-M courses) are the main target group for the project. Young refugees with insecure status of stay are given schooling in Hamburg in the two-year in-school training course "VJ-M", which aims to take them to the level of secondary school leaving certificate. Most of the students in VJ-M classes have little knowledge of German, and some of them come from families with a poor educational background. The project provides support provisions for transition management at the relevant schools. It provides regular counselling directly at the school location, in cooperation with the schools. These counselling sessions are held either in the class group or in individual interviews, depending on the subject. This counselling is based on an intercultural approach. It starts in a school class, mostly on the first school day of the last year of school. Brief counselling sessions held at the school are then continued with the participants at the external location of the project. A systematic cooperation relationship is built up and continued with the schools concerned.

A comprehensive series of workshops is held at a selected school location, with the final year classes in cooperation with their teaching staff, on transition from school to work. The school teaching staff are involved in this project with specific teaching courses. The project is thus a fixed part of the school programme. Regular meetings are held with everyone involved to ensure close exchanges between school and project.

A workshop series comprises three units (vocational orientation; experience of the world of work; job application training), each of which is made up of several modules. The workshops are conducted in close cooperation with the respective teaching staff. Design of the workshops is based on the individual needs and learning levels of the respective classes and the individual students. The goal of the workshop series is to give the students specific ideas of their work perspectives after leaving the school, and to draw up a realistic vocational plan.

The workshop programme is complemented by innovative approaches to work with parents and work with role models.

2. Placement and support for young people in appropriate programmes

In parallel to the workshops and short counselling sessions at the schools, the students also have access to individual training and employment preparation counselling/coaching. Experience shows that individually adapted placement often takes more than just one school year. This form of counselling is therefore available not only to current school students, but also to students who have already completed their schooling.

Student get placements in keeping with their abilities in training and or employment, with supporting or remedial teaching. The project staff help to find individually appropriate internships and training companies. They also provide support once training or employment has started, up to the completion of the probationary period, in order to avoid drop-outs. They maintain constant, direct dialogue in order to clear up any conflict situations at the workplace and avoid possible future conflicts. Either the company or the participant can call on the project to mediate in any conflict. The project also raises awareness in the companies identified for training, by counselling and support for intercultural opening, and for issues of discrimination on the grounds of religion or ethnic origin.

3. Social advice and support

The main focus of counselling is on social issues and social work and teaching, which are key elements in the project. They address matters related to rights of residence and work permits, and also financial issues; they also address the individual psychosocial situation of the students. They take a holistic view, so that counselling can be designed to fit the life situation of the student. They work with resource-based orientation, to help the students find ways to stabilise their life situation, which is essential for their integration in the labour market.

4. Most important milestones
<ul><li>One of the key factors is active involvement of the teaching staff in the project work. This cooperation helps to identify the individual needs of the students better, and to draw up realistic vocational training plans in good time. This cooperation with the teaching staff enables the target group to get a much better sense of the relevance of vocational integration in everyday school work. It makes it possible to strengthen and maintain the individual abilities of the students, which in turn helps to stabilise the target group. This project helps to close the gap in transition management for less qualified young people.</li><li>An innovative module in this project is that young refugees (former students at the school) who are already in further programmes/training, etc., are invited to the school classes as experts. They report on their educational career, and can act as successful role models for the students to plan their own vocational progress. The visits by these "role models" can be prepared in regular teaching (preparation of questions, finding out about the guest's vocational area in advance, etc.).</li></ul>
5. Most important hurdles:
In some cases the young refugees are prevented by their poor housing situation from making full use of their learning potentials. The housing situation may be problematic because of a large number of people from different origins living in the accommodation without enough rooms for them to be able to withdraw. There are always two sharing a room, and families have little more space. Any existing mental conditions may become worse due to the unfavourable housing conditions.
Many of the young people receive funding from social security. But there is a special condition in the German system under the Asylum Seekers Act, which regulates the granting of (reduced) social benefits for certain foreigners. The resulting financial disadvantage for the target group means that these young people are often not able to eat a balanced, healthy diet. They are short of money for school materials, and they can make use of remedial teaching only where it is available free of charge.
6. Networking partners (local, which types of organisation)
The most important networking partners, and their roles, are as follows:<ul><li>Jobs Agency and Hamburg Ministry of the Interior: clarification of individual rights of stay and work.</li><li>Safe Haven Network "FLUCHTort Hamburg PLUS II": cooperation in case-specific work and cooperation by joint networking.</li><li>"Networking Migration Hamburg": active participation of the project in networking to improve access of refugees to the labour market.</li><li>**Hamburg Institute of Vocational Education** (HIBB), together with three vocational training schools H15; G19; G20: These schools currently provide refugees and asylum seekers with teaching, and have a need for counselling, support and coaching on vocational orientation, job application training, or support to prevent drop-outs from training.</li><li>Counselling agency flucht•punkt and law firm Steindamm 91: joint work on questions arising from social counselling, rights of stay and work, and debt regulation.</li><li>Pedagogical/therapeutic Centre: joint handling of questions from the teaching and psycho-social areas (e.g. traumatisation).</li><li>Chamber of Crafts and PlusPunkt gGmbH: support in setting up new contacts with companies.</li><li>A large number of contacts have been built up in the past with Hamburg companies, and that is a good basis for placement in internships, training and employment. These are being maintained and expanded.</li></ul>

Franziska Gottschalk, basis & woge e.V.

4.3 Local authority concepts for language promotion

The Hamburg Ministry of Labour, Social Affairs, Family and Integration set up a programme in 2008 for supplementary language teaching, paid for by funds from the Hamburg budget. Certain "integration courses" conducted by organisations in Hamburg and funded by the Federal government, also include refugees and asylum seekers, and the funding of their places is provided by the City of Hamburg. This ensures that refugees and asylum seekers can be integrated in the existing courses. This programme is exemplary in Germany.

1. Country/City
GERMANY Hamburg
2. Project/organisation
Hamburg Ministry of Labour, Social Affairs, Family and Integration, Hamburger Strasse 47, 22083 Hamburg. Martin Garske, martin.garske@basfi.hamburg.de. Tel. +49 40 48 63 6017. The Ministry takes the lead role in implementation of the Hamburg Integration Action Concept.   **Flüchtlingszentrum – Zentrale Information und Beratung für Flüchtlinge gGmbH** (Refugee Centre – Central Information and Counselling Centre for Refugees) is a non-profit organisation run by Arbeiterwohlfahrt (national industrial welfare organisation), Caritas and the German Red Cross. The programmes of the Refugee Centre target refugees, asylum seekers and people with unsecured status of stay in Hamburg. Those seeking counselling receive individual and comprehensive advice on asylum questions and law relating to foreigners, and on work, qualification and training, and support in individual clarification of perspectives. Those interested in returning to their countries of origin are given individual advice on the possibilities and prerequisites for voluntary return to their home countries.   Flüchtlingszentrum   Zentrale Information und Beratung gGmbH   Adenauerallee 10, 20097 Hamburg, Germany   Contact: Lotfi Ben Brahim   Valentin Günther   Tel.: +49 40 – 284 079 115   Tel.: +49 40 – 284 079 117   benbrahim@fz-hh.deGuenther@fz-hh.de
3. Illustration of practice
Initial situation   Participation in German courses for immigrants with long-term right of stay in Germany was regulated by law for the first time from 01/01/2005 (AufenthG). Thus from 2005 onwards, new immigrants with insufficient knowledge of German have a right to participate in an integration course. If their German knowledge is insufficient, their participation can even be officially ordered (by the Aliens Authority, or the organisations for basic social security of job seekers – this includes immigrants who have been in the country for a long time and still have integration needs).   The integration course is split into a German language part, comprising a basic course and a more advanced course, and a social knowledge part (orientation course) to give knowledge of the laws, culture and history of Germany. There are general integration courses with 600 teaching units ("normal learner courses") and integration courses for special learning groups such as women, or parents, or illiterate learners, comprising 900 teaching units. The orientation courses comprise 45 teaching units. The courses are funded by the Federal Office for Migration and Refugees (BAMF).

However, the law avoids reference to migrants who have no residence permit or only a short-term right of stay (residence permit must be valid for more than one year, or must have been in existence for at least 18 months). That means there is no provision for asylum seekers and tolerated persons.

Since spring 2008 there has been a regulation in Hamburg to close this gap – since the beginning of 2009, immigrants with insecure status of stay, who do not have access to the integration courses, can participate in German courses. The "German courses for refugees" programme is funded as additional language promotion from the budget of the City of Hamburg.

Implementation

The "German courses for refugees" programme provides 500 places for participants in the first 3 budget years, whereby parents with children aged 3 years or more have priority.

The Refugee Centre was given the task of handling this project, learning counselling, and placement in the German courses.

In this context, the staff of the Refugee Centre first check the participation entitlement of people expressing interest; then they provide learning counselling and explain the scope, type and goals of the course. Then a grading test is conducted in accordance with the specifications of BAMF for integration courses. Course placement based on the test result is done by the Refugee Centre. Placement is made exclusively with Hamburg course organisers that have given their written declaration of willingness to cooperate in the "German courses for refugees" project and have given their assurance that they will comply with all the quality and procedure rules stipulated by BAMF for conduct of integration courses. Placement is effected rapidly, and where possible close to where the refugee is living.

In the event that the refugee has to make a longer trip to get to the course, a travel expenses grant is given and paid out monthly by the Refugee Centre for the duration of the course. Placement is effected taking account of any need for childcare. The costs of childcare are borne by the project.

The course participants are also given counselling by the staff of the Refugee Centre. Participation in the courses is free of charge for the refugees. When they reach level B1 (Common European Framework of Reference), the costs of the German Test for Immigrants (DTZ) are also borne by the Refugee Centre.

4. Most important milestones

To the best of our knowledge, this project is unparalleled in Germany in its form and scope. Other states of Germany have expressed their interest in using this approach.

The Refugee Centre itself is an organiser of a sub-project within the Hamburg network FLUCHTort HAMBURG PLUS (SAFE HAVEN HAMBURG PLUS) and cooperates closely with the network. There is close coordination between the Refugee Centre and the training sub-projects of the network, with the goal of making the transition as seamless as possible from the German course for refugees to other programmes, in particular the other German courses of the network project, and vice versa.

5. Most important hurdles:

Unlike the integration courses described above, the German courses for refugees comprise only 300 hours.

A requirement for participation in these courses is that the person is registered as resident in Hamburg, and has a right of stay or tolerated status with validity of at least 6 months, or a residence permit pursuant to Section 25 para. 5 for not more than 1 year. Thus right of access to the integration courses of BAMF excludes participation in this project. Where right of residence is confirmed, the hours completed in the framework of this project are not counted towards the integration course hours of the BAMF programme.

6. Networking partners (local, which types of organisation)
• Networks FLUCHTort Hamburg (Safe Haven Hamburg) • Chancen für Flüchtlinge (Opportunities for Refugees) • Hamburg organisers conducting the integration courses

Lotfi Benbrahim, Zentrale Information und Beratung gGmbH

The programme is an important additional module in the range of funding programmes already provided by the network projects. Combination with the language courses provided in the networks, differentiated for various levels, gives a chain of support which satisfies the widely differing levels of knowledge of the participants.

4.4 Training for employment and for living in Hamburg

Other modules are qualification programmes which build on the first language programmes. They are likewise a part of the support chain, and are illustrated below. Success is dependent on the programmes being flexible for the different starting levels of participants, and accompanied by individual coaching and systematically adapted language teaching, aimed both at the elements that are particularly relevant to refugees and to their employment prospects (Beckmann-Schulz et. al 2007). It is also important to develop and give training in the basic skills needed for communication at the workplace (Beckmann-Schulz et. al 2011).

1. Country
Germany HAMBURG
2. Project/organisation
Vocational skill training for refugees "Vocational skill training for refugees" is included in various projects by verikom: 　　"AQUABA for refugees" was a networking project run by basis & woge e.V., the international Diakoniecafé why not? and verikom – Verbund für interkulturelle Kommunikation und Bildung e.V. (Intercultural Communication and Education Association). 　　That has led to development of the project "Opportunities for refugees", a network run by basis & woge e.V. and verikom in cooperation with the Hamburg Vocational Education Institute (HIBB). 　　"COACH" is a part of the SAFE HAVEN Hamburg PLUS II network. Contact: verikom, Norderreihe 61; 22767 Hamburg; Phone: +49 (0)40-350177233/36 Project management "AQUABA" for refugees: Katerina Hibbe; hibbe@verikom.de Project management "Opportunities for refugees": Barbara Feige; feige@verikom.de Project management COACH: Katerina Hibbe; hibbe@verikom.de

verikom – Verbund für interkulturelle Kommunikation und Bildung e.V. is a non-profit, state recognised organisation for counselling and training for migrants. verikom is one of the city's integration centres, and is funded by the Hamburg Senate as a regular provision. verikom conducts language courses (integration courses), literacy and computer courses, events and further education programmes, and promotes active engagement of migrants and refugees in their districts and in the labour market, with various projects. The counselling programme of verikom includes general advice for migrants and refugees, language learning advice, and intercultural counselling for victims of domestic violence and forced marriage.

3. Illustration of practice

Since 2001, verikom has been involved in Hamburg networking in various projects, for vocational integration of refugees whose right of stay is unsecured.

In the first years of this work, training measures were developed specially for female refugees. They included basic training for the areas of health care and teaching, and also multiplier courses for IT and languages (e-qualify). The AQUABA project was then developed for refugees.

At present verikom is working on two sub-projects, in the framework of the Hamburg network "SAFE HAVEN Hamburg Plus II" and Opportunities for refugees". They are part of a modular system run by a number of Hamburg organisations to promote vocational integration of refugees.

The goal of both these projects is to improve the labour market opportunities for refugees. They use a carefully coordinated chain of support measures, starting with literacy courses and beginners' language courses, and moving on to Europe-wide recognised certificates of German language ability, and computer courses, giving the refugees ideal entry to the training modules, and to appropriate further qualifications. These programmes are supported by social counselling, support in applications, and coaching for applications for and use of internships. Empowerment of the refugees is a key factor in the work, both in coaching and in the teaching programmes.

Finally, a key part of the projects is "**Vocational skill training**". This component was developed in the qualification projects by verikom towards the end of the second EQUAL funding period (2005 – 2007) (e-qualify and basic training pedagogy). Those responsible for the current funding programme of the Federal Ministry of Labour and Social Affairs made some changes in the programme and the concepts. The goal was to ensure that participants, most of whom were subject to the "right of stay" regulation at the time, were prepared for the labour market as quickly as possible, after they had been excluded from the employment market for many years by the regulations under foreigners law and labour law.

After this first trial period, the Vocational skill training programme was further developed in the project AQUABA for refugees (2008-2010), funded from the Hamburg ESF programme, and is now used again in the project "Opportunities for refugees".

The Vocational skill training programme gave participants an introduction to important aspects of the labour market, and at the same time improved their presentation skills and their self-confidence. The vocational skills training included identification of competencies and vocational orientation, labour market research, preparation of application documents, training for application situations including video recordings and presentation exercises, vocational German language teaching with exercises in writing, speaking and in vocabulary, communication for the world of work including telephone and voice training, and information about the German employment market. The programme also included several weeks of IT training for preparation of digital documents, and training for employment market research. Participants also did a four-week internship in the primary labour market, as an integral part of their course. Before, during and after the internships, monitoring and support was provided both to the interns and to the companies where they were placed.

182

These training programmes are conducted twice a year, and have been constantly further developed and adapted to the respective needs in terms of contents and individual learning situations. The main emphasis was on internal differentiation, orientation for action and practice, intercultural learning, and orientation towards the special life situation of refugees. Participants were given practical preparation for the world of work, by their own exploration of vocational fields, by targeted telephone and communication training, by research exercises and role play. Possibilities of social engagement were also presented in this framework, for example by civic and cultural units, by library visits, and by visits to trade union offices.

The training materials were mostly developed specially for the course. The methodology was based on the recommendations and teaching principles set out in the "Manual on second language training with asylum seekers and refugees", which was developed in the second EQUAL funding period together with transnational partner organisations of SAFE HAVEN Hamburg PLUS.

The training took an intercultural approach. The communication forms, social values, modes of working, and also materials and conflict solution methods, were analysed from this perspective. Specific "intercultural training" was conducted to raise awareness of participants, and to build their confidence in handling differences and coping with forms of discrimination.

Two further methodological modules contributed to empowerment: the forward-looking group coaching, and a form of 'mind based stress reduction' which was specially developed and adapted for this target group. That provided a means of psycho-social stabilisation by means of mental training, to cope even with very difficult life conditions.

The current Hamburg ESF project "Opportunities for refugees" supplements vocational training by a preliminary German language course at level B1, in order to achieve more equality in the level of language skill of participants, and to improve their chances of integration in the labour market.

4. Most important milestones

Continuous learning supervision, tests and evaluations after the end of internship and training, both with the teaching staff and with participants, were used to ensure constant monitoring of quality and effectiveness of the programme for everyone involved. Nevertheless, evaluation of the success of vocational skill training is often hard to achieve with participants directly after the end of the course, because there are still many obstacles to access to the employment market in Germany for this target group.

However, it was clear from project-internal evaluations that participants gained not only knowledge of the contents of the course, but also greatly increased their self-confidence. The vocational skill training accompanied by counselling and coaching gave the refugees new perspectives, and helped to stabilise their situation. During the internship, the refugees were often able to see that they could be active, useful and respected members of society. For this short period, they were able to put aside the forced passivity imposed on them in terms of employment, and that enabled them to gain in strength and sense of being recognised.

Some of the former participants in vocational skill training from previous projects have now found employment or a training place, or have successfully completed their training.

Cooperation with a number of companies, which made internships available for the target group of refugees, made it possible to achieve the first steps towards intercultural opening of the labour market and awareness raising for the life conditions of people with unsecured right of stay.

5. Most important hurdles

Refugees with unsecured right of stay are living in difficult circumstances – uncertain perspectives of stay, and constant fear of being deported, toleration status often extended only for a short period at a time, often difficult, cramped housing situation in refugee accommodation, precarious financial situation (Asylum Seekers Benefits Act), lack of recognition of qualifications and certificates, exclusion from many areas of life, lack of participation possibilities, limited labour market access, and experience during flight, in some cases with traumatisation from experiences then – these are just some of the problems that participants had to struggle with.

On average, only about one third of participants have a work permit. One of the reasons for that is that refugees often do not have a passport, without which they will not normally be granted a residence permit. That sometimes leads to frustrating experience, if participants are offered a job following their internship in a company but the Foreigners Authority refuses to grant them a work permit. This shows the paradoxical situation that one authority helps refugees with an employment market programme, and another prevents the long-term success of this programme by putting obstacles in the way.
6. Networking partners (local, regional, national level)
Employment Agency and Ministry of the Interior: clarification of individual conditions for rights or residence and work. Hamburg alliance FLIGHT MIGRATION education – work: active participation of the project in networking to improve the access of refugees to the labour market. Counselling organisation flucht•punkt and refugee centre Hamburg: joint response to questions related to social counselling, rights of residence and work, and debt management. Chamber of Trades: support in making new contacts with companies.
7. Products available in which language? Place of finding – link to web-sites
Beckmann-Schulz, Iris et. al, passage gGmbH (2007): EQUAL LANGUAGE. Manual on Second Language Training with Asylum Seekers and Refugees. Hamburg. www.fluchtort-hamburg.de

Katerina Hibbe, verikom

Language skills are a key component for success in vocational learning and activities in the world of work today. Experts in vocational second-language teaching and vocational education and training for migrants refer to the need for additional support, supplementing the regular provisions of vocational education and training, so that the programmes and measures can be aligned better to individual needs and increase the prospects of success for participants with different mother tongues (Bethscheider et al. 2010).

Experience from practice also shows that vocational education and training is not only relevant for the employment market, but also has an important social function, helping people to develop their own strengths and to play an active part in society. Vocational education & training and policy are always more than simply qualification and policy for labour market integration. Involvement in vocational education and training also has a socialising effect on participants.

5. Summary and recommendations

Ten years of practical work in vocational integration of asylum seekers and tolerated refugees in Hamburg has resulted in a great deal of knowledge, giving in-depth insights into the life situation of refugees.

Many business companies have recognised the potentials of young refugees, and see their high level of motivation and multi-lingual skills as an advantage for

184

the company. At the same time, it is evident that certain ethnic groups are subject to rejection. That is shown by discrimination in the labour market. A study by IZA (Institute for the Study of Labor) at the University of Constance has shown in a field test that applicants with Turkish names received fewer positive responses from employers than applicants of German origin (Kaas, Manger 2010).

The future Action Plan of the City of Hamburg sets out a clear change in direction in its integration policy[27]. It defines itself as "the Global City of Hamburg", underlining enhancement of the intercultural processes of opening up in administration, and emphasising the diversity, shared values and solidarity of its people. It highlights a "We-Concept" (rather than a "Them-and-Us-Concept") to work for an improved welcoming culture towards immigrants. Participation of refugees with perspectives of right to stay is likewise defined as a cross-sectional task. This policy of the City of Hamburg is exemplary for the whole of Germany. The new action plan calls for social inclusion of all individuals for social participation on a basis of equality; it will in future have to be measured by how far it succeeds in setting up integrational and vocational training concepts which are appropriate to make full use of the diversity of the users. It has to ensure that it deals with diversity and heterogeneity in such a way that it takes account of the specific life situations of refugees and asylum seekers more than in the past, because it is evident from analysis of practice and the development of the biographies described here that there are still significant exclusion mechanisms to be eliminated. That will require funding for practical work, and more intervention at institutional level.

Recommendations

The following recommendations are given for stabilisation of the programmes available in Hamburg and to improve the vocational integration of young refugees:

Monitoring – educational report on life situations of refugees

In keeping with the specifications currently applicable in the Hamburg Action Concept, "Monitoring" of integration policy measures and the social and educational reporting puts the focus on migrant groups having secured status of stay. It

---

27 The future action concept is being prepared by the "Integration" steering group chaired by a senior executive of the Hamburg Ministry of Labour, Social Affairs, Family and Integration. The guidelines for this concept have been the subject of public discussion in Hamburg since March 2012.

does not take account of asylum seekers or persons with 'tolerated' status, and those having leave to stay (refugees). Our experience shows that there is a need for development of a suitable data concept in order to analyse quantity and quality of the programmes available in Hamburg, and to identify any inequality and disadvantaging of these groups. Particularly with respect to educational planning, we believe it is important to collect data regularly on the educational participation of refugees in the various districts and schools, and to use the data for evaluation. The goal should be to prepare a qualitative, problem-related educational report, giving indications for action for the policy makers in education and vocational training in Hamburg.

Improving the transition system for young lateral entrants

In 2011 the Hamburg Senate put forward an Action Concept for implementation of the reform of vocational education and training in Hamburg (Doc. 19/8472 of 18.01.11). The transition from school to work is defined as a cross-sectional task for all school forms, but this concept does not take account of the training programmes BVJ-M and VJ-M, and it still fails to consider the specific learning conditions and needs of tolerated refugees. The VJ-M/BVJ-M programmes need to be harmonised in the transition phase 'from school to employment'. The changes in the legislative framework conditions, and the change in the concept of Hamburg's integration policy mean that the educational programmes should be changed in terms of their facilities, their curriculum and their timetable. A report on the educational situation of young refugees in Hamburg has been prepared by *Maren Gag* and *Prof. Dr. Joachim Schroeder* (Hamburg University), focusing on the development and public presentation of the "Refugee Monitoring" concept, and aiming to set up a monitoring process with regular reporting (Gag/Schroeder 2012). The report summarises the consequences of reform of vocational education for refugees living in Hamburg. It presents problem analyses on the structural and educational matching issues of the relevant courses, and illustrates organisational, administrative and legal difficulties based on the educational careers of young refugees. The recommendations set out there are to be used for restructuring the courses.

What should be kept?

The network structures need to be kept, because experience in the Hamburg projects shows that they are viable, and that they help refugees without secured status of stay to participate in education and labour market integration programmes. After all, refugees are particularly dependent on stability of social relations, in view of their own biographical discontinuities. Interlinking of formal and non-formal educational courses in combination with specific counselling and support makes it easier for them to participate, because work is proceeding continuously on optimisation of the communication structures between the players and the relevant institutions. Funding is needed to consolidate the implementation phase and support these processes.

Raising awareness in Job Centres and Employment Agencies

A study by the Federal Ministry of Labour and Social Affairs, examining the effectiveness of the methods set out in the Social Code and treatment of migrants by the regular social services shows that the main problems for placement are inadequate knowledge of German among unemployed people receiving benefits under SGB II. At the same time, it is found that only 55% of respondents who indicated problems in spoken communication in German had attended a language course. It is necessary to make more use of the action reserves available at Job Centres and Employment Agencies to remedy this situation (Institute for Employment and Qualification 2009). The question of whether tolerated refugees and asylum seekers should be allocated to the Job Centres or to the Employment Agencies is dependent on the exact legal details of their status.[28] As this legal situation is extremely complex, it is important to conduct long-term awareness raising measures and continuing education of advisers and placement officials at these institutions, so that the people affected can make use of their rights to counselling and placement, and use the promotion instruments available.

Hamburg calls for changes at Federal level

Most of the legal standards relating to improved vocational integration of refugees are decided at Federal level. So appropriate amendment proposals have to be made to the Ministry of the Interior and the Ministry of Labour and Social Affairs. It would be desirable for Hamburg to advocate the removal of legal barriers, to facilitate labour market access for refugees without a residence permit, and to prepare the relevant initiatives in the Bundesrat.

---

28 passage gGmbH (2009): Integration by employment and training. Advice for counselling and placement of refugees and persons with right of stay.

ANNEX

Mapping City HAMBURG

Formal VET System	Do have Asylum-Seekers and Refugees[29] access to VET (if/if not and how)	Structural obstacles – factors for success
"Dual system": Most of the vocational training is done in the framework of the Dual System. The training takes place at two locations – in a company and in a vocational school. As a rule it takes three years. The companies bear the costs of in-company training.	There are no further requirements for access to training in the dual system – it is in principle open to anyone. Migrants must have secured right to stay for the duration of the training. Work permit is needed. Participation of asylum seekers and refugees depends on their status and many details regarding individual *characteristics* (duration of stay, legislation on which the status is based...).	In the past, refugees and asylum seekers were systematically excluded from education and the labour market, but a paradigm shift in policy has been launched with the introduction of the "right to remain" regulation and the legislation for transposition of the directive into practice. However, it only goes part of the way, because participation depends on the duration of stay, and differs depending on status ('tolerated' status, residence permit, right to remain, etc.). Implementation of the carefully tailored funding programmes is proving successful, and is indispensable. The regular services at the Job Centres and the Job Agency have not yet adjusted to changes in legislation – these changes recognise specific disadvantages for refugees, and give them access to the labour market policy instruments (depending on their status). Business companies are not yet convinced, so there is still a lot of persuasion work to be done. In addition, business companies are faced with major bureaucratic obstacles in obtaining work permits for refugees and asylum seekers.

---

29   The terms refugees and asylum seekers in the context of the project include: individuals who have received a residence permit on probation according to the statutory "grandfather clause" (Altfallregelung); asylum-seekers; and "tolerated" persons (Geduldete).

Full-time vocational training schools (Berufsfachschulen): Give their students an introduction to one ore more vocational profiles, or take them to a vocational preparation (one-year programme) or help their students to obtain the higher school leaving certificates. There are schools for commercial professions, and for foreign-language professions, for craft trades, for household management and social care professions, for healthcare professionals and for artistic vocations.	Free access for refugees and asylum seekers if – enough German language competencies, – the required school leaving certificate is available – a work permit is not needed.	Funding is available to refugees and asylum seekers under the Federal Education Funding Act (BAföG) if they have had legal right of stay or tolerated status in Germany for four years or more (Art. 8 BAföG), provided that the young people are not living at home with their parents.
University sector (Hochschulbereich)	Access is available.	Funding is available to refugees and asylum seekers under the Federal Education Funding Act (BAföG) if they have had legal right of stay or tolerated status in Germany for four years or more (Art. 8 BAföG), provided that the young people are not living at home with their parents.
Transitional system for lateral entrants subject to compulsory schooling at the Hamburg Institute of Vocational Education	A special course is provided for migrants where the language of the country of origin is not German (preparatory year for migrants – VJ-M), where their status of stay is provisional (leave to stay or tolerated status); this course takes two years for full-time participants.	This course is equipped with fewer resources (lower assessment of needs – basic lessons, basic frequency); that means disadvantages compared with other lateral entrants.
Hamburg Vocational Training Programme (Hamburger Ausbildungs-programm, HAP)	The Hamburg Vocational Training Programme (HAP) is mainly for young people who cannot obtain in-company training due to individual disadvantages, but who are expected to be capable of successfully completing company training with support, and can achieve rapid transfer to such training. This programme is open to refugees and asylum seekers.	The age limit is 24 years.

Second labour market pro-grammes	Access is possible for a limited group who receive benefits under the provisions of the Social Code. Allocation is via the Job Centre.	Practically no chance of getting a job in the regular labour market after completion of the programme.

Non-formal VET System	Do have Asylum-Seekers and Refugees access to VET (if/if not and how)	Structural obstacles – factors for success
Advice and counselling: Help desk and information centres at Diakonie (church organisation); Help desk for guidance (organi-sation funded by the Land of Hamburg); Clearing unit for those in need of special support (organisation funded by the Land of Ham-burg).	Specific offers for Asylum seekers and refugees.	
Integration courses: Language training and learning in the German social context (645 hours)	A sub-group of refugees is eligible for participation, due to the offer by the City of Ham-burg to fund "supplementary language programmes" and thus to open up the integration courses.	Regularly NO, only for mi-grants who come to Germany staying permanently (compul-sory participation pursuant to Sections 44 and 4a Residence Act [AufenthG]); minimum framework of integration bene-fits. 1 euro per lesson to be paid by participant.
Advice, training, placement SAFE HAVEN Hamburg (FLUCHTort Hamburg): Net-work of 8 sub-projects gives advice, guidance, coaching, vocational training, placement in education and workplaces. Target: asylum seekers and refugees. Training for multipliers. Target: public institutions e.g. labour office … (Federal ESF programme lim-ited to 3 years)	Specific offers for asylum seekers and refugees. With the "Federal ESF Programme on labour-market support for migrants with a refugee back-ground and refugees with ac-cess to the labour market", the Federal Ministry of Labour and Social Affairs has launched a programme which is intended to support the labour market integration process.	The tried-and-tested model of development partnerships of the EQUAL programme was therefore taken up once again. The various players in migra-tion and labour market policy work together at local level in the context of the networks (non-governmental organisa-tions, job placement services, chambers of commerce and crafts, and trade unions are involved as well as the respon-sible authorities). This leads to cooperation between institu-tions which previously often worked in parallel or even at cross purposes.

		The programmes within the network are based on the life situations of participants and are interrelated to provide a chain of support, and to enable the refugees to go through a series of programmes that are as precisely "customised" as possible, taking account of their individual circumstances. Evaluation of the past funding period for the whole of the programme in Germany shows that it obtained positions in education and work for more than 50% of participants. A major structural problem is that there are not enough training programmes with a longer period of funding, to compensate for qualification gaps due to long waiting times and long interruptions in educational careers. Immediate entry into dual training is not possible for many of the young refugees, and in particular for adults who want direct access to the labour market.
Opportunities for refugees: 2 projects, one of which works with young refugees and asylum seekers and cooperates with 3 vocational schools (ESF programme of the Land of Hamburg limited to 2-3 years)	Specific offers for asylum seekers and refugees. The Hamburg ESF programme also launched a call to create projects in this field and for this target group. A first project (3 sub-projects) was completed at the end of 2010 after 3 years. The next period starts in March 2011).	The project is planned and implemented as a programme to complement the sub-projects at SAFE HAVEN Hamburg. The networks work in close cooperation with one another.
Additional language training: German courses for refugees (Flüchtlingszentrum)	Specific offers for asylum seekers and refugees. Most refugees have access, with certain restrictions – they must have been living in Germany for more than 6 months, number of lessons reduced (300 hours), priority to parents with children aged 3 years or more, to help them learn the German language and to give	The number of hours is not sufficient. Very good complementary programme, supporting the work of the networks. A positive feature is the linking of courses to the local area, ensuring provision close to place of residence.

	support to them when they go to school.	
Supplementary language teaching: language courses for learning work-related German, for participants who do not receive benefits under the provisions of the Social Code (Regenbogen Plus project with the Turkish Community in Hamburg)	This project is just starting. The participation of refugees and asylum seekers has to be arranged.	Problem: the number of hours is not sufficient to get access to the labour market and/or vocational education.
ESF BAMF programme "German language for work" (Berufsbezogene Deutschförderung), project group passage, Hamburger Adult Education Institute and IBH, in various parts of the city and in various segments of the world of work – caring/social professions, hotels/restaurants, office/trade, industrial	Access possible for refugees since 01/01/2012. Allocation via SAFE HAVEN Hamburg.	In some cases long waiting periods.
Central recognition office (Zentrale Anlaufstelle Anerkennung, ZAA, at the Diakonisches Werk): advises and informs on issues of recognition of foreign professional certificates and qualifications. There is a grant programme run by the Hamburg Ministry of Economics and Labour Affairs which can fund appropriate further training and additional qualification courses on application.	Access is open to refugees. But it should be noted that many of them do not have any of the necessary documents, because in many cases they had to leave their country of origin without papers due to a situation of war.	The Federal Government is planning legislation for recognition of foreign professional qualifications (Recognition Act), to enter into force in 2011. Hamburg has already started setting up the relevant unit, for a structure to provide the necessary advisory service and to look after the procedure for the migrants. It remains to be seen exactly how the recognition process will work. The key factor for successful implementation will be appropriate adaptation programmes – these are currently available only in a few vocational fields (for example an additional "Medicine" course with specialist language teaching, with an internship in a hospital, preparation for review of equivalent status). A major problem is that recognition conflicts with other legislation in some respects. There are also

		specific obstacles for third-country nationals (for example, a doctor from a third country will never get full recognition *[Approbation]*, but at most a specialist work permit which is limited in time and place, as regulated in the Federal Medical Practitioners Ordinance *[Bundesärzteordnung]*).
Job promotion – advice and placement by – Job Centre – Agency for Labour	Responsibility for job promotion depends on the responsibility for granting benefits for cost of living. If the applicant is entitled to Unemployment Benefit II pursuant to SGB II, the Job Centres are also responsible for job promotion (Section 14 SGB II and Section 22 para. 4 SGB III). If the applicant is entitled to benefits from the Social Department pursuant to the Asylum Seeker Benefits Act, that does not lead to exclusion. The Agency for Labour is then responsible.	The granting of educational vouchers is a responsibility of Agency for Labour or Job Centre. The criterion for decision is whether a programme is "necessary" (not whether it is appropriate). There is little success in practice so far in this area.

III.1
Refugee Monitoring: Research status, conceptual basis and implementation proposals, taking the example of the City of Hamburg

Maren Gag, Joachim Schroeder

Means of control in the transnational educational area

The establishment of a transnational European educational area makes it necessary to develop new concepts for control of educational policy and for analysis and evaluation of control practices. Earlier control theory, up to the 1980s, was very much concentrated on national state controls, and saw the state as the central controlling body in society. Today it is necessary to respond to transnationalisation processes, and to clarify what means of control for the educational sector can be identified or needs to be developed beyond national borders. Control theory distinguishes between three central means of control (Willke 2001):

- *Power*, in the form of legally binding regulations, for example EU regulations in the vocational education and training sector;
- *Money*, in the form of project funding or credit allocation;
- *Knowledge*, in the form of creating and disseminating knowledge from evaluation studies, quality management or implementation research.

These three means of control are interdependent, contextual and process-related, and they are functionally dependent on individual societal sub-systems (political, economic, academic). At the same time, they can be framed as the theoretical starting point for solution of control and coordination problems in complex social systems.

Following this approach, it needs to be clarified what control instruments are appropriate for use in the transnational educational area of international and supranational organisations. The EU is not entitled to conduct its own independent educational policy, but it can make suggestions in the general education sector, and can even set up programmes in the vocational education sector; it can support educational programmes at national level while respecting the principle of subsidiarity (means of control: *Power*). It can also work through the funding of projects and activities both at European and at national level to set priorities on the educational agenda, thus having a major influence on national educational policy (*Money*). It is increasingly putting *knowledge* at the centre of its efforts as the means of control – for example, the Lisbon Strategy introduced a new form of coordination, which practically institutionalises reciprocal learning between member states (Parreira 2006).

There are three main tools used for generating 'knowledge' in the European educational sector (Ioannidou 2008):

- Regular monitoring and educational reporting;
- Peer review; and
- International performance comparison (e.g. PISA).

All three of these tools have gained importance in the past decade, and are used intensively by the EU and the OECD to support control efforts in the educational sector and to exert an influence on national educational policy. All three tools are also used to examine the impact of migration processes in the educational sector. However, due to the specifics of European asylum and refugee policy, these tools are at most rudimentary and locally developed for asylum seekers, people with tolerated status and refugees, but not in such a way that they can provide effective and useful support to local, national and overall European control policies. The present paper outlines a procedure for closing this gap. It is to develop, test and evaluate tools for regular monitoring

- with respect to specific *migrant groups* (asylum seekers, tolerated persons and refugees);
- by means of continuous *educational reporting* (as a major foundation for education policy control);
- in the *European educational area* (which is to be understood as a transnational area).

Monitoring and educational reporting

The term *monitoring* means systematic recording, observation and control of processes and events by means of objective observation and recording tools. It is increasingly used in the educational context – both by academics, referring to the development of tools for systematic observation of educational processes, and by politicians, where the object is to identify gaps between expectations and realities and to identify possibilities of targeted intervention. Educational monitoring includes indicators and benchmarks which permit systematic and long-term observation of educational processes and direct comparison between the desired status and the actual status.

196

A basic tool for educational monitoring is the preparation of *educational reports*. That means thematic reporting with systematic, regular publication of various information on the educational system, using data both from official statistics and from surveys and educational research. The purpose is to help describe what is happening in education, and to lay the foundations for knowledge-based system control and system infrastructure. Regular educational reporting makes it possible to compare what is happening in individual countries, and thus contributes to transparency in the educational sector. It helps to show the results of education, identify needs and disadvantages, and puts the policy makers under pressure to justify what they are doing and to take action. And, not least important, it provides control-relevant knowledge for political decision making processes.

The OECD, for example, has a long history of compiling statistical information on educational systems, in particular with the work done by CERI, and disseminates a wide range of country studies and comparative thematic educational reports. The EU also makes use of such tools – for example monitoring and benchmarking of national progress – for achievement of joint European goals. Particularly in the educational sector, where the EU has only relatively limited regulative power, this is to help "develop an evaluation and feedback culture, so that lessons can be learned from previous successes and failures, and they can generate regulative effect" (EU Commission 2001, p. 29).

Tools of this kind are already being used at municipal and local levels, too. For example, some tools for *ethnic monitoring* have been developed for local educational and integration management, to examine the quantity and quality of programmes and identify their geographical distribution and ongoing inequality and disadvantages of migrants. *Ethnic monitoring* collects data regularly on a district and school basis to determine the educational participation of various population groups, and to make assessments on this basis (Radtke 2003). The aim is to increase the transparency of organisational activities related to the schools, from cultural supervision down through educational administration to the individual educational institutions. It is characteristic of this approach that educational reporting is linked with the use of social data (available in many places from poverty research and in the form of a municipal "social atlas") and with data from children's and youth services. The goal is to produce a qualitative, problem-related educational report, to help the political decision makers in their decisions and actions.

In Germany, a number of inter-state initiatives have been launched with the implementation of the Federal Government's National Integration Plan, to advance the development of common indicators and to standardise monitoring processes in the various states, in order to facilitate evaluation of the targets set by the states for projects aimed at improving integration and education policy.[1]

The problem – refugees are left out[2]

The specifics of European asylum and refugee policies mean that the tools for quantitative and qualitative data collection are at most rudimentary for the group of asylum seekers, tolerated persons and refugees – they are not appropriate for effective support to municipal, national or overall European control policies. While positive experience has been gathered with *ethnic monitoring*, mainly in some of the large European cities, the group of asylum seekers, tolerated persons and refugees is mostly not included in these projects. Integration policy mostly puts the spotlight on migrant groups having secured status of stay. And it is often difficult to collect the necessary data on refugees – most countries have specific regulations for refugees in terms of access to social benefits, so they are often not included in the usual procedures of social reporting. It may therefore be assumed that the foundations have not yet been laid for regular *refugee monitoring*; experience and insights from migration research can be used, but need to be adapted for this target group.

Monitoring specifically related to refugees is an urgent requirement, particularly because of significant changes in German refugee policy. Refugees with 'tolerated' status are increasingly being included in integration policy measures. The conditions required for refugees to be permitted to work or to enter training are dependent on duration of their residence, and differ depending on their status. This important development was triggered by implementation of the joint European initiative EQUAL (2001-2007). Following that, in 2008 the Federal Ministry of Labour and Social Affairs set up the "ESF Federal programme for labour market support for persons with right of stay and refugees with access to the labour market". It achieved substantial success in the first funding period – more than 50% of the participants which it covered were able to get placement in training

---

1   Integration policy has made substantial progress in recent years. Three Integration summits launched by the Federal Government showed that government had also realized that Germany is an immigration country, and that it is up to governement and civil society to deal with the facts as they are. The National Integration Plan of 2007 contains noumerous self-commitments, and sets up the ambitious goal of achieving mearsurable improvements. A great many concepts have been formulated, and in many areas also tangible steps undertaken for intercultural opening.

2   "Refugees" in this context means immigrants who have *fled* to Germany, rather than persons formally recognised as "refugees"; thus the term used here includes asylum seekers, 'tolerated' persons, and persons having a right of residence on humanitarian grounds.

or employment (Johann Daniel Lawaetz Foundation et al. 2011). A second period has been running since November 2010 with 28 networks (about 230 individual projects), providing regular counselling, coaching, placement and public relations work at regional level.

Nevertheless, it is evident that inclusion of refugees in education and employment is still an experimental field. There is need for improvement particularly in the use of regulatory tools, in order to achieve sustainable support. The municipal integration concepts in Germany also show that as a rule they are related exclusively to immigrants who live legally and permanently in Germany. This integration policy guideline, which is supported by valid residence law (Section 43 I AufenthG) is an obstacle to new integration initiatives that are promoted by the Federation and individual states for refugees, tolerated persons and asylum seekers. These persons do not have a legal right of residence, but they do have an official document which certifies their legitimate stay (toleration) and hence the legality of their presence, and often they have been tolerated in Germany for many years. As long as these legal reforms, aimed at educational participation and labour market integration of people with precarious right of stay, are in conflict with the dominant mainstream, further efforts are still needed to keep highlighting the life situations of refugees as a hidden group among the immigrants, at least in the present stage of discourse in society.

Inventory of refugee monitoring in five European cities

Cities and metropolitan regions tend to attract migrants and refugees because they have better chances there of finding work, or getting into training or study programmes. They are also centres for asylum seekers and newly arrived migrants who come to join their families. And cities are not only attractive in terms of work productivity, but also because they have networks of ethnic communities, which are used as a support structure and as bridges for integration. That also applies for transnationally organised families already living in the cities. The arrival of migrants and refugees contributes to greater diversity in the urban population, and at the same time it makes great demands on municipal integration policy, to meet the needs of different population groups, to provide equivalent integration opportunities for all, and to support peaceful co-existence between the indigenous population and the new arrivals. Co-existence in diversity, which has a long tradition in European cities, is associated with a constant process of reflection on local strategy development for involvement of all groups of the population, taking account in particular of disparities and lines of difference, i.e. there is a need for constant examination of how far specific sub-groups or specific sub-issues are taken into account. That applies in particular for ensuring the basic right to education and training for young people. Refugees are particularly disadvantaged due to many years of restrictive policy, preventing them from taking up their rights to education, and setting up regulatory barriers to acquisition of education and training, so that they often have major gaps in their education and training careers.

This subject was taken up in the European project group "Integration of refugees into the European educational and labour market: Requirements for a target oriented approach", involving researchers and players from vocational education and training institutions in Hamburg, Glasgow, Göteborg, Florence and Thessaloniki, which tracked the educational pathways and employment careers of refugees with insecure status of stay and examined the impact of locally based integration programmes.[3] The objective is to clarify in European comparison if and in what way the *target group* was able to benefit from participating in a training and employment programme, and whether integration was achieved in the various segments of general education, vocational education and higher education, and in the employment market. Particular attention is thereby given to the development of subjective potentials of the refugees, by examining how they were able to pursue development of their educational goals.

The preliminary considerations here are to be started in Hamburg in the spirit of a pilot project in a discussion on targeted monitoring of this specific migrant group of asylum seekers, tolerated persons and refugees, and steps for implementation are to be examined. Experience gained is to be transferred to other locations.

Conceptual foundations of educational reporting

Regardless of requirements for lifelong learning, youth is a vital life stage for acquisition of educational qualifications, for stepwise approach to the world of work, for crystallisation of wishes for the vocational future, and for entry into the employment system. Educational researchers point out in the international education discussion that today people need about fifteen years of education and training to acquire the fundamental educational level needed for successful activity in a globalised world (Schroeder/Seukwa 2007). It is particularly difficult for refugees to complete this long period of education, because they live at different places in different countries in the course of their biographies, and cannot complete this

---

3   This project is funded by the Lifelong Learning programme (Leonardo da Vinci – Partnerships) and coordinated in Hamburg by Prof. Dr. Louis Henri Seukwa – Hamburg University of Applied Sciences. Maren Gag – passage gGmbH Hamburg and Prof. Dr. Joachim Schroeder – Johann Wolfgang Goethe University Frankfurt/Main are participating partners.

period of education in the institutionally formalised sequence without interruptions. In Germany they were excluded from vocational education and training for many years and, though there has been a re-structuring in the formal regulatory system by means of legislative changes, that does not mean that there has been a systematic paradigm shift in the practice of government and administration. It is therefore desirable that participation of refugees in education and training and in the labour market should be taken up as an indicator in measurement of integration policy in Hamburg and in the educational reporting.

Different routes can be taken for preparation of a report on the life situation and educational situation of refugees. It can use a *descriptive* approach, presenting data-based developments in the educational system and in neighbouring areas and institutions relevant for education, in order to show long-term developments and impacts of political measures; or it can use a *problem-oriented* approach, seeking to show the requirements for action and control by government. But in either case it must be *internationally compatible*, in order to ensure comparability between the EU member states and thus at least to permit data-based framing of a European education policy.

Educational reporting is normally based on structural, process and result data. The goal is to establish integrated educational analyses which

- process the structural data and thus describe the supply side of formal and non-formal education;
- give indications of take-up and participation, type and extent of educational participation of the target group;
- collect findings on short, medium and long-term effect and performance of the educational programmes, and thus of possible individual educational processes, and thus determine their output or outcome.

These conceptual basics are needed for regular *Refugee monitoring* with respect to general and vocational education and labour market integration, as they are for any other form of educational reporting. The necessary data concept first has to be prepared in comparison with the specific life situations of the target group. Educational reporting as a specific form of social reporting can not only consider the social conditions and institutional responses (system perspective), but also has the task of reporting on subjective expectations for institutions and subjective satisfaction with them (stakeholder perspective). Reporting which is based only on the conventional educational systems would completely miss the point of reporting on these problems, because what is important here is to analyse the close relationship between social situation, life situation of the target group and educational programmes. What is urgently needed is an approach based on life situation, including formal and non-formal programmes available within institutions and outside of them (Isoplan Consult 2005; Schroeder/Seukwa 2007).

Access to socio-structural data on asylum seekers, tolerated persons and refugees is often possible only to a limited degree, even for the authorities. In particular, collecting such data is hindered by the different systematisation principles applied in the different authorities and institutions (social authorities, housing and health authorities, labour administration, education authorities, urban development authorities, etc.). Many of the authorities do not have the necessary localised data and evaluation frameworks. Differences in geographical definition of the areas, and differences in organisational principles of the areas are problems for integrated data processing (no. of cases considered, alphabetical system, district reference, etc.). The available data are often out-of-date, incomplete, insufficient or incorrect, so that all in all they are not able to provide useful results. That is highly problematic for reporting which is not designed on a one-off basis, but is intended for systematic ongoing reporting, especially as continuous monitoring requires dependable, standardised, regularly collected data, to identify lines of development and gaps in current programmes and performance, and to permit forecasts for forward planning.

A suitable system of social indicators is needed in order to permit long-term, systematic observation of social phenomena and problems (social monitoring). Data and indicators can only be collected inductively (by plausibility). Thus before indicators are defined to give information on education, labour market, vocational qualification, etc., there first has to be agreement on what data are suitable and available, in order to examine the desired thematic fields. Typical *quality criteria* of socio-cultural data are: factual correctness, accuracy, precise localisation, inter-district comparability (*system used*); all desired data are to be collected and published independently of government institutions and organisations (*autonomy*); only long-term, regular surveys permit identification of changes in social situations (*regularity*); if possible social indicators should reveal problematic developments in good time (*timeliness* as an 'early warning system').

A wide range of *data sources* can be used for educational planning, whereby a distinction is to be made between the system perspective and the stakeholder perspective. The system perspective means that programmes and services of institutions are the subject of analysis, e.g. costs and funding of the institutional programmes, their facilities and equipment, their staffing or the qualifications of the professionals. The stakeholder perspective examines usage behaviour and individual educational processes: Who takes up what programmes and in what way? What expectations do users have of the institutions? How satisfied are they with them? How can the educational processes be analysed and presented? What statements can be made about the educational processes and their impact? Educational reporting is based on official statistics (microcensus, random samples); data of administrative implementation, surveys and user analyses, for example on the acceptance of social services and institutions; qualitative information (management reports, organiser reports). According to information obtained so far, refugees have not been involved in such surveys at all, and are not included in data collection.

In working out a possible *data concept* it is necessary to clarify what core data ("must-have" data) are absolutely essential and therefore have to be collected if the database is to have any use at all, and what supplementary data ("should-have" data) contribute to a more differentiated picture, help to support the data concept and – unless there are major collection difficulties standing in the way – help to increase the significance of the database. And finally, what additional data ("can-have" data) should be collected, rounding off the database and giving value-added for specific indications, provided that their collection does not raise problems or could be used to the disadvantage of the refugees. Data are collected at different levels via these surveys, i.e. data records are collected with information on structures and types of programmes of institutions, and also on (aggregated) groups of persons (e.g. their sex or age), and thirdly on individuals. A systematic approach is also needed for this purpose, for example to show the validity and scope of each data group.

For purposes of educational planning and taking account of the available data, their accuracy, reliability and original collection purposes, the possibilities are then to be specified for *processing, evaluation* and *presentation* of the data. Although it is a general goal of social reporting to show various forms of social inequality, selective impoverishment, exclusion and marginalisation, this can be done in such a way as to identify and open discussion on socio-economic polarisation, socio-demographic structural changes, socio-cultural heterogenisation and socio-geographical segregation. Thus data evaluation and presentation can be done in terms of socio-geography (social atlas, local profiles, district reports) or socio-culture (sociotopes, environment analyses), and life situation related ranking, indexing or target group evaluations can be made (e.g. equality reports). Selection and specification for a presentation form is effected firstly on the basis of content reasons (depending which of the indicators is best able to give information on the relevant questions and inter-relationships). Another relevant issue is what resources in staffing and equipment are needed to obtain the data. And data presentation should also be suitable for continued inputs, and facilitate constant updating, to avoid simply taking short-term snapshots of the current situation which would be open to dispute.

Educational reporting must present its arguments on an empirical-descriptive basis, but at the same time show disparities in access to educational programmes. It has to draw attention to normative issues and problems, to raise awareness for developments which could otherwise go unnoticed and not be addressed in social and political debate. But reporting itself cannot make decisions on how much inequality a society can permit, tolerate and endure, or how emerging disparities can be dealt with in political terms, or what steps can be taken to compensate and to minimise inequalities. That can only be done in open discussion by professionals and politicians. So a task of the data concept is to show what strategies and organisational forms can ensure *communication via the data*.

Indicator development and refugee-sensitive monitoring in Hamburg – proposals for a data concept

The Hamburg Senate has for many years given concrete integration perspectives to asylum seekers and people having longstanding tolerated status, by means of continuous financial and advisory support through the network projects known under the name of FLUCHTort Hamburg (SAFE HAVEN Hamburg).[4] In this context, and in the context of changes in the legal framework conditions, the network together with the Hamburg alliance 'FLIGHT MIGRATION Education Employment' called for a revision of the Hamburg Integration Concept by the Hamburg Ministries and the Integration Advisory Council. The necessity of doing this was recently underscored by a public meeting with numerous experts at Hamburg City Hall, and confirmed by the policy makers present there from administration and parliament.[5] On the basis of this real integration policy change, it is proposed that indicators should be set up for each of the goals formulated, to ensure long-term monitoring of goal achievement in these action strategies.

The proposals set out here are related to the 'state of the art', as currently used in practice in Hamburg, hoping to raise awareness of the fact that modifications in favour of this group will be possible in the ongoing process of indicator development and reporting. We realise that qualitative monitoring in particular can be extremely expensive, and have therefore limited ourselves to proposals which could be classified as "minimal solutions" from the experts' viewpoint.

Whether or not social integration can be achieved is decided particularly in the social area and in the housing districts. The set-up of the infrastructure in the *social area* is a key factor in success or failure of integration processes. At the same time, there is a need to keep the whole of the city in view when considering participation in education and employment, to examine access opportunities to institutions and

---

4 The EU initiative EQUAL launched a significant development. A number of network projects were implemented in Hamburg under the leadership of passage gGmbH: Training initiative for asylum seekers and refugees (2001-2005); SAFE HAVEN Hamburg – vocational integration for refugees (2005-2007); SAFE HAVEN Hamburg Plus (2008-2010), funded from the ESF Federal programme for labour market support to people having right to stay and refugees.

5 See documentation of event (September 2010) www.fluchtort-hamburg.de.

the accommodation situation in the framework of public-sector youth services. As it is in any case difficult to access the socio-structural data of asylum seekers, tolerated persons and refugees, we see the implementation of data collection tools and the assessment of structural data and findings as complementary.

Proposals for reporting at state level

For some years now, complex processes have been ongoing in Germany at the level of the individual states, to implement a unified system of integration monitoring with the aim of developing a tool based on core indicators, compatible with monitoring at Federal level and at European level. The inter-state working group on "Indicator development and monitoring" of the Conference of Ministers Responsible for Integration presented the results of a pilot study with participation of seven of the German states in February 2011. The extensive set of parameters and indicators includes basic demographic data on a range of integration relevant issues, and these were subjected to practical testing in the states involved. The results were interpreted on this basis, and recommendations were drawn up for nationwide monitoring in all the states (Statistical Office Berlin Brandenburg 2010). There is no provision for separate reporting on 'Refugees'; only 'Residence right' and 'Duration of stay' are included as parameters.

This set of indicators, which is quantitative in nature, is likely to be the basis for future reporting by the states, so the proposals for 'refugee sensitive' monitoring are linked to it, in order to minimise the development effort to set up the necessary data collection tools. Based on knowledge of the life situation of refugees, relevant comments are given below on selected indicators, and supplementary proposals are made, related mainly to the status of educational market and labour market participation of refugees.

Indicator	Definition	Relevance	Data source
Population	Number of people with/ without migration background, broken down into German nationals with migration background, EU nationals, and non-EU nationals, and into appropriate age groups.	Refugees, tolerated persons and asylum seekers mostly come from third countries (1); breakdown of countries of origin would be relevant. In terms of age groups, it should be considered that some of them are underage unaccompanied refugees who need special support (2). Goal: to get more accurate knowledge of flight backgrounds, life situations in	(1) In combination with the category "non-EU nationals" breakdown of countries of origin (Central Register Office). (2) In combination with age category, data collection from youth services on the proportion of underage unaccompanied refugees.

Indicator	Definition	Relevance	Data source
		the countries of origin, etc., to take account of cultural/religious specifics.	
Foreigners by residence status	The category relevant for refugees is "third country nationals" with limited residence permit and with toleration. The category of "limited residence" includes a subgroup of refugees covered by right of stay (Section 104a AufenthG), but where this is by no means secure.	Residence status in detail is particularly important for granting of a work permit and for access to educational funding programmes. Granting of residence permit and toleration permit employment and participation in education only under certain conditions. The recommendation of the pilot study is taken up here to include residence permission in data collected. Goal: to make better use of scope for use of education rights, support in access.	Central Register Office
Recipients of benefits under SGB II	Concerns German/foreign employable benefit recipients under SGB II (basic security for job seekers), breakdown by age.	This category includes only a small sub-group (with right to stay under § 104a AufenthG and others). Most receive benefits under AsylLG. We suggest this data should also be collected. Goal: to make use of scope in taking up funding tools, to compensate for disadvantages.	Basic security from social security offices of district and Ministry of Social Affairs and Family
Housing space per family member	Relates to housing space per family member in families with children under 18 years old, calculated per individual person.	The housing situation of refugees living in homes is not taken into account. Goal: to compensate for disadvantage, especially to get different accommodation for families with children and adolescents. Under current conditions schooling and participation in education and employment is difficult.	"Support and housing" programme and Ministry of Social Affairs and Family

There are a number of other indicators which would be relevant to filter out more precise data on the specific life situations. The example of the indicator 'school students by school type' shows that data collection cannot be realised, because a distinction is made only between "with" and "without" migration background, and in any case the status of residence is not recorded at the schools. The First Hamburg Education Report is designed to pursue an "inter-disciplinary data collection strategy, in order to permit networked and continuous monitoring of transitions in the educational system and to permit an overview of the problem situations" (City of Hamburg 2009). On this basis, further indicators are also proposed, also on a complementary basis.

Indicator	Definition	Relevance	Data source
(A2) Demographic development of population / foreign population and persons with migration background	Distinction between Germans and foreign nationals and population with migration background.	Sub-group of foreign population has special support needs – specifically refugees and asylum seekers. Goal: to make the sub-group of refugees/asylum seekers visible in a differentiated way. Reference to sub-group.	Ministry of the Interior, and qualitative (see below)
Family and life forms	Distinction between life forms as spouses, cohabitation and sole parents – reference to disadvantage due to 'social capital'	Among young refugees there is an increasing proportion of underage unaccompanied refugees (as life form); this group normally has no 'social capital'. Goal: to reduce special disadvantage.	Youth services of districts
(C4) Special educational needs / high proportion of those with special needs have migration background	Reference to large proportion of school students with migration background among those requiring support	Due to their flight biographies, a proportion of the refugees/ asylum seekers probably belong to those with special needs. Check to what extent there is a proportion of refugees/asylum seekers that can be helped by external counselling provision (trauma coping, learning assistance, etc.). Goal: To provide support appropriate to life situation, and to manage transitions better.	At school locations
Lateral entrants without knowledge of German language up to grade 9/10	Not mentioned in report	Children and young refugees frequently join the school as lateral entrants due to their flight biography. Check to what extent chil-	Data collection at regional school locations and school information centre

Indicator	Definition	Relevance	Data source
		dren from refugee families or of asylum seekers can be given additional external support in preparatory classes. Goal: To ensure support appropriate to life situation, to manage transitions better.	
(D) Vocational preparation schools (BVS)	Not covered	At school locations H15, G8 and G20 there are currently a large number of refugees, tolerated persons and asylum seekers concentrated in VJM classes (preparatory classes for migrants). Goal: Targeted transition management, optimisation of training opportunities.	Data collection at school locations
Languages of origin	Not covered	Refugees often have a number of languages of origin. Goal: Make this resource visible for lifelong learning and the world of work.	Data collection at school locations

Supplementary information is to be obtained for a number of different indicators by means of qualitative surveys, mainly to be conducted on a social geography basis. Interlinking of the two data collection levels is to create an improved basis for systematic inclusion of refugees in educational planning. They are useful additions to check the effectiveness of support measures. It is suggested that the expertise of the stakeholders should be added to the following fields of activity:

Traineeship programme of the Hamburg Senate

The Senate (i.e. the Government of Hamburg) has explicitly opened this programme for this sub-group.

The programme should be checked to see what participation actually happens.

– How many of the participants are young refugees?

Tailor-made programmes

For some ten years now, the Senate has been involved in co-funding by various Hamburg Ministries (Ministry of Education and Vocational Training; Ministry of Labour, Social Affairs, Family and Integration; Senate Chancellery; and previously the Ministry of Economic Affairs and Labour) for implementation of tailor-made support programmes for tolerated refugees (adolescent and adult). There are extensive case studies from the various funding periods, and detailed reports and other project publications which can be used for collection of data.

a) How are the results of the network projects FLUCHTort Hamburg (passage gGmbH) to be assessed (2010-2014)? Answers to the following questions are to be filtered out of project reports and discussions with experts:
What is the percentage of young refugees who are reached by the programme? How many of them have been placed in schools and dual training? What methods and tools were successful in the practical work? What obstacles are there in transition to training/ the labour market?
b) How is the experience gained in the network project "Opportunities for refugees" (basis & woge e.V.) to be assessed (2011-2012/13)? The project is co-operating with HIBB (Hamburg Institute for Vocational Training) and provides school-integrated programmes for transition management.
What is the percentage of young refugees who are reached by the programme? How many of them have been placed in schools and dual training? What methods and tools were successful in the practical work? What obstacles are there in transition to training/ the labour market?
c) The experience gained at the clearing office for those in need of special protection (refugee centre) should be used:
What are the problems and needs of those who seek advice there?
d) The evaluation of supplementary language promotion by opening of the integration courses (BSG funding via refugee centre) should be used:
What is the age structure of participants? Is the programme compatible, i.e. is it designed for integration in a systematic chain of support?

Proposals to take account of social area reporting

Every Hamburg district has an office which is responsible for 'integrated social planning', which collects and processes data and draws up social area descriptions, to provide a planning basis for further social area management. A whole range of proposals is set out below related to the needs of refugees, in order to supplement the data collected at state level and to add qualitative aspects. Experts from the local institutions, such as schools, social services, youth services, or other organisers of youth provisions, often have a lot of detailed knowledge about the life situations of refugees, and this has to be systematically collected and compiled in order to make use of it for further planning. The collection of quantitative and qualitative data in the following fields of activity would provide useful additional insights into the life world of refugees from the perspective of the social area.

Transition from school to employment

In connection with the conduct of regional education conferences, valuable cooperation and dialogue forums are set up in the districts, characterised by diversity of the bodies involved together with the general schools. Awareness raising for special difficulties in the transition from school to employment can be effected from the 8th year of schooling. So the following data should be collected in the relevant classes at school:

What is the percentage of refugees among the school students?
Which countries do they come from? Are there any ethnic groups which need special protection? (Roma?)
What follow-up perspectives can be developed?
What obstacles are there?

Social benefits / basic security to SGB XII and SGB VIII (Social Security Code XII and VIII)

For many tolerated persons and refugees, access to integration promotion programmes is dependent on the type of public funding they get, so it is advisable to collect differentiated data on this.

How many people receive benefits under Section 2 AsylbLG[6]?
How many receive benefits under Section 3 AsylbLG?
How many receive support under KJHG[7] (benefits under §34 and §35 SGB VIII)?

---

6   Asylbewerberleistungsgesetz (Asylum Seekers Benefits Act), reduced cost of living payments.
7   Benefits under the Kinder- und Jugendhilfegesetz (Children's and Young People's Support Act) are governed by SGB VIII.

Educational support

Due to the specific situations in countries of origin, some of the refugees migrate alone and arrive in Germany without their families, as underage unaccompanied refugees. The youth services and youth support agencies have a particularly important role to play in these cases. In order to get networking in the social area or beyond it at the earliest possible time, and to arrange the perspectives for further progress as effectively as possible, it is necessary to collect the following data in the districts:

How many refugees receive educational support?
How many of them are underage unaccompanied refugees?

Health

Refugees often have health problems due to trauma experienced in war situations. These psychological impairments often have a negative impact on their acquisition of education and their participation in the employment market. So the following questions are relevant:

Are trauma experiences known?
What other impairments are known?

Housing

In connection with data collection at central level (see above), it would be useful in qualitative respect to include staff from the housing accommodation in surveys, and also to hear from the refugees, asylum seekers and tolerated persons themselves.

Are access opportunities to counselling used?
Are the programmes in the social area adequate?

Social infrastructure and fields of action – potentials and deficits

Social institutions which are explicitly concerned with refugees, and also NGOs that have a key bridging function for integration are particularly important in the direct housing environment. It is important to identify them, in order to set up new cooperation links where appropriate:

What institutions are there?
What self-help organisations are there? What do these organisations offer?
What other informal groups or faith communities are there in the district?

Outlook

Targeted examination of life situations is particularly important in the case of young refugees and asylum seekers in Hamburg, taking the perspectives of social and educational reporting, and from the perspective of the social area. This would give more detailed knowledge of their life situations and permit sound assessment of their disadvantages and their educational needs. That would create the conditions to make targeted educational planning for this target group among the migrants in Hamburg. It is advisable to use the indicators and tools suggested here as long as refugees and asylum seekers are still treated separately in municipal integration policy. The selection and procedure explained here with the example of Hamburg can give some ideas and trigger similar thinking in other cities, in order to achieve implementation in Germany and in other European countries.

III.2
Refugee Monitoring in Hamburg – first steps taken!

Maren Gag, Joachim Schroeder

The academic discussion on establishment of a transnational European educational area is particularly important in view of increased mobility of refugees, who have no regular access to education or the job market due to exclusion mechanisms. Discussion was held within the European partnership on the question of what educational steering instruments should be developed, and what steering media can be identified in VET (Vocational Education and Training) beyond national borders, giving a transnational dimension to educational careers. However, the instruments for asylum seekers, persons with "tolerated" status and refugees are rudimentary at most, due to the specific features of European asylum and refugee policies; a concept was therefore developed in Hamburg to examine the impact of migration processes on refugees, specifically in VET (Gag, Schroeder 2011).

The following sections describe and comment on the first steps in implementation of the *Refugee Monitoring* concept in Hamburg. The central focus is on procedures to prepare a VET report on the situation of young refugees in the Hamburg transitional system from school to vocation, on the contents and on the recommendations derived from reporting (Gag, Schroeder 2012). The last section analyses the multiple elements of Hamburg stabilisation strategy, aimed at implementation of monitoring and educational reporting on this marginalised group in Hamburg. The concept and implementation strategy may also serve as examples for other European cities.

1. Lack of educational monitoring of the target group

The use of tools for systematic monitoring and regular educational reporting has now been introduced in Germany at the level of the Federation and of individual Laender, and in a number of municipalities, as a standard method to improve steering in various policy areas. Inter-state initiatives have also been launched in the context of implementing the Federal Government's national integration plan, in order to move forward with development of common indicators and to harmonise monitoring processes, to evaluate the goal setting of the Laender for improved integration and education policy.

It is urgently necessary to monitor specifically the target group of refugees and asylum seekers[1], especially in view of key changes in German refugee policy. Tolerated refugees are increasingly being included in integration policy measures. At the same time, it is becoming clear that the participation of refugees in education and employment is still an experimental field. In particular, there is a need for considerable improvement in the use of the standard instruments, in order to provide effective support. It is also apparent in the municipal integration concepts that these are generally aimed exclusively at immigrants who live in Germany legally and on a permanent basis. This integration policy guideline, which is supported by currently valid residence law (S. 43 I Residence Act [AufenthG]) prevents recent integration support initiatives for refugees, tolerated persons and asylum seekers funded by the Federation and the Laender. They have no legal status of residence within the meaning of the Residence Act, but they have an official document which certifies their legitimate status ("toleration") and thus their legal residence in Germany, which has in some cases already lasted for many years. As long as the legal reforms of recent times, which are aimed at educational participation and labour market integration of people with precarious status of residence, are still in conflict with the dominant political mainstream, continued efforts are needed to make the life situations and conditions of refugees visible, at least at the present stage of the debate within society, because at present they are a hidden group among immigrants.

Regardless of the need to facilitate lifelong learning, youth is still a vital lifestage for obtaining educational qualifications, for stepwise approach to the world of work, for the establishment of concrete ideas on vocational future, and for entry into the employment system. Reference is made in the international discussion of education to the fact that today about fifteen years of education and training are needed to obtain the basic educational status required for action in a globalised world (Schroeder/Seukwa 2007). It is particularly difficult for refugees to complete this lengthy period of education, because their biographic development means they live in different places, in different countries, and they do not have the time to complete the institutionally formalised sequence of educational steps without interruptions. In Germany they were denied the right to vocational training over many years, and the new ordering of policy with changes in the law has not yet brought about a systematic paradigm shift in policy and administrative practice; it is therefore desirable for participation of refugees in education and the labour market to be taken up as an indicator for the assessment of integration policy in Hamburg and in educational reporting.

---

1   The term "refugee" is not to be understood in the legal sense of persons recognised as refugees, but as immigrants who have *fled* to Germany, that is asylum seekers, persons with "tolerated" status and persons with leave to stay granted on humanitarian grounds.

The specific characteristics of European asylum and refugee policy mean that in Germany the instruments for quantitative and qualitative data collection are at most rudimentary for asylum seekers, tolerated persons and refugees, but not in such a way as to give effective and practical support to the local, national and overall European steering policies. In some major European cities, positive experience has already been gathered with *Ethnic Monitoring*, but asylum seekers, tolerated persons and refugees are normally not included in these projects. The requisite data on people who have fled from their countries of origin is often difficult to collect, and most of the German Laender have specific conditions for access of refugees to social benefits, so this is often not included in the usual procedures for social reporting. Thus it may be assumed that the basic conditions have not yet been created for regular *Refugee Monitoring* – this certainly applies at least for Hamburg; experience and insights from migration research can be used, but have to be re-adapted to this target group.

The *Refugee Monitoring* concept was drawn up in connection with the many years of integration policy efforts for participation of tolerated refugees and asylum seekers in the Hamburg networking project FLUCHTort Hamburg (SAFE HAVEN Hamburg) and the related partner projects; its aim is to achieve continuous monitoring of the effectiveness of an extended integration policy in Hamburg (Gag/Schroeder 2011). The goal is to implement a monitoring process and regular educational reporting which includes the group of refugees in Hamburg. The proposals for a pilot project were put forward at a workshop discussion in Hamburg in June 2011, with participation of numerous experts from authorities, schools and refugee facilities. The central result was the decision that instead of a comprehensive educational report, which would at present hardly be feasible to prepare, individual reports should be published in an "unstructured sequence", covering subjects of immediate concern. Great interest was expressed by the principals of a number of vocational schools, which are the locations of the educational programmes for refugees and are affected by the reorganisation of the school/vocation transitional system, and they would like to work on preparation of a theme-based educational report of this kind, which would be the first of the series.

2. Reporting – the situation of young refugees in Hamburg's school/employment transition system

The transition system from school to employment was fundamentally restructured in Hamburg in 2011, but young refugees, often entering Germany as unaccompanied minors, and getting into the school system by lateral entry as asylum seekers or as tolerated persons, attend schools outside of this reformed system.[2]

They attend two vocational preparation programmes located at vocational schools, exclusively aimed at young people with migration background, defined as follows in the law:

- The vocational preparation year for migrants (BVJ-M) whose knowledge, skills and abilities in the German language are not sufficient to participate with prospects of success in the educational programmes of the BVJ (vocational preparation year); the BVJ-M lasts two school years in full-time attendance (§2 (2) APO-BVS).[3]
- The preparation year for school students whose language of origin is not German, and whose stay in the territory of the Federal Republic of Germany is of temporary nature, particularly on the basis of leave to stay or toleration (VJ-M); the VJ-M lasts two school years in full-time attendance (§2 (3) APO-BVS).

At year end 2011/2012 there were more than 750 young refugees in Hamburg, concentrated in special-needs classes at nine vocational schools. Forecasts indicate that this figure could double in the coming years. The specific needs of the target group, the lack of data and of tools for data collection, and the impossibility of planning immigration face the educational service and the vocational schools with great challenges – they are trying to plan admission to the school system without long waiting times and to plan education in a flexible way in accordance with needs and to ensure appropriate provision of teaching. The structural difficulties cannot be compensated by existing positive approaches and specific knowledge of refugees at certain school locations. The reform of the transition system has made the inadequacies of this form of schooling particularly clear, and some of the problems have been made worse by the new organisational structure.

The core of the reform is the reorganisation of the transition from school to vocational activity, focusing on preparation for vocational training (AV) by implementation of dual places of learning (curricular orientation towards the dual system and the conditions of vocational training in Hamburg) and by support in the transitional phase.[4] But, regrettably, the relevant documents and concepts do not examine whether it is legally possible for young people going into vocational schools without knowledge of German, and in particular for refugees and asylum seekers, to start and maintain and successfully complete participation in the reformed AV

2   Bürgerschaft (Parliament) of the City of Hamburg, Communication by Senate to Bürgerschaft: Measures for implementation of vocational training in Hamburg, docs. 19/6273 of 2/7/2010 and 19/8472 of 18/01/11.

3   APO BVS = Training and examination regulations for Vocational Preparation Schools, 22/07/2011.

4   Bürgerschaft (Parliament) of the City of Hamburg, doc. 19/8472.

system; they do not consider whether this possibility is permitted by organisation and plausible in terms of its content.

The legal restrictions, which were specifically the basis of the introduction of the VJ-M, have successively been removed in the legislation at Federal and state level in recent years. After one year of stay in Germany, young refugees and asylum seekers are increasingly given more opportunities to make use of their rights to education and to participate in training and in the job market. After one year, they have a subsidiary right of access to the labour market, and after four years they have unrestricted access to the labour market. With this in mind, further development is needed in terms of function and design of the BVJ-M and VJ-M courses at vocational schools, especially as the Hamburg Senate explicitly includes this target group in new orientation of the Hamburg action concept for immigrants.

2.1 Procedure for preparation of report

In order to implement the pilot project, a number of preliminary talks have been held with head teachers, heads of department and some teachers to collect initial assessments of the difficulties in implementation of reform of the transition system in education courses for refugees. The relevant documents (Hamburg Parliament documents, curricula, ordinances) have also been collected, and also statistical material. We have drawn up a survey concept on this basis and presented it at the vocational schools. Contacts were made with all five vocational schools where such courses were provided in the survey period (October to December 2011).

A total of thirteen teachers participated (mostly heads of classes) and six school head teacher and heads of department at three school locations. As mentioned previously, the intention was *not* to evaluate the pedagogical work in the two courses, but rather to identify assessments and experience of the teachers with respect to implementation difficulties in the reform of the transition system from school to vocation and problems of fit of the education courses to the needs of young refugees. We held problem oriented discussions at the participating schools in two separate groups – in the first discussion round we talked to the head teachers of the schools and the heads of department for these courses, with a particular focus on the organisational, infrastructural and school policy problems. In the second round we talked to the teachers in these courses, focusing on pedagogical matters.

The range of subjects covered the specific support needs of young school-age refugees with unsecured status of stay, the curriculum and arrangements for teaching, the importance of learning a second language, vocational orientation, cooperation with external players, the perspectives for stay of the school students, the role of the school administration and supervisory body, the available materials and human resources, and the supply and demand for continuing education of teachers. The interviews were conducted on the basis of guidelines which we developed for structuring, but in the course of the interviews we naturally permitted deviations from it.

Following the interviews at the schools, further interviews were conducted with persons having various functions in the organisation and implementation of courses for refugees – two representatives of the Informationszentrum (IZ) (Information Centre) at the Hamburger Institut für Berufliche Bildung (HIBB) (Hamburg Institute of Vocational Education), which advises young people on education courses and programmes of the vocational schools, taking special account of young people with and without junior high school certificate and young migrants. The IZ is an establishment of HIBB and is responsible for the Hamburg state vocational schools, as an institution of the Hamburg Schools and Vocational Education Ministry. A representative of the Landesinstitut für Lehrerbildung und Schulentwicklung (LI) (Hamburg Institute of Teacher Training and School Development) was also involved, holding responsibility for the transition phase from school to vocation in the department of 'Vocational Education' (LIF 23), and from February 2012 the schools supervision unit at HIBB responsible for such programmes at HIBB (HI 16, Unit for Transition School to Employment).

All the interviews were recorded and in parallel to this notes were taken, and subsequently a transcription was made. The first evaluation step was that we reconstructed the subjects which were mentioned frequently or only occasionally in the interviews, and thus obtained an overview of the material as a whole. We then set out what we thought would be an appropriate structure for the report, and allocated the transcription extracts to the relevant subject areas. We had previously agreed with the interviewees that we would not include verbatim and/or named extracts from the interviews, but would present the evaluations given in a generalised, summary reporting mode. This approach was designed to identify the problem areas in the redesign of the transitional system and to generate proposals for further development.

This evaluation step enabled us to derive a number of recommendations, but we felt that an extension of reporting was needed to embed the results in overall contexts. Firstly, because we wanted to capture some of the impact of the reform on the young refugees themselves. But it was not possible to conduct interviews with them because this report was prepared without the provision of any kind of funding. Analysis of the subsequent situation would in any case have been premature at the time of the survey, because there were hardly any students who had completed the new courses. That is why we made use of biographical reconstructions compiled in the course of the many years of practical experience of the

Hamburg networks. They give impressions of the life situations and conditions of young refugees and asylum seekers in Hamburg, who have received preparation and support in the projects. They show different courses of educational and employment biographies, whereby participation in an education programme was one of the stages in their individual development. They also show a clear influence of the structural policy standards on the chances of individuals to make use of their development potentials. We also prepared an overview of the status of research, and gave comments on the available empirical studies on the life situations and educational careers of refugees living in Hamburg.

Finally, we felt it would be useful to include at least a brief comparison with the educational policy measures in other major cities (Berlin, Cologne, Munich) for assessment of results and formulation of recommendations.

2.2 Summary: content of educational report and recommendations for implementation

The report published in May 2012 analyses the impact of the reform of the school/ employment transition system on young refugees living in Hamburg. It presents analyses on issues of structural and pedagogical fit of the education and training courses for asylum seekers and tolerated persons. It also examines the practice of allocation and placement of the young people and organisational, administrative and legal difficulties. The analyses are put in concrete form using the educational biographies of refugees who have gone through the Hamburg school system. These biographies have been reconstructed in the framework of various research work and in practical networking. We also considered how such courses are organised in other cities in Germany, in order to get some ideas for practice in Hamburg. Finally, we summarise the results of the analysis and present recommendations for changes in the education programmes.

The report demonstrates that numerous difficulties arise in everyday school operations because of the considerable problems of pedagogical fit between the courses, with insufficient equipment, with educational goal conflicts, with inconsistent curricular concepts, with lack of flexibility and coherence in the examination rules, and with shortcomings in implementation of vocational preparation and language support; all of this is due to the fact that these programmes are not tailored to the learning status and life situation of the young people. There are also additional factors which have an impact on implementation of the courses – they include the organisational and administrative position of the courses at HIBB, the complex legal conditions applicable to the situation of asylum seekers and tolerated persons. These problems reduce the achievement of the educational goals of the current Hamburg Senate, which declare that "no-one should be left behind", and "no qualification without prospects of employment". On the contrary, there are massive obstacles in the way of such young people making use of their right to education, as they are on the margins of society in various respects. The conclusions drawn from this by the authors of the report are as follows:

A separate educational programme needs to be kept at the vocational schools for further concept improvement and for organisation of an appropriate vocational preparation programme for this target group, giving young lateral entrants without knowledge of the German language and with insecure status of stay opportunities to catch up on school qualifications and to enter the Hamburg education system with the option of follow-up programmes, and enabling them to achieve seamless transition to the world of work; this programme needs to be re-organised in its structure and curricula, and should have the same resources as the training preparation programme (AV).

Detailed recommendations are as follows

Firstly: extend the age limits for school attendance

Compulsory schooling and the right to schooling are at present linked with age and with attainment of legal status of majority, as prescribed in the Education Act. That should not be applied to this group. Instead, rules should be set up to take account of the individual's time actually spent in education. The period of compulsory schooling set out in the Hamburg Education Act, that is eleven years of school attendance, should be extended to include young refugees, asylum seekers and migrants, to that they can achieve their potentials despite gaps in their educational careers resulting from migration.

Secondly: set up a VET programme which is flexible in time and modularised in content

A two- or three-year "AV-M" should be set up for equal opportunities of young refugees, asylum seekers and migrants, with the same formal goals as the AV but a completely different organisational structure (flexible module principle). A good fit is needed in the educational programmes for the individual developments for rights of stay, social obstacles, and diversity of starting conditions for learning. In order to achieve that, the vocational schools need school policy conditions enabling them to provide different education and qualification modules adapted to teaching migrants, so that they can obtain qualification credits and get certification for them – *language modules* (literacy, basic German language education, promotion of languages of country of origin, German at the workplace); *basic modules relevant to everyday life* (coping with everyday requirements, going to official departments, health, housing, financial skills, how to deal with discrimination and racism, etc.); *basic modules relevant to the world of work* (key skills for industry and commerce); *practical modules* (stage-by-stage dualisation of places of learning at workshops / vocational schools and placements within the primary employment market); *examination modules* (time-limited preparation for examinations, in order to obtain school leaving certificates); *transition modules* (intensive school and social support for transition to employment).

Thirdly: adjust organisational framework of VET programme

The Hamburg Department of Education should provide sufficient resources for the education programme to take on a realistic bridging function, enabling young refugees, asylum seekers and other young people with migration background to pursue their educational path.

- *Clarification of responsibilities:* It is necessary to compensate for the delay in reforms for the BVJ-M and VJ-M programmes by setting up goal agreements which define the areas of responsibility more clearly.
- *Removal of distinction between "BVJ" and "VJ":* The distinction between the two educational programmes BVJ-M and VJ-M is already removed de facto in a number of vocational schools, because it is difficult to make a precise distinction in status of residence between two groups of migrants, and because it causes problems in school organisation, and makes no sense in terms of teaching. Separate programmes for refugees and migrants with secured status of stay are no longer justifiable due to the changes in the legal framework conditions, and should therefore be abolished in the law as soon as possible.
- *Fair measurement of needs:* In order to achieve equality in terms of measurement of needs with other standards applicable for educational programmes in the Hamburg school system, the basic frequency and basic number of hours of teaching should be set at the same level as for vocational training preparation (basic frequency: 13, basic hours: 30) and training support (4 basic hours per ten students). The curriculum provides for a total of 1,475 basic hours for AV (one year), so 2,950 module hours should be estimated for "AV-M" (two years).
- *Revision of examination regulations:* The examination regulations in the AV programme for acquisition of junior secondary school certificate are based on the assumption than a nine-year general education course has been completed in Hamburg. This standard cannot be applied to lateral entrance. It is therefore

necessary to develop an examination which corresponds to their needs and the subject matter of a course which covers two or at most three years, which is conducted on a modular basis, and which has a large proportion of practical elements related to the world of work. As the vocational schools now already take on new students continuously in the course of the school year, the examination dates also need flexibility in timing.

- *Revision of curricula*: In the course of merging the two programmes BVJ-M and VJ-M, the currently valid curricula should be developed into a joint curriculum, which is tailored to the life situations of refugees and asylum seekers. This should be done independently of whether a modularisation system is applied in the new organisation of AV-M. It is recommended that the curricula already developed in other states of Germany should be carefully studied and adapted to the conditions in Hamburg.
- *Preparation course*: Entry into vocational preparation should be preceded by a module for language/literacy development, giving the students the basic language skills, as is also included in the framework for integration of immigrant children and young people in regular school classes. The scope should be based on the specifications of the Federal Office for Migration and Refugees and on the integration courses for young adults, and should comprise 960 teaching units.

Fourthly: ensure placement and support

In order to set up an educational programme appropriate to life situation, it is essential to hold a detailed survey and get an accurate description of the individual life situations of the young refugees, so that corresponding social interventions can be provided for stabilisation.

- *Data collection on life situations and skills:* In order to achieve the most systematic and comprehensive clarification of the up-to-date, individual life situations of students, it is recommended to work at first-point-of-contact institutions, youth assistance services, schools and the IZ of the HIBB , using standardised or mutually harmonised survey methods, which make it possible to find out what happens to the students after completing their programme. To make placement in training or employment easier, it is suggested that the experience gathered, at least in the employment-related sector, should be documented in the form of portfolios. The work experience gathered could thus be made more visible, and would optimise the chances of follow-up employment.

- *Learning support and social monitoring*: It is vitally important to develop or provide the expertise for advice or support to clients at the planned youth job centres. As with the other reform projects in Hamburg, individual learning support staff and social workers should be integrated into the programme, to take account of the special needs of refugees and asylum seekers. The preparation of young refugees for training can be improved by close links between teaching and intensive counselling and support.

Fifthly: strengthen and expand school organisation cooperation structures

Changes at structural level are needed to minimise disadvantage effects and to ensure that young refugees can make use of their educational rights, and that nobody is left behind.

- *Cooperation*: Networking should be expanded and cooperation links with the relevant organisations should be institutionalised in order to facilitate handling of teaching paradoxes due to complex and difficult legal situations, and to improve cooperation with external refugee services and players. Apart from improved cooperation of the teaching staff with refugees institutions in individual cases, the youth job agencies should ensure that they include refugee specific counselling within the planned counselling centres ("under the same roof"), and get the necessary funding to secure this, in order to stabilise the situation.
- *Expert Council*: Establishment of an Expert Council is proposed in order to make use of synergy effects; it should support the changeover process of the transition system for this target group and it should input into the public debate and to political forums the results of future monitoring in refugee and migration work, with the participation of external experts from academic circles and out-of-school practice. Other cities in Germany could also be involved here.

Sixthly: implement targeted continuing VET campaign

Targeted human resources development among teachers and other teaching staff working at the vocational schools is needed for reform of the two education programmes addressed here. The teaching and management staff of these programmes should be included in this skill building initiative. School related and inter-school support measures should also be provided with the participation of various departments of the LI.

- *Language support and basic education*: Comprehensive, long-term teaching provisions have to be set up in particular for appropriate implementation of literacy support, to counteract the shortage of teaching staff with skills in teaching German as a foreign language in the VET sector.
- *Quality development*: Inter-school cooperation should be strengthened in order to include 'new' school sites in the exchange of experience and to improve quality development. That requires provision of sufficient resources in the form of working time and supporting staff for cooperation and expert services. Reorientation of the programmes could be supported by examination of existing approaches, concepts, tools and teaching materials for refugee-sensitive schooling and support.

Seventhly: institutionalise refugee-related education reporting

It is recommended to implement regular empirical educational reporting to examine the educational policy targets of the Senate related to young refugees, and to document results. This should also continuously show the obstacles for the target group to access and continuation, and transition to vocational training, and indicate prospective needs for action and control to school administration and policy makers. Suitable data collection tools and indicators are provided in the annex to the Education Report (May 2012), to aggregate data on a non-personal basis. Data collection should be carried out by the planned youth job centres, and the Institute of Education Monitoring should include the results in future education reports.

3. Stages on the way to stabilisation

To illustrate the stabilisation strategy pursued by the FLUCHTort Hamburg network for sustainable establishment of the monitoring concept, the following texts show some details from the practical activities for mainstreaming, associated with implementation of the Monitoring concept, and aimed at establishing a binding reporting system in Hamburg (and elsewhere). At the present time it cannot be expected that specific results will be demonstrated and successes reported. The objective is rather to show what tools and methods are suitable, and on what paths initiatives can be launched, stages pursued, and existing networking structures expanded.

3.1 Reform cannot be implemented without active participation of the vocational schools

The school management and teaching staff at the sites concerned are an important basis for implementation of the proposed reform changes which go with the recommendations in the education report. In other words, a reform without commitment on the part of the vocational schools is not realistic, because operationalisition of individual proposals for a range of school organisation requirements and pedagogical and methodological changes at the school call for a decisive will for reform in order to achieve complete re-orientation. A key foundation stone in this process was laid with the result of the Workshop Discussion in June 2011, where the concept of *Refugee Monitoring* was presented to experts in Hamburg and to representatives of the Hamburg authorities, and on this occasion the project was taken up as positive by some of the school principals, to play an active part in preparation of a (first) educational report. A concept group, comprising a number of school principals and a representative of the LI, already gave active support to the working process of reporting, and was also the first forum dealing with results, and using them as a practical correction device for further procedure. A first milestone was that reporting and the recommendations derived from it were given a positive assessment, and seen as support for their own efforts vis-à-vis their own institution to call for reform processes for the two educational programmes.

Two working tools provided with the education report illustrate by way of example simple data collection methods with which (1) life situations can be determined in the course of the educational process, and (2) indicators which could be used as the framework for determination of data for a long-term monitoring process, in order to build follow-up reporting on that:

- A profile sheet (1), which collects and updates data on the person, place of residence, status of stay and work permit, school certificates obtained (in country of origin or in other countries), on language knowledge, and on collection of their social benefits, should be used in a standardised way by everyone involved in the schooling and support process, particularly in order to record their transition to further programmes and their progress.
- Selection of the proposed indicators (2) for 'refugee sensitive' monitoring ensured that the necessary effort for development of the tools and the work effort for data collection are kept to a minimum, and that the survey design is adapted to the processes which are regularly used in Hamburg for reporting:

Indicator	Relevance / Goal
Students required to attend vocational school	To get more detailed knowledge of refugee backgrounds, life situations in countries of origin, etc. To take account of cultural/faith backgrounds
Students at each site, on entry and exit from the educational programme	Make better use of scope for use of educational rights, get support for admission. Pay attention to securing of status of stay in the process, because that can give more educational rights
Recipients of benefits under SGB II (Social Code) or Asylbewerberleistungsgesetz (AsylLG) (Asylum Seekers Benefits Act)	Make use of scope to get funding, in order to compensate for disadvantages
Housing situation	Eliminate disadvantages, finding different accommodation especially for families with children and young people. These conditions make it difficult to ensure school attendance and participation in training and the employment market
Forms of family and living	Reduce disadvantages for the increasing proportion of under-age unaccompanied refugees
Special educational needs/high proportion of young people with migration background who need funding	Ensure support in keeping with life situation, arrange transitions better
Lateral entrants without knowledge of German up to Grade 9/10 (in preparatory programmes at primary and district schools, for transition to standard classes)	Ensure support in keeping with life situation, arrange transitions better
Language of origin	Make resource for lifelong learning visible, make world of work visible, create support programmes
Health	Support in provision of appropriate support offers
Subsequent: placement in dual training, placement in funded training, placement in school education, placement in counselling	Gain in knowledge of operation of reforms and determination of needs for change
Cooperation with external partners	Strengthen stabilisation strategy

3.2 "Reward effort by providing places"

Those were the words of the Mayor of Hamburg, when he visited FLUCHTort Hamburg in March 2012 to find out about the successes and problems of networking for vocational integration of refugees and asylum seekers. In the course of the discussion, contributions were made not only by the network partners, but also by two employers and two trainees, reporting on their experience in training.

This subject is on the political agenda in Hamburg, as shown by the Mayor's statement and by the new orientation of the Hamburg Action Concept for integration of immigrants in favour of participation of refugees and asylum seekers. So the conditions are good to demand the necessary reforms of the educational programmes BVJ-M and VJ-M. It is necessary to identify numerous people responsible for the specialist aspects, and policy decision makers within the administration, and other relevant persons outside of the institutions, in order to get problem analyses on the educational situation in Hamburg's transition system into the experts' debate and to persuade people of what is needed. Comprehensive reorientation of these educational programmes and the acceptance of reporting may be seen as specific indicators of the political will to redirect the Hamburg Action Concept for integration, in favour of participation of refugees and asylum seekers, on an inter-disciplinary basis.

The FLUCHTort Hamburg network not only has to do a lot of persuasion work in the coming period, but also to develop cooperation with numerous players in VET, the employment market, the Hamburg Ministries, and also with stakeholders in practice and research, to move the subject forward in the expert and academic debate. The Hamburger Aktionsbündnis für Bildung und Beschäftigung (Hamburg Action Alliance for Education and Employment), comprising high-ranking representatives of Ministries, the Job Centre, social institutions and the Confederation of Industry, is involved in the vocational integration of disadvantaged young people at the political level in Hamburg, and their support is also needed. Their attention must be drawn to this target group, because the aim in Hamburg is "not to lose any of the young people in the transition to training".[5]

3.3 Closing research gaps – Refugee Monitoring in the social space

In the course of discussion about the necessity of monitoring for refugees in Hamburg, a research group has also been set up with the HafenCity University (Urban Planning) and the University of Hamburg (Educational Sciences), to develop a research project together with the departments integrated in three Hamburg districts for 'Integrated Social Planning' and passage.

The planned project is to operate under the working title of "FLUCHTORT STADT" ("SAFE HAVEN CITY"), and develop and test a social space monitoring process, examining activities in employment, education and residence. The goal is to determine and analyse the life situations of refugees in the residential

---

5   Bürgerschaft der Freien und Hansestadt Hamburg: Einrichtung einer Jugendberufsagentur (Establishment of a youth jobs centre) doc. 20/4195 of 15/05/2012.

areas and to derive action approaches from that. Data-based observation of areas will be used to track selected statistical and socio-economic data and thus follow the development of specific areas of the city, and to make an assessment on the basis of a specially designed index method, in order to identify special problem situations. Qualitative data will be collected on an exemplary basis on participation of refugees in urban social life in three districts in Hamburg, and this will be supplemented by comparison with other cities in Germany that have already agreed to participate: Berlin, Munich, Bremen and Leipzig. The perspective of the cities gives further important requirements for action, because integration of refugees is an important basis for peaceful co-existence between indigenous and immigrant population. In addition, ethnic diversity is increasingly seen as a potential for social, cultural and economic development in cities, in an ever more globalised world. This diversity can be used by the districts to secure location benefits for themselves versus other cities. Considering the burden on public budgets, it is also advisable for the municipalities to avoid producing additional costs by non-integration, that is by excluding sub-groups of the urban population with migration background.

This project is thus based on the status of existing research work in Hamburg and can at the same time close a research gap, because the life situation of refugees in German cities has in the past been practically ignored by research. The approaches for action to be formulated here can also lead to improved integration and participation in the social area, and transfer to other major German or European cities, which are currently the primary immigration destination of many international refugees because of their political and economic characteristics.

The academic discourse is of the greatest importance for urban practice, because it is reflected more comprehensively, the development of perspectives is subjected to critical analysis, and because recommendations for implementation and reform projects are supported by theory-based approaches. A research project on the *city* as a living space, and on the right to participation of refugees and asylum seekers, can make an important contribution here, particularly in the context of the new integration policy orientation of the City of Hamburg, which aims to include this group.

New stimuli can also be established at other locations in Germany by participation of additional cities. That means the work of the networks based there, which is funded together with FLUCHTort Hamburg from the Federal ESF programme for persons having a right to stay, can be expanded and useful synergy effects can be obtained. The Federal thematic network *Asylum*, which currently interlinks 28 funded project groups, with 230 individual projects, is an important forum for exchange of experience and transfer of proven models from practice and research.

3.4 Summary

The process for implementation of continuous monitoring and reporting on the life situation of refugees is being accomplished in small steps in Hamburg. Despite the integration policy acceptance of the subject of refugees and asylum seekers, which are no longer to be separated as a specific group among the migrants in Hamburg, the authorities react very sceptically to the demand to examine the effectiveness of integration policy reorientation. Many arguments are put forward for this – due to the difficulty of insufficient data available to the authorities, conditions for data protection in the import and export of inter-ministerial assessments, and lack of transparency in existing educational reports so that their thematic coverage cannot be extended. And it may also be suspected that there are concerns about too much collection of data on the life situations and conditions of the refugees living in Hamburg, due to structural exclusion mechanisms, the elimination of which is likely to require expenditure of additional funds.

The Hamburg network is following a political strategy of establishing equality of opportunity, for the benefit of refugees and asylum seekers in Hamburg and in other German and European cities (and regions), and is thereby following up on the guidelines issued by the EU for harmonisation of monitoring systems and common development of output and result indicators, calling for better evaluation of the measures in the member states at EU level. These guidelines are also to be seen in the context of the Europe 2020 goals, which set out specific strategic goals and measures in the various policy areas, to achieve promotion of employment, education and training, and combating poverty with more collaboration between the various fields of policy. Migrants/persons of foreign origin and the members of minorities are explicitly mentioned as a target group for *social inclusion* in the member states.[6] Thus the introduction of a monitoring system for refugees in Hamburg and elsewhere not only contributes to improving structure for the respective educational and consulting work, and to sound educational planning, but also provides additional knowledge to shape a European educational area where refugees and asylum seekers are already moving around within Europe.

---

6   European Commission: European Social Fund (ESF) 2014-2020, Proposed Regulation. Brussels 2012; Communiqué of the European ministers responsible for vocational training, the European Social Partners and the European Commission: the Bruges Communiqué on enhanced European Cooperation in Vocational Education and Training for the period 2011-2020. Version of 7 December 2010.

IV.
The reception and introduction of asylum seekers and new arrivals in Gothenburg. Successes and failures in the development of a new system

Eva Norström and Anna Norberg

1. Introduction

This paper investigates the reception of asylum seekers and new arrivals (those who are granted leave to remain) in Gothenburg for the period of 2000-2011.[1] Furthermore, it analyses issues which influence the integration into educational and vocational programmes and the labour market. The paper is built on qualitative methods, mainly the more than 50 interviews and consultations carried out with representatives from all parties involved. Interviews with refugees have been about their life story. We are grateful for the good will and interest that we have met from all those we have contacted.

The paper begins with a presentation of Gothenburg, the second largest city in Sweden (part 2), followed by an overview of the *Swedish Migration Board* (Migrationsverket), SMB, the examination of asylum applications and the reception of asylum seekers (part 3). The overview will be short as the possibility for asylum seekers to work is limited. It is, however, clear that there is a link between future integration and the social conditions while waiting and therefore some space will be given to describe the reception conditions. The responsibilities of the *Public Employment Service* (Arbetsförmedlingen), PES and the possibilities created for *new arrivals* will then be elaborated (part 4), followed by short sections about the situation of undocumented people (part 5), the role of NGOs (part 6), and the experiences of five refugees who were granted leave to remain in Sweden (part 7). In the last part (8) the reception and integration of asylum seekers and refugees will be analysed and discussed.

---

1 The paper is a shorter version of a report commissioned by the European Social Fund in Sweden (www.esf.se/sv/english).

231

2. Gothenburg

Gothenburg is situated in Västra Götaland, a region with 49 municipalities and 1.5 million inhabitants. With a strategic position at the mouth of the Göta River, the city has been an important trading centre since the 12th century. It has the largest port in Scandinavia. Around 70 per cent of Scandinavia's total industrial capacity is located within a 500-kilometre radius of the Gothenburg Region. The University of Gothenburg has 38,000 students and Chalmers University of Technology has around 11,000 students.

On December 31st, 2011the population of Gothenburg was 520,000. 115,000 were born abroad (22.4 per cent). Of the 183 nations represented, the six most common countries of birth were Iran, Iraq, Finland, FRY, Bosnia/Herzegovina, Poland, and Somalia.

The City Council is the supreme decision-making body. There are 10 City Districts with their own Committees who make political decisions about basic compulsory education, care of the elderly, child welfare, local culture, recreation, social support and support for the functionally impaired.[2] The City employs about 47,000 people, of which about 33,000 work in the district committees.

3. The reception of asylum seekers

The head office of the SMB is situated in Norrköping, 160 km south of Stockholm. Around the country there are some 40 regional offices. It is possible to seek asylum at six of these offices.[3] Of the roughly 3,400 employees about 700 work on asylum cases and another 1,400 work with reception matters. The SMB is organised as shown below:

---

2   See Appendix 2 for more detailed information about the 10 districts.
3   Malmö, Göteborg, Norrköping, Stockholm, Märsta, and Gävle.

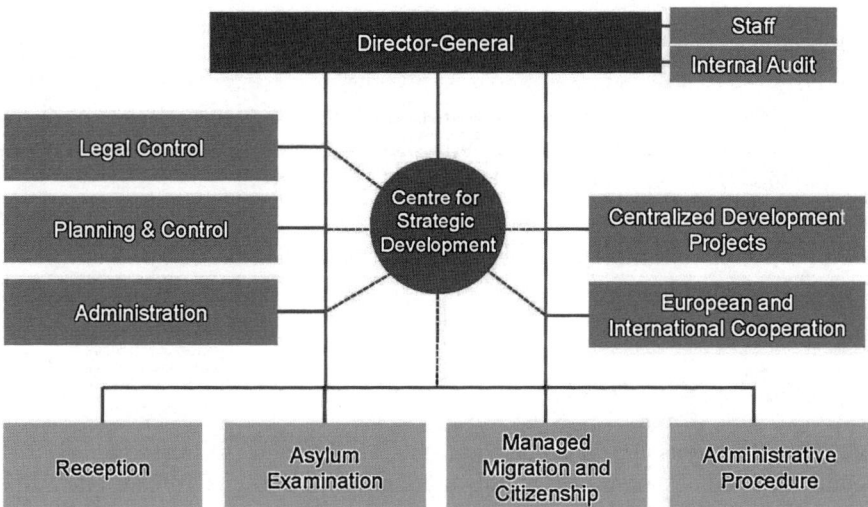

Source: SMB

One regional office, situated 30 minutes by public transportation from the Gothenburg city centre handles all asylum applications in Gothenburg and five neighbouring municipalities. Here the asylum seekers meet with the officers from the *Asylum Examination Unit* and from the *Reception Unit*. The average number of asylum seekers registered in Gothenburg during 2000-2011 is 1,900/year (SMB head office). [4] Below, the steps from the first SMB to a legally binding decision.

The SMB has the main responsibility for the Asylum Examination and the Reception of asylum seekers, by ordinance of the Swedish Parliament and Government.[5] It answers to the Ministries of Justice and Employment. Through the work of the SMB, practice is established concerning decision-making: collective knowledge, experiences, interaction with different parties, negotiations, scope and freedom of action, etc.[6] One area of critique has been long decision-making periods. In order to deal with this, *Shorter wait* was introduced in 2009, starting as a project in

---

4   See Appendix 1 for some statistics, national, Västra Götaland and Gothenburg. For further information about the asylum rules and different grounds for leave to remain see: www.migrationsverket.se/info/443_en.html.

5   Förordning (2007:996) med instruktion för Migrationsverket and Lag (1994:137) om mottagande av asylsökande m.fl.

6   According to the Swedish Constitution, a minister cannot micromanage an authority. The authorities answer to the government.

Gothenburg. *Shorter wait* is now part of the ordinary national system.[7] An asylum investigation should be carried out within one week of the application and the average examination time should be no longer than three months in the first instance. By 2012 the average examination time in the first instance had been cut from nine to just over four months. In the second instance, waiting time is much longer; therefore, the total waiting period is still prolonged.

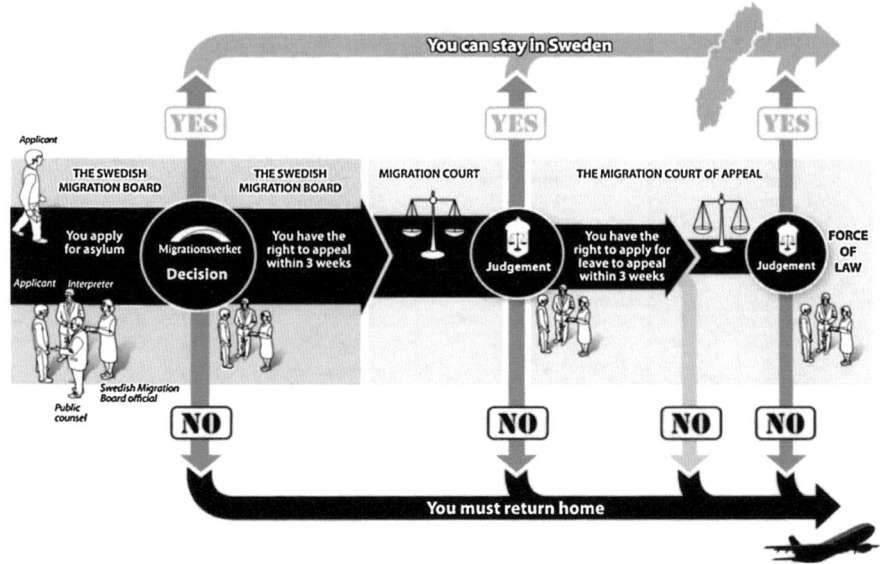

Source: SMB

3.1 The Asylum Examination

It is the task of the Asylum Examination Unit to offer fair and efficient procedures to asylum applicants, illustrated by the chart below.

---

7   At the same time the SMB decided to use the working model *Lean* (a set of management practices based on the Toyota Production System). See *Lean thinking* by Womack and Jones (2003).

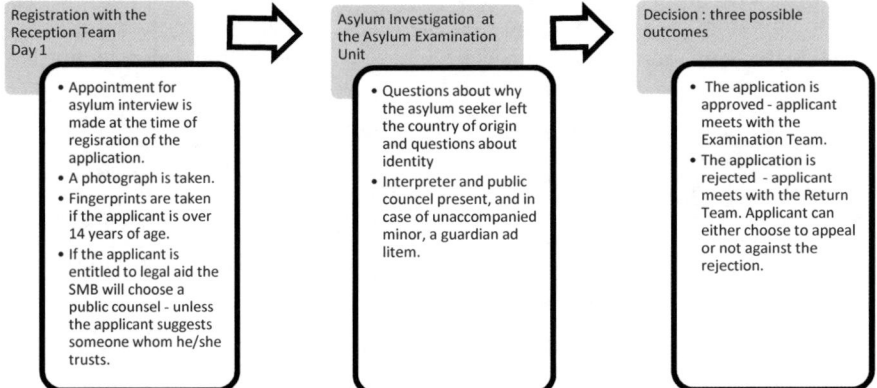

A large number of the rejected cases are appealed and re-examined, first by the SMB and then by one of three Migration Courts (Migrationsdomstol), as illustrated below:

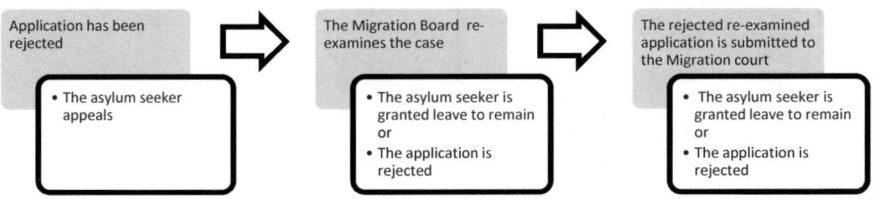

It is possible to make a second appeal to the Administrative Migration Court of Appeal (Migrationsöverdomstol) in Stockholm. A reestablishment support is available on returning to some countries.) If the applicant does not comply with a rejection, he/she may be put under supervision or be transferred to a detention centre.

3.2 The Reception of asylum seekers

The Reception Directive (European Parliament and Council Directive 2003/9/EC of 27 January 2003), laying down minimum standards for reception of asylum seekers, ensures asylum seekers a decent reception. An asylum seeker arriving in Sweden is thus subject to certain rights and obligations, regulated in the *Act on the reception of asylum seekers*.[8] They are valid from the submission of the ap-

---

8   Lag (1994:137) om mottagande av asylsökande m.fl. (Act on the reception of asylum seekers and others).

plication for asylum until the applicant has obtained leave to remain or has been refused and left the country.[9] The Reception unit is divided into three parts, Reception, Examination and Return. The main activities within the reception are outlined below:

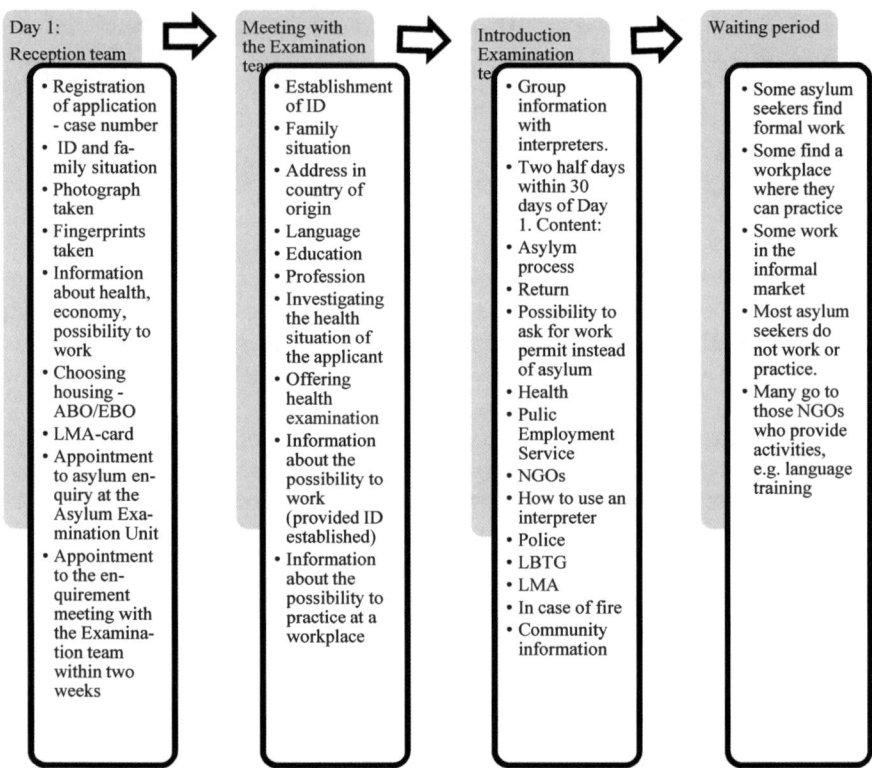

Day 1: Reception team	Meeting with the Examination team	Introduction Examination team	Waiting period
• Registration of application - case number • ID and family situation • Photograph taken • Fingerprints taken • Information about health, economy, possibility to work • Choosing housing - ABO/EBO • LMA-card • Appointment to asylum enquiry at the Asylum Examination Unit • Appointment to the enquirement meeting with the Examination team within two weeks	• Establishment of ID • Family situation • Address in country of origin • Language • Education • Profession • Investigating the health situation of the applicant • Offering health examination • Information about the possibility to work (provided ID established) • Information about the possibility to practice at a workplace	• Group information with interpreters. • Two half days within 30 days of Day 1. Content: • Asylum process • Return • Possibility to ask for work permit instead of asylum • Health • Pulic Employment Service • NGOs • How to use an interpreter • Police • LBTG • LMA • In case of fire • Community information	• Some asylum seekers find formal work • Some find a workplace where they can practice • Some work in the informal market • Most asylum seekers do not work or practice. • Many go to those NGOs who provide activities, e.g. language training

The applicant will be interviewed about his/her health, family, education, social situation and asked to prove his/her identity. The SMB will arrange suitable *accommodation* (ABO), mostly in residential areas in self-catering apartments. Since 1994 asylum seekers may arrange their own living (EBO).[10] Predominantly this means moving in with relatives or friends already residing in Sweden.[11]

9   Sweden does not make International conventions national law, but adjust existing laws.
10   ACT 1994:137.
11   Rebecca Lennartsson (2007) discusses experiences and strategies while waiting in EBO. Some grounds given for choosing EBO is the proximity to relatives and friends. See: www.temaasyl.se/ Templates/Page.aspx?id=1667.

In 2012, about 60 per cent of the asylum seekers in Sweden chose to live in ABO. There are, however, no ABO possibilities in Gothenburg. Asylum applicants live in EBO, mainly in six areas in Gothenburg.

In recent years voices have been raised to put restrictions on the EBO possibility.[12] Voices of concern from municipal officers are common, not only concerning overcrowded housing and lack of contacts with the Swedish majority but also concerning the situation of children, development of poverty and the informal labour market: "EBO causes problems and for sure politicians at the national level could have done something about the black job market that has emerged" (Municipal officer, 2012). NGOs in Gothenburg talk about lack of space for personal integrity, which in turn affects the situation for young people, especially girls growing into women. Also homework, sex life of adults, the possibility to rest, and peace and harmony in the family are affected by over-crowding. During the period of the first instance of the asylum examination EBO might work, but a rejection often means a much prolonged period of cohabitation, often leading to difficulties for both host family and their lodgers. In December 2008 the *Swedish National Board of Housing, Building and Planning* (Boverket) issued a report about EBO, to a large extent endorsing the findings of other critics.[13]

The *Act on **Health Care** for Asylum Seekers and Others* regulates the county councils' responsibility for providing asylum seekers and others with health and dental care in accordance with special agreements between the State and Local Authorities and Regions.[14] All asylum seekers are offered a *health assessment*. Asylum seeking children are offered the same health care as a child residing in the country. Adult asylum seekers are offered treatment that cannot be deferred, maternity care, care for abortion and contraceptive advice. An interpreter is summoned if medical staff are unable to communicate with the asylum seeker.[15]

---

12 This has been endorsed by municipal politicians and discussed in media. E.g. www.dn.se/nyheter/
    valet-2010/anders-lago-positiv-till-andringar-i-ebo-lagen, and www.gp.se/nyheter/ledare/1.6760
    88-serien-om-integration-harda-nypor-i-hjallbo.

13 www.boverket.se/Om-Boverket/Webbokhandel/Publikationer/2009/Asylsokandes-eget-boende-
    EBO---en-kartlaggning/ There are also other studies which indicate that the problems defined
    by NGOs and municipal officers would best be taken seriously, e.g. Brekke (2004) studied asy-
    lum seekers in ABO Among other things, he showed the negative effect that waiting has on the
    concept of time, and of not knowing when the decision is going to be made or whether the ap-
    plication is to be accepted or rejected.

14 Lag (2008:344) om hälso- och sjukvård åt asylsökande m.fl.

15 Administrative Procedure Act (Förvaltningslag 1986:223) regulates the way cases are handled
    by the administrative authorities. It specifies that a public authority should use an interpreter
    'when needed'. The Health and Medical Services Act (Hälso- och sjukvårdslag 1982:763) states
    that health care must be provided with respect for equality and human dignity meaning that
    people who do not understand or speak Swedish are entitled to the same access as others to
    proper health care, information about their illness and the care they are receiving.

In Västra Götaland approximately 50 per cent of the asylum seekers consented to undergoing a health examination. One big problem is the difficulty to reach asylum seekers living in EBO. From 2012 the assignment to reach everybody is centralised to the *Adult refugee unit* within the primary health care in Gothenburg (versus earlier nine health centres receiving refugees for medical examination).

Under certain circumstances asylum seekers are *exempted from the obligation to have a work permit* (AT-UND).[16] It is required that the asylum seeker can prove his/her identity, and that the application for asylum will be considered in Sweden. In conjunction with new legislation on labour migration entering into force in December 2008, the applicants need to assist in clarifying their identity.[17] Many asylum seekers have no proper documents and the possibility to AT-UND is in reality limited.[18] Working during the waiting period is an important factor in order not to lose ones skill during the waiting period, a big worry for many asylum seekers. "I was not allowed to work for many years and I lost my competence. I had to start all over again". (Refugee, June 8).[19] Work is also important in order to find relief from the anxiety of possible rejection, and from worry about family members in the country of origin or in refugee camps. Working opens possibilities for the future; the applicant gains experience of Swedish working life, and because a steady job means that the applicant may have a possibility to apply for a work permit.[20] Those who cannot find formal work or are not allowed to work often lose hope and self-esteem.

All asylum seekers may look for job-practice without payment. If an asylum seeker finds a place to do job-practice, the SMB will sign a contract with the

---

16   c.f. EU Directive 2003/9 EC, Art.11.

17   Nya regler för arbetskraftsinvandring: www.regeringen.se/sb/d/10026/a/105151. Prop 2007/08:147

18   The result of the new system is that a significantly lower number of those who sought asylum from 2009 have received AT-UND. Throughout 2008, for example, 17,000 AT-UND were issued. The corresponding figure in 2009 was 3,000 (SMB Annual Report 2009). 72 asylum seekers in Gothenburg had found a job in June 2012.

19   The research project *Behind closed doors* found that unaccompanied young people with good school background were preoccupied by the loss of knowledge in mathematics, physics, chemistry as well as geography and history. Participatory observations showed that they were met with lack of understanding for their worries both from personnel at the group homes and the schools (Norström, Gustafsson, Fioretos 2011).

20   Under certain circumstances those who are rejected and have a job, may "change tracks", and apply for a work permit when the decision on expulsion is no longer subject to appeal (res judicata). This is possible if the person has been working for at least six months and is offered continuation of the employment for at least one year. The employment has to meet basic requirements to qualify as ground for a work permit (www.regeringen.se/sb/d/9685/a/90346).

employer concerning insurance, working hours and such. The employer is not allowed to pay the asylum seeker. In June 2012 there were 30 asylum seekers in Gothenburg with a contract for job-practice.

The educational and professional background of the asylum seeker is mapped by the SMB. For the majority of the applicants it does not mean much, seeing that they will not be able to study or work during the waiting period. *Vocational training is not available for asylum seekers.*

Until 2011, **Organised Activities**, OV, arranged by the SMB were available to asylum seekers between 18 and 64 of age. OV was based on a principle of normalisation, i.e. asylum seekers should be a natural part of the society in which they reside. The activities primarily consisted of Swedish language training, but also learning English and computer skills, management of refugee reception centres and other activities that contributed to a meaningful existence during the waiting period. In November 2004 nearly 20,000 asylum seekers were entitled to participate in OV. 43 per cent of them participated. More than 5,000 classes in Swedish language training were organised around Sweden. As of January 1, 2006 all asylum seekers between 18 and 64 were offered personalised activities 3 hours per day.

In December 2011 the SMB decided to close OV completely, also SFI (VCA nr 223/2011): "As of January 2012 SMBs no longer provide teaching in Swedish for asylum seekers as organised in the past."[21] This is criticised by several of the interviewed sectors. All interviewed NGOs suggest that lack of activities, training (vocational or other) and employment during the waiting marginalises the individual. SMB staff do not have daily contact with the asylum seekers and as there is no formal reporting to the SMB from the schools. Thus many problems are left unsolved. In case of a rejection of the application focus will be on motivating the applicant to return. The time waiting for return can be long and voices have been raised within the SMB that from a health perspective it can be devastating to be unoccupied.

Asylum seekers with no personal means to support themselves are offered a **daily allowance** to cover expenses for food, clothing and footwear, leisure activities, personal care and other consumables, health care, dental care and pharmaceuticals. This allowance has been SEK 71/day since 1994.[22] The SMB may

---

21 Asylum seekers are encouraged to learn Swedish using the internet: www.digitalasparet.se, www.lattlast.se, www.8sidor.se/start

22 71 SEK is around 8 EUR. Those asylum seekers who cannot find work or for some reason do not have money, can apply for a daily allowance. The Government Report (SOU 2009:19) suggests an increase in the daily allowance to 80 SEK/day with a possibility to increase the sum to 120 SEK/day if the applicant participated in activities. Lobbying for higher allowances is ongoing. E.g. see www.dn.se/debatt/asylsokandes-ersattning-har-blivit-skamligt-lag (DN August 3, 2012).

grant extra allowances for costs that are necessary for a decent life, e.g. for glasses, winter clothing, food supplements, disability or baby equipment.[23]

The Examination Unit will offer all applicants two half days of **introduction to the Swedish society** in language groups with interpreters. The introduction meetings are held once a month and the applicant will normally be invited within one month of arrival. Representatives from different authorities in Gothenburg are invited to present their areas or work. E.g. the PES present its mandate and the SMB inform about the asylum process, rights and obligations AT-UND and job practice, the rights of children, schools, LGBT, and social orientation.[24] NGOs talk about their activities. Written material in the different languages is handed out. The introduction is an important activity, which is proved by high attendance. It is, however, unclear how much is received and remembered and almost all persons interviewed spontaneously talk about the difficulty of understanding, or absorbing, information when in a completely new situation, and most definitely if in distress For those who are quickly given leave to remain it is reasonable to believe that the SMB introduction is of higher value. For those who wait for longer periods, informal information from hosts and neighbours together with personal experiences in their everyday lives become more important.

Since July 2006, municipalities have been responsible for accommodation and reception of asylum seeking **unaccompanied minors**. In Gothenburg around 150 unaccompanied minors live with relatives. There are three group homes: one for 16 children, always with at least four asylum seekers, one for six young people of 16 – 21 years of age, and with permission to stay, and one for young people over 18 years of age, with permission to stay.

Under a special agreement and with a clear allocation of responsibility, Sweden's municipal authorities and county councils, together with the SMB and the National Board of Health and Welfare, have joint responsibility for separated minors. The SMB is responsible for examining the minor's asylum application, for matters related to assistance, matters related to return, and for signing agreements with municipal authorities.

Since January 2002, asylum seeking children and young people have the right to education, preschool and child care on the same terms as children resident in Sweden. Compulsory school attendance does not include asylum seeking children and there are no reliable statistics showing to what degree these children attend school. "The children are forgotten in the system" (NGO, 2012). The SMB pays the municipalities for the children's schooling, but does not know how the children

---

23 SOU 2003:89, www.regeringen.se/content/1/c4/14/29/ed702141.pdf.
24 LGBT – Lesbian, gay, bisexual, and transgender.

are doing. One reason for this is that confidentiality is observed between the different authorities. (SMB officer, 2012).

4. The introduction of refugees and others granted leave to remain

In 2007 the *Swedish Integration Board*, SIB, issued a report (Integrationsverket 2007:05) about the outcomes of the introductory activities for the newly arrived. Although the focus of the activities was on the needs of the individual the report showed that, within all areas evaluated immigrants had an inferior situation than those born Swedish. It was estimated that it took an average of seven years before just over 50 per cent of the new arrivals had work, and after around ten years 60 per cent were self-reliant.[25] Furthermore, the SIB report argued that there was insufficient expertise in the municipalities and that the methods used were not effective.

In 2006, Sweden changed government and in 2007 the SIB was closed. Since then, there has been no coherent evaluation taking into account the results of the different actors working with introduction. The government appointed a commission to consider a new and more resourceful system and with the *Act on establishment activities for certain new arrivals* the responsibility of settlement issues concerning certain new arrivals shifted from the municipalities to the PES.[26] The goal is to enable all new arrivals to find their way into the Swedish labour market as soon as possible. Quota refugees and newly arrived between 20-64 years of age are subject to the law. New arrivals working full-time, studying at a high school or who cannot participate in activities more than 10 hours a week (rehabilitation activities included) are excluded.

4.1 Areas of responsibility

The reform brought new areas of responsibilities to the *County Administrative Boards* (Länsstyrelse), the *County Councils* (Landsting/Region), the SMB, the Municipalities, the PESs and the *Social Insurance Agency* (Försäkringskassa).[27] A new actor was introduced, namely the *Introduction Guides*.[28]

---

25 Cf Statskontoret (2012:22, p. 30).
26 Prop. (2009/10:60). Nyanlända invandrares arbetsmarknadsetablering – egenansvar med professionellt stöd. Lag (2010:197) om etableringsinsatser för vissa nyanlända invandrare.
27 www.forsakringskassan.se/sprak/eng.
28 An introduction guide works at a Pilot Company contracted by the PES. The introduction guides support new arrivals to carry out the activities in the introduction plan.

4.1.1 The County Administrative Boards

The 21 County Administrative Boards serve as regional representatives of the government. Their responsibilities include facilitating cooperation between the above mentioned operators, NGOs and companies engaged in the introduction of new arrivals. Since 2007, the County Administrative Boards negotiate with the municipalities on the number of new arrivals that each municipality is committed to receive. 269 of 290 municipalities in Sweden (44 of 49 in Västra Götaland) have made agreements about receiving refugees. In Västra Götaland this means 26,000 new arrivals, for Gothenburg alone 850 individuals.[29]

4.1.2 The County Council

The County Council is responsible for all health, medical and dental care under the *Health and Medical Care for Asylum Seekers and Others Act* (SFS 2008:344). A new arrival has the same rights as any other inhabitant in Sweden. In short, the county councils are responsible for:

- People with special needs (elderly, with disabilities, pregnant women, separated minors, victims of torture or rape, etc.)
- Asylum seeking children – same right to medical care as resident children
- Adult asylum seekers – care that cannot be deferred (maternity, abortion care & contraception advice).

4.1.3 The Swedish Migration Board

When an applicant is granted leave to remain in Sweden the Examination teams meet with the now *new arrival* for a *settlement meeting,* normally within 7-10 days of the decision. The system presupposes that the PES is present at this meeting. In Gothenburg, however, the distance from the PES, situated in the centre of Gothenburg, to the SMB is perceived as far and the PES argues that it is more efficient to have records of the settlement meeting sent by post.

The new arrival is given a residence permit card, valid for five years. ABO residents have to move as soon as possible, EBO residents are free to stay where they are. New arrivals in Gothenburg are informed about the difficult housing situation in Gothenburg. In reality the difficulty of finding a place to live is so severe that on an average between 2,500 and 3,000 new arrivals in Sweden are stuck in the accommodations of the SMB.

---

29   Source: SMB August 15, 2012 and the County Administrative Board, Västra Götaland.

At the settlement meeting, information is given about the possibility to ask the PES for support in finding a municipality where housing is available, as well as prospects of future work. Such a request must be made within six months from the time permission to stay is granted, and the new arrival must accept the first offer given.[30]

4.1.4 The Municipality

Although the municipalities are no longer in charge of coordinating the introduction of new arrivals between 18 – 64 years of age, they still have a whole range of responsibilities, e.g. practical support, social service and assistance, arranging SFI and SO, schooling and care of children with special needs.

In 2010 the Gothenburg City Council organised the *Establishment Unit*, serving all new arrivals in the whole of Gothenburg with both individual and family matters (Document 2010 nr 180). Together with the PES, primary care, and other actors the unit ensures that new arrivals with reduced performance receive all appropriate interventions.

Swedish for Immigrants and vocational training

According to the Education Act (Skollag), the municipality is obligated to ensure that Swedish for Immigrants, SFI, is offered to those who reside in the municipality and lack basic knowledge of the Swedish language.[31] In Gothenburg 9,000-10,000 individuals regularly participate in SFI. 2012 around 10-15 per cent are new arrivals with an introduction plan.

SFI in Gothenburg is outsourced to 10 different companies and also offered by three Folk High Schools.[32] Some companies offer Swedish for academics, the disabled, those with impaired hearing or SFI to blind and deaf immigrants. All companies have a wider range of educational activities than just SFI. The Folk High Schools are independent and supervised by the Swedish National Agency for Education (www.skolverket.se). The municipality pays for those who are referred to their SFI programmes.

---

30   In April 2012, 97 new arrivals had applied for housing in Gothenburg, 13 had been offered housing. Seven had accepted the appointed flat. 15 had found housing themselves and 63 were waiting (information via mail from the PES head office in Stockholm, August 7, 2012).

31   Skollag (2010:800). See chapter 14 § 6.

32   ABF, Cuben Utbildning, Eductus, Folkuniversitetet, Göteborgs Tekniska College, Hermods Iris Hadar, Lernia, Sveas, Studium (part of the Education administration in Gothenburg municipality), Folkhögskolan Angered, Finska (mångkulturella) folkhögskolan, and Göteborgs folkhögskola.

SFI is studied in four levels:

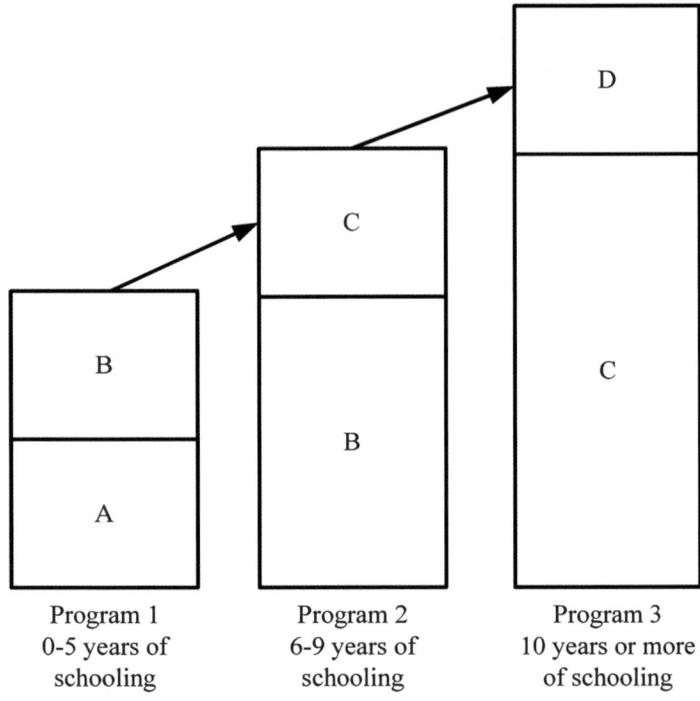

| | Program 1
0-5 years of
schooling | Program 2
6-9 years of
schooling | Program 3
10 years or more
of schooling |

In Gothenburg SFI for immigrants with higher education is offered by Folkuni-versitetet and Lernia. Individuals with higher education are referred to a selection group and relevant documents may be directed for validation etc. The mapping consists of all experiences of the individual; formal, non-formal and informal. After having finished SFI A and B the participant will continue in a "career group".[33] Job practice and coaching is part of the programme. At the end of the programme, the students will be qualified for admission to university and other higher educational programmes. The number of new arrivals participating in this programme is very low (9 or 10 individuals out of 300). One reason is that many new arrivals have to deal with more immediate needs, such as housing and family

---

33 There are different groups for different professions: 1.physicians and nurses, 2. other medical staff such as veterinarians, psychologists, chemists, bio-medicine etc. 3. lawyers, social workers, etc. 4. artists, designers and cultural workers, 5. economists, 6 pedagogy and 7 natural sciences, IT and technology.

matters. Another reason is that many have lost competences and motivation. They have the possibility to return to higher studies later on.

Vocational SFI was launched in Gothenburg in 2002/2003. It is mostly offered in combination with vocational training at high school level. Examples of vocational SFI are courses for entrepreneurs, industrial workers, warehouse workers, health care and occupations involving food. More than 70 vocational training programmes are offered at high school level by 16 different adult educational organisers in Gothenburg.[34] 15,000 students participate in these programmes. Around 65 – 70 per cent of the students have a mother tongue other than Swedish. Only few of them are new arrivals. The City Committee for Adult Education in Gothenburg has, however, decided that the vocational SFI for new arrivals provided by the municipality will stop in the autumn of 2012 (§ 60 Projekt 101). The Employment Service will then resume responsibility for vocational SFI for new arrivals.

Social Orientation, SO

As of December 2010 the municipalities must offer SO at a minimum of 60 hours to all new arrivals.[35] An established curriculum is given in the mother tongue of the new arrivals. SO classes are carried out in dialogue form, drawing on the personal experiences of the participants both from the country of origin and from their time spent in Sweden. Gothenburg created this model in 2008. Study material for nationwide use of the model has been developed together with the County Administrative Board in Västra Götaland. In Gothenburg new arrivals participate for three hours per week, to a total amount of 72 hours. Most new arrivals have not had much contact with Swedish society or with Swedes; "Swedes are an abstraction, not human beings of flesh and blood" (Municipality officer, 2012). They have mainly been referred to compatriots for information and are thus often prone to misunderstandings and rumours.[36]

---

34 Business and Administration, Child care and recreation, Construction, Crafts, Electricity and energy, Food, Health and social care, Hotels and restaurants, Introduction to academic studies, Industrial work, Media, Natural Resources, Service & Consulting, Technology, Transport, Vehicle etc.

35 See SOU 2010:16. Utredningen om samhällsorientering för nyanlända invandrare.

36 Internal and external evaluations show that the participants of the SO programme are happy with the outcome and that their understanding of the function of authorities and the role of officials within the public functions has increased extensively. Sennemark & Moberg (2009 and 2010).

"The Refugee Guide — your route to the Swedes and the Swedish language" is a voluntary meeting place, run by the municipality, where Swedes and immigrants can meet and get to know each other. The Refugee Guide Project in Gothenburg started in 2003 and was made permanent by the municipality in 2007. It is seen as an important social aspect of integration and a question for the future: "the Gothenburg we have today has not landed overnight but is based on decisions made 20-30 years ago. Similarly, what we do today affects what it will be like in 20-30 years" (Municipality officer, 2012). The participants are new arrivals between 20 and 65, their relatives, young people with no parents in Sweden and children together with their families. Those who are interested in the project can register and be matched (man-man, woman-woman, and family-family) on the basis of shared experiences and wishes.

The project aims at supporting meetings between people. The underlying understanding is that it is hard to establish social contacts with Swedes, as well as to find work and that therefore social contacts and knowledge of Swedish social codes may help. Time and effort is put into finding "ordinary" people, to provide information and offer the opportunity to get involved. "Voluntary meetings open up new possibilities and the opportunity for personal friendship" (Municipal officer, 2012). The Refugee Guide Project also provides information about the project in the classrooms of SFI and SO. There is also cooperation with the unit responsible for unaccompanied minors. Networking with Swedish young people and families is an important part of the preparations for adult life:

The segregation in Gothenburg is a problem. It is wrong. Instead, it is necessary to create natural opportunities to meet one another. For example, all newly arrived students go to the same school in Lindholmen, where there are no other students. For one year they are isolated up on the hill (the school is actually situated on the top of a hill). They feel put aside. The adolescents coming to our activities always ask how to meet Swedish adolescents. "They are everywhere and yet nowhere!" (NGO, 2012)

In May 2012 there were 1,500 immigrant households participating, 250 households waiting for a Swedish contact and 100 Swedish families/individuals available to be matched.

4.1.5 The Public Employment Service

It is the responsibility of the PES to coordinate the work of all involved in the introduction of new arrivals and to assist in finding a place to live – if the new arrival so wishes. From December 2012 to April 2012 the PES had registered nearly 11,000 individuals throughout Sweden since the introduction of the establishment reform in December 2010.[37] 690 individuals were registered for an Introduction Plan in Gothenburg on April 30, 2012 (i.e. 7 per cent of the total number in Sweden).[38]

The PES supports the new arrival in making his/her own introduction plan, give study and/or vocational guidance and when relevant help, with starting up a business and support *step-in-job*.[39] The new arrival will be offered the support of a Pilot Company procured by the PES. 89 per cent of the new arrivals had received a work preparatory or labour market policy activity (December 2010 – April 2012). The PES decides on introduction benefits. From the individual point of view the process can be summarised as follows:

---

37   9,651 new arrivals had a plan in April 2012. 51 % were men. 434 had left the introduction activities
      with a job. This low number is perhaps due to the fact that the system is new, but it is also relevant to
      think about the target group itself, its situation and its needs, from a holistic point of view. (PES
      report to the government, June 15, 2012, and www.arbetsformedlingen.se/Globalmeny/Other-
      languages/New-in-Sweden.html.)

38   In Västra Götaland 729 women and 795 men were registered between December 2010 and April
      2012. Activities in Gothenburg, April 2012: Employments 5, New start jobs, 13, Entry recruit-
      ment incentives 12, Work experience placements 8, Trial opportunities 8, Practical skills en-
      hancements 10, Projects with labour market policy orientation 29, Labour market trainings 11,
      Preparatory training courses 132, Sundry 462. Total 690.

39   A person is entitled to a step-in-job, or recruitment incentive, if he/she has obtained a residence
      permit within 36 months of requiring such a job. Citizens of an EU/EEA country are not entitled
      to this support. Recruitment incentive means that the employer will get a grant for the salary
      equating 80 per cent or maximum 800 SEK/day. A requirement is that the new arrival is partici-
      pating in SFI.

247

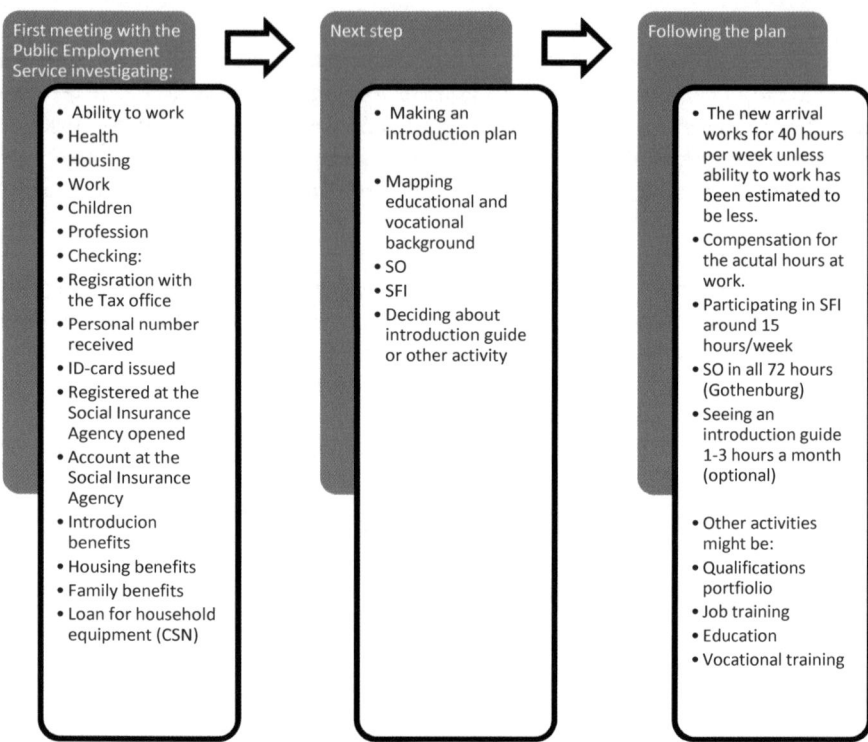

First meeting with the Public Employment Service investigating:	Next step	Following the plan
• Ability to work • Health • Housing • Work • Children • Profession • Checking: • Regisration with the Tax office • Personal number received • ID-card issued • Registered at the Social Insurance Agency opened • Account at the Social Insurance Agency • Introducion benefits • Housing benefits • Family benefits • Loan for household equipment (CSN)	• Making an introduction plan • Mapping educational and vocational background • SO • SFI • Deciding about introduction guide or other activity	• The new arrival works for 40 hours per week unless ability to work has been estimated to be less. • Compensation for the acutal hours at work. • Participating in SFI around 15 hours/week • SO in all 72 hours (Gothenburg) • Seeing an introduction guide 1-3 hours a month (optional) • Other activities might be: • Qualifications portfiolio • Job training • Education • Vocational training

Introduction plan

An introduction plan contains activities that will help the new arrival to learn Swedish as quickly as possible and to find work. The professional and academic background, ambitions, interests and talents, and assessment of qualifications from previous employment will be mapped. All certificates of education, skills and work experience are compiled in a Merit Portfolio. The new arrival meets with a mentor/tutor on several occasions and together they decide what/if anything more is required to meet Swedish standards.

An investigation of the new arrival´s capacity to participate in activities in an establishment plan begins during the first establishment meeting. An introduction plan should be individualised and designed based on the individual circumstances and needs.[40] The activities will as far as possible be adapted so that the individual can attend full time. Where this is not possible the extent of the intro-

---

40   Nyanländas etablering – reformens första år (Arbetsförmedlingen, 2012-02-22).

duction plan will be reduced. This is substantiated by a medical certificate. A part-time introduction plan can include 75, 50 or 25 per cent of full time. If the capacity is judged to be lower than 25 per cent, the individual is rejected the right to an establishment plan. When planning the introduction activities, the PES shall consider the individual's resources and take into account current health status and family situation. The individual's family relationships, age, previous education and work experience may not be a barrier to participation in full time introduction activities.[41]

The Introduction Guide

In June 2012, 77 per cent of the new arrivals in Sweden have accepted the services of an introduction guide. The service shall be designed according to individual needs and offered in the new arrival's language. If the Pilot Company does not have introduction guides speaking a required language, there is an obligation to arrange for an interpreter. The introduction guide's duties include supporting the new arrival in gathering and presenting experiences such as language skills, education, working life, knowledge of the Swedish society and building personal contacts. The new arrival may expect support to carry out and develop the introduction plan as well as when it comes to making choices of studies or vocations, helping to look for jobs and contacting employers. In addition to individual meetings many introduction guides provide different types of group activities, such as field trips, seminars, language training, coffee shops, and courses and "open-house activities".

The right to a guide lasts for 24 months within a timeframe of 36 months. It is possible to switch Pilot Companies. At the introduction interview with the PES the new arrival is informed about the possibility to choose a Pilot Company.[42] On the website of the PES in Gothenburg there are 47 options. The new arrival finds the following sectors and languages:

Sector	Number of Pilot Companies		Language	Number of Pilot Companies
Administration, Economy, Law	23		Albanian	20
Agriculture	36		Arabic	40
Body and Beauty care	40		Dari	26
Building and Construction	43		English	47
Computer/IT	45		French	30

41 Prop. (2009/10:60) Nyanlända invandrares arbetsmarknadsetablering – egenansvar med professionellt stöd.
42 The law on free choice systems (SFS 2008:962).

249

Sector	Number of Pilot Companies		Language	Number of Pilot Companies
Culture, Media, Design	44		Mongolian	15
Educational work,	45		Persian	36
Health Care	45		Russian	25
Hotel, Restaurant, Catering	44		Somali	33
Industrial Manufacturing	44		Sorani	25
Installation, Service, and Management, Maintenance	43		Spanish	30
			Tigrinya	23
Management	41			
Remediation/Waste Management	41			
Safety work	40			
Scientific work	38			
Selling, Purchasing, Marketing	44			
Skilled trades	45			
Social work	45			
Technical work	42			
Transport	44			

Validation

One of the tools available for new arrivals is validation of education and practical skills. The government defines validation as "a process that involves a structured assessment, evaluation, documentation and recognition of knowledge and skills that a person possesses, regardless of how the knowledge and skills were acquired" (Ds 2003:23). Some of the goals are to contribute to the supply of skilled workers and professionals, to create a better functioning labour market (increasing the employment rate), and to avoid unnecessary training. Concerning validations the PES cooperates with three other authorities.[43] Direct cooperation with industry organisations is also available.

One evident problem is that many new arrivals lack documents proving educational qualification and professional experiences. In the municipal adult educa-

---

43 The Swedish National Agency for Higher Education (Högskoleverket), HV, The Swedish Agency for Higher Education Services (Verket för högskoleservice), VHS, and The Swedish National Agency for Higher Vocational Education (Yrkeshögskolan), YH, responsible for all matters concerning higher vocational education in Sweden. This includes evaluating the demands for qualified workers, deciding on programmes for higher vocational education, and taking responsibility for the assessment of foreign higher vocational education. YH is the national coordinator for the European Qualifications Framework. From January 2013 a new authority, Universitets- och Högskolerådet, will be established. One responsibility will be the assessment of foreign higher education.

tional programmes there are alternative possibilities; one is that some upper-secondary schools have validation programmes where personal skills are appraised during several weeks followed by the making of individual study plans. Another option is, e.g. that a new arrival with experience of health care work starts vocational training to become an assistant nurse. During the course it will be evident what skills the person already has and training in these skills can be excluded from the person's study agenda. Validation of skills can also be made through around 25 different models used by industry organisations to validate around 140 different professional capacities. These validations are sorted under the supervision of YH. Should the validation lead to a professional certificate, this will be issued by the organisation.

In validation, the method Merit Portfolio, mentioned above, is used in order to map the qualifications of individuals. In Gothenburg, new arrivals work up to13 weeks to create the Portfolio, listing all their personal formal and informal competences. The new arrival reflects thoroughly on his/her experiences, individually and in groups, and compares them with what is needed for a certain profession. Validation could be the next step.

Some feel that the introduction plan would benefit from early validation, say within weeks of the permission to stay. "An early validation would help the new arrival to settle. Where in Sweden is there work within the trade in question? Are there educational, vocational and housing possibilities in that area?" (Company making validations, 2012). Other voices are hesitant to early validations, e.g. a report from a validation project called VINN.[44] The aim was to help create a sustainable platform for the assessment and documentation of newly arrived immigrants' skills and competences based on models for validation developed within different sectors of industry. The report shows that there are many difficulties involved in the validation process. First of all, it is difficult to say exactly what is evaluated. The new arrival has learned a trade within other frameworks than those of a Swedish working place. Studies show that validating is closely connected to social, cultural and linguistic situations that a new arrival cannot possibly have any knowledge of. One risk here is that experiences and competences are validated in relation to the Swedish context, not in relation to the actual skills of the individual. Another risk is that differences are constructed as deviations or proof of incompetence. In both cases, the person is placed at a disadvantage. The VINN report also confirms that, in many cases, new arrivals are attributed template-like and negative characteristics, and that presumptions often influence validations. Adding to this difficulty, in the first steps of validation

---

44 The project was run by The National Agency for Higher Vocational Education, the PES and 16 branch organisations. Report (Diedrich 2011).

only a few practical elements were evaluated before making a decision about even continuing the validation or not. It is as if it would be enough to assess a filigree jeweller's skills based on how he looked at the metal.

Early validations demand interpreters who are knowledgeable within the validated trade. It is hard enough to find skilled interpreters in Sweden and even harder to find interpreters with knowledge in trade language and practice.[45] The VINN report discusses this problem and also the problem of the role of the interpreter, which in some parts of the valuation process tends to move to the role of a translator. This is problematic because the interpreter loses his/her 'impartiality'. In order do find solutions for the problems connected with the use of interpreters in validation, a pilot project was created, "Validation interpreting", with the aim of developing training for interpreters in professional vocabulary, theory and practice in woodworking, metalworking and in other professional fields, e.g. health care.[46]

The development of validation methods is closely connected with needs within specific sectors or when money is allocated, e.g. from the government. One example: since 1998, around 5,000 persons in Gothenburg have been validated in relation to secondary education in health care. It is estimated that when individuals have been able to continue their studies based on previous skills it has halved the time needed to become qualified.

One more example comes from the Tibro Training Centre. TTC provides validation of knowledge and professional assessment of employability in the furniture industry. The methods developed have been shared with others and today there is an industry-related basis for validation. The furniture industry offers very good examples of what validation is all about. Among the new arrivals with experience from that field, there are many with no formal education. A properly conducted validation will measure their competences, thus providing a platform for planning the future. Is it possible to get a job at once? Are supplementary studies necessary? Are language studies necessary, for example, of the professional language?

Interviews with experts of validation show that there is a strong wish to develop national norms for validation and standardisations in different industries.[47] "There is enough knowledge today to develop a unified form for those parts of validation that are common to all industries" (Company making validations, June 28).

---

45 See www.tolkprojektet.se for more information about community interpreting in Sweden.

46 See www.tolk.mariestad.se and www.valideringstolk.se.

47 A delegation from *Nordic Network for Adult Education* launched a report in 2008 focusing on contributing to validation receiving national legitimacy, and with validation opportunities based on quality and equivalence.

National norms would strengthen validation legitimacy and employers would know the exact value of a validation certificate.

In order for the new arrival to benefit from the system, it is important that the PES has full control over the Pilot Companies, the Merit Portfolio and of applicable validation possibilities. The new arrival has two years at his/her disposal and there is no margin for things going wrong in the introduction, although validation is open for everyone looking for work and thus can be conducted after the introduction period. Standardised validation methods would also strengthen the procurements that are made by the PES. Procuring this service is difficult. The procurers need to know the industries and how to gauge the quality of the validation. A low bid might in fact mean that the validation provider lacks sufficient resources. One suggestion from the field is that the PES hires experts, first to ensure that the quality requirements are realistic and measurable, and then to do much needed follow-ups. In the long run, the fact that no monitoring is performed inhibits the development of validation methods.[48]

New arrivals need to be guided to professions in which (and where) it is possible to find work. For these jobs, manpower may be recruited from new arrivals that already have experience of the trade and from those who have an interest in learning the trade. One problem here might be the feeling among some interviewees that only few officials within the public sector seem to be well informed about the different possibilities and the work of the Agency for Higher Vocational Education (Company making validations, June 28).

Introduction benefits

When the introduction plan has been made together with the employment officer and while the plan is being carried out, the new arrival has a right to an introduction benefit, even if he/she is still in ABO. The PES will decide on the benefit after an application has been submitted. While preparing the introduction plan the new arrival receives SEK 231 per day, five days per calendar week. When taking part in the introduction activities, the maximum sum is SEK 308 per day, five days per calendar week, depending on the extent of the introduction plan and if the new arrival is working within the plan. Supplementary introduction benefits may be granted if the new arrival has children or rental charges for a flat with a lease or sublet lease accepted by the landlord.

Absence from the introduction activities has to be approved; otherwise, deductions are made from the introduction benefit. Reasons for approved absence

---

48 The interviews give at hand that the difficulties facing the procurers at the PES are similar to the difficulties procuring interpreter agency services (www.tolkprojektet.se).

can be a visit to the doctor, the death or illness of a close relative, a funeral, moving, visiting an administrator in the municipality, or doing a driving test when a driving licence is required for the intended occupation.

4.2 Observations

In June 2012, a report was issued by the Swedish Agency for Public Management (Statskontoret 2012:22) – The introduction of new arrivals – a follow-up of the authorities' enforcement of the Establishment Act.[49] The overall assessment in the Report (2012:22) is that the authorities and municipalities need to improve the coordination of their activities. Lack of childcare for example jeopardises the possibilities for both parents to benefit fully from the introduction activities. A coordination problem on another level is the gap between the payment from the SMB and the introduction benefits. During this period the new arrivals have no other option than to turn to the municipality for economic support.

Municipal officers and NGOs in Gothenburg say that although many new arrivals are perfectly fit, there are also many who are in a bad state because of psychological problems from trauma and worries with family still in the country of origin or in refugee camps. There are also down-to-earth problems such as the difficulties of finding housing in Gothenburg and long queues to child care. New arrivals mostly continue to live in sublet apartments. And when they get an apartment of their own they might well feel obliged to house asylum seeking relatives. Several years of cramped living with worried people is not good for anyone's health and integration, especially not for children who tend to carry the worries of the grownups.[50]

As mentioned earlier, the PES in Gothenburg does not participate in the settlement meeting at the SMB. From an administrative point of view this may seem rational, "it saves time and the new arrival may not yet be ready for PES". On the other hand, from the point of view of the individual it might not to be rational at all. Many of the interviewed officials and NGOs point out that the

---

49 The Swedish Agency for Public Management provides the Government and Ministries with relevant documentation for reassessment and rationalisation decisions. Matters relating to the organisation, governance and development of public administration are covered by the Agency's remit in the area of administrative policy.

50 NGOs testify that children in their programmes take grown-up responsibilities when the parents fail. "Talking about the family situation is a very difficult subject for the children and when it comes to unaccompanied minors there is an almost palpable anguish in the room" (NGO, 2012). This observation is consistent with other studies of unaccompanied minors (cf. Norström and Gustafsson, 2010 & Gustafsson and Norström & Fioretos, 2012).

system is dealing with persons who, for some reason or other, have applied for asylum. This means that there are traumatised and run-down people among the new arrivals. A whole new life with many demands is waiting for them and it would be better to establish a personal contact with PES already when the asylum seeker is granted leave to remain. The reason for an introduction officer to be present at the settlement meeting is not so much to make full mapping of the educational, vocational and work experiences as to create an opportunity to build trust.

A point mentioned in the report (2012:22) is that many new arrivals have not made an introduction plan within two months of having received a residence permit, which is the requirement. The report's message is that the processes leading to the new arrival's finding work and participating in social life must be carried out "without delay", while the quality of these processes must still be maintained. This may be true, but it needs to be discussed how to interpret "without delay". It depends on what is included in a proper introduction plan. At the PES the new arrival is interviewed and informed about various options. Much effort is put into making this part of the process fruitful. The Merit Portfolio can take up to 13 weeks according to the PES, and is part of actually understanding what options may be available to the new arrival. Making a definite plan before that might not be constructive. It seems as if a good way to work is to be very meticulous with the Merit Portfolio and to make sure that formal, non-formal, and informal working experiences are considered.[51] Non-formal and informal experiences most often belong to the category "silent knowledge" and might need time and courage to be truly mapped. It might also be good to practice at a work place to gain knowledge of Swedish working culture and professional language before making a deeper validation, as shown in the evaluation of the VINN project. Accepting that the first steps may take time is a necessary part of investing for the future. "To force people into a job as quickly as possible is not always right. A paid job that is wrong for the person does not bring freedom. There are already many people competing for unskilled work; why force educated people to enter that race when they could do so much better given the proper support?" (Municipal officer July, 2012).

The new arrival is offered the support of an introduction guide. From May 2010 the *Act on freedom of choice* is mandatory vis-à-vis the new arrivals.[52] There are 47 options on the website of the Employment Service. True freedom of choice demands knowledge of the alternatives available. In fact, it is almost impossible to make an informed choice in this case. It is possible to change Pilot Companies. However, a wrong choice does not extend the 24-month period

---

51 www.meritea.se/ and www.botkyrka.se.
52 Lag (2010:536) om valfrihet hos Arbetsförmedlingen.

available for the new arrival. Initial mapping includes questions about housing, economy, the family situation and health, but whether these areas are to be integrated in the preparation for the possibilities at the labour market or not depends on how the introduction guide works. The PES holds regular meetings with the Pilot Companies and their guides, but there is no supervision or structured quality control of Pilot Companies.

The PES needs to develop its monitoring of work-related activities and the services they procure regarding introduction activities. This is generally agreed on within the whole field and is one of the recommendations in the Report (2012:22).

Coordination and cooperation on an everyday level with *all* actors involved would not only strengthen the individual, as shown in a report *Without health no establishment* from the County Administrative Board (Länsstyrelsen, 2011), but it would also strengthen the introduction system if the knowledge and engagement that is to be found amongst the different actors could be of assistance on a collective level.

5. Undocumented migrants and asylum seekers in hiding

In Sweden, as in other Western countries; there is an informal labour market where people such as asylum seekers, refugees in hiding from expulsion and migrants without residence permit look for work. Migrants with no documents may have entered the country legally, but overstayed the allowed duration or they may also have entered irregularly, e.g. as victims of trafficking.[53] New categories of undocumented emerge from time to time. One example from Gothenburg is that established immigrants, who have old parents but are denied family reunion in Sweden, see no other option than to bring these parents to Sweden nonetheless.

It is unclear how many undocumented people there are in Sweden, but different sources suggest 10,000-50,000 individuals, of which 2,000-3,000 are children (Socialstyrelsen, 2010).[54] In Gothenburg NGOs seem to agree that there are at least 2,500 to 3,000 undocumented individuals, although some of the migrant organisations say that this estimation is much too low.

In her doctoral thesis Geographer Erika Sigvardsdotter (2012) shows that, as a rule undocumented migrants live in a vulnerable position with extremely limited

---

53 According to the Swedish Aliens Act, the main principle is that foreigners must have a residence permit to stay for more than three months, as long as they are not EU citizens, who are covered by the EEA agreement.

54 Journalist Kaisa Viitanen and photographer Katja Tähjä document the everyday life of people without legal documentation in Europe in *Undocumented Lives* (www.undocumentedlives.com).

access to healthcare, education, insurance against work injuries and other social functions. Gender researcher Maja Sager (2012) discusses in her doctoral thesis how waiting in limbo without social rights, combined with the risk of expulsion, has an impact on asylum seekers' lives on many levels; employment, family life and social life. She argues that their potential for collective political action is constantly undermined, practically and symbolically. Either they are dismissed as criminals because they have entered in an unofficial way or they finally may stay on humanitarian grounds, not political. The result is a de-politicisation of the voices of the undocumented. Sociologist Helena Holgersson (2011) shows in her thesis that undocumented migrants in Gothenburg lack the possibility to become visible in the public room and to demand social and economic rights. Being cut off from society and rights raises feelings of total isolation. It is difficult and dangerous to be an undocumented migrant in Sweden, completely at the mercy of other people's kindness and compassion. Between 2007 and 2009 Social Anthropologist Shahram Khosravi studied "illegal" immigrants and the informal economy in Sweden.[55] He shows that there is a constant exploitation of undocumented persons on the Swedish labour market. Often they end up in occupations where they do not meet other workers (e.g. cleaning offices at night). They do not learn Swedish, their working experiences are not documented and they will not get any work references. This means that it is difficult to get access to the formal labour market even after permission to stay in Sweden is granted. Khosravi (2010) also finds that the health condition of undocumented is of concern. Due to lack of medical treatment illness becomes severe and prolonged.[56]

Labour market

Sweden has not ratified the ILO and UN International Convention on the Protection of the Rights of All Migrant Workers and Members of Their Families (1990). It is still a crime to work in Sweden without permission. The trade unions LO and TCO require decriminalisation of the undocumented while increasing the punishment for employers who hire such persons.[57] They suggest that employers who exploit

---

55 The project was part of a European research project "Trafficking for forced labour in industries other than the sex industry across Europe", University of the West of England.

56 Also see *"Illegal" traveller* (Khosravi 2010).

57 LO is the central organisation for 14 affiliates which organise about 1.5 million workers within the private and the public sectors. www.lo.se/home/lo/home.nsf/unidView/943717B4077AAF1 AC1256E4B0033629CTCO (The Swedish Confederation for Professional Employees) comprises 15 affiliated trade unions. The 1.2 million members of these unions are professional and qualified employees within private and public sectors who share a major responsibility for important functions in society. www.tco.se/Templates/Page2____2319.aspx.

undocumented persons and pay unfair wages or no wages at all shall be liable to damages. The European Trade Union Confederation ETUC is committed to the undocumented and believes that they should have the same rights at work as everyone else. The undocumented mostly work in construction, in agriculture and in the cleaning industry (Working Life 2008). In an article in which four undocumented cleaners are interviewed, the Swedish Building Maintenance Workers' Union writes about what they call the non-existent cleaners: They are "invisible" but still clean in public places, public services and schools. They earn less and have the worst working conditions in the cleaning industry. They are exploited by unscrupulous employers (Fastighetsfolket 3/2008).

A trade union centre for the undocumented is open once a week in Stockholm. The centre is a collaboration between LO, TCO, nine other unions and the network for the undocumented in Stockholm.[58] There are many other networks giving support to undocumented persons, e.g. *No one is illegal – for a world without borders.*[59]

In June 2009 the European Parliament and the Council decided on minimum standards on sanctions against employers who hired undocumented third-country nationals.[60] The directive has led to changes in the Swedish legislation, for example that employers who hire undocumented third nationals will have to pay a fee if detected (SOU 2010:63). For the undocumented workers it did not change much; they still have no rights to organise themselves. From NGOs in Gothenburg we hear about ways to get around the rules. This also affects asylum seekers with permission to work. For example, the employer may hire a person for one day a week in a legal manner and will therefore be able to manage any controls from the authorities, while the individual actually works full time or more for the same low wages as before and with no legal rights. The undocumented are in an even worse situation as they do not know whether they will have a job from one day to the other and if they complain they know they will have nothing. The lowest wage we have heard of is SEK7.50 an hour. "They are worn out and have occupational injuries. There is seldom any protective equipment for this category" (Nurse, 2012).

Health

Health care for undocumented persons has been a subject of concern for many years in Sweden. NGOs, public authorities and unions have been very active in

---

58 www.fcfp.se/.
59 www.ingenillegal.org/no-one-illegal-world-without-borders.
60 Directive 2009/52/EC of the European parliament and of the Council of 18 June 2009 providing for minimum standards on sanctions and measures against employers of illegally staying third-country nationals.

promoting better rights to health care for the undocumented as well as better training of staff, since knowledge of the existing rights has proved to be low.[61] The undocumented do not exist officially, and legally they constitute a residual category. Yet, they are present among us; this discrepancy is particularly evident in the health care sector where their official and administrative absences are set against their bodily presence (Sigvardsdotter, 2012). The UN Special Rapporteur on the Right to highest attainable standard of health, Paul Hunt, wrote in his UN report (2007) that the prevailing bias against undocumented migrants in Sweden amounts to discrimination under international human rights laws.[62] UNICEF has pointed out that it is common that undocumented children live with constant worry and are afraid to become ill. The result is that many children and young people avoid doing anything they believe might increase the risk for accidents or illness.

In several places in Sweden there are clinics where medical staff work voluntarily to give as much care as possible to those in need, but with no rights within the regular system. One such clinic is the *Rosengrenska Foundation* in Gothenburg, an independent network of different types of voluntary medical staff who help refugees in hiding (www.rosengrenska.org.). Through a hotline, refugees in hiding have contact with health care providers within or outside the usual care). "The number of old people visiting Rosengrenska is growing. In 1998, most of the refugees were young families. Now, there is a mixture of three generations" (Nurse, 2012).

Some county councils have taken their own decision on which benefits to be applied to the undocumented. One example is the Sahlgrenska University Hospital in Gothenburg. In June 2006, its Board of Directors decided that "the hidden refugees and other patients without a contract or insurance shall receive emergency or other immediately necessary care at the hospital regardless of ability to pay."[63]

As mentioned, critique of the system has been severe from many different parties in the Swedish society. The report *Health care according to needs and on equal terms – a human right* (SOU 2011:48) proposes that asylum seekers and undocumented persons, regardless of age, must be offered subsidised health care by the county council in the area where they are staying.[64] Care should be offered to the same extent and under the same conditions as to residents. The report also proposes that asylum seekers and undocumented persons should be offered subsidised complete dental care until they are 19 years old. From July 1st, 2012

---

61 "Right to health care initiative" (www.vardforpapperslosa.se/english.asp). 35 organisations have signed in since 2008, some of them can be found on www.vardforpapperslosa.se/organisations.asp.
62 www.vardforalla.se/files/vardforalla/paul_hunt_mission_to_sweden.pdf.
63 www.sahlgrenska.se/upload/SU/omrade_barn/BUP/Flyktingbarnteamet/PM_asyl_flyktingar.pdf.
64 Vård efter behov och på lika villkor – en mänsklig rättighet (SOU 2011:48).

undocumented migrants and refugees in hiding will have the same rights to health care as asylum seekers. Individuals under 18 years of age will have complete rights to health and dental care as well as to medication. Adults will receive subsidised health care and dental care that cannot be deferred, plus drugs prescribed in connection with this, maternity care and health assessments. The county councils will still have a right to provide care at a higher level.[65] This is considered a step forward by the organisations.[66] The lobbying for better conditions will, however, most likely continue, seeing that asylum seekers have limited rights to medical treatment and that many undocumented persons suffer from diseases that need treatment.

6. Non-Governmental Organisations

NGOs play an important role in the reception and introduction of asylum seekers and refugees, especially those who do not find jobs directly or for other reasons need support. Here, we have collected main experiences from the 14 NGOs that were most often mentioned by other actors in the field. There are many more NGOs in Gothenburg.

NGOs do not receive any money for general activities directed to asylum seekers. Funding for this purpose was once available from the SMB, but was frozen when all other activities were stopped. Asylum seekers are increasingly looking to the NGOs for support. They lack activities. "The total waiting time becomes very long when you are on the outside" (NGO, 2012). Without a social registration number it is not possible for the asylum seeker to participate in activities commonly offered in Gothenburg. The asylum seekers therefore go to NGOs for language training, social orientation, assistance with documents they do not understand, support getting medical help, food, finding family members, and someone to talk to. The participants in different activities "feel isolated, have poor psychological health, live with stress and are often helpless because of the lack of orientation and no social network." (NGO, 2012) Although NGOs try to meet these needs they are critical of the lack of financial support and of the SMB for freezing its own activities.

Most NGOs do not distinguish between projects for asylum seekers and new arrivals. They work with open doors and people are only asked to sign up for outings or other activities that need more thorough planning. "The situation of

---

65 Betänkande av Utredningen om vård för pappersslösa m.fl. (SOU 2011:48). PM om överenskommelsen om vård, 2012 (www.regeringen.se/content/1/c6/19/59/63/b61531f0.pdf).
66 www.vardforalla.se.

asylum seekers is based on exclusion; this is not necessarily bad, but all need the ability to understand the society they live in." (NGO, 2012).

The majority of the asylum seekers are poor. During the first instance a single person receives just over EUR 200/month and during the appeal around EUR 150/month. "They become very poor and are forced to take illegal jobs. Black jobs are the new modern slavery, people working for between 10 and 30 SEK/hour, never knowing if they have a job the next day" (NGO, 2012). Many of the workers on the black labour market are young men with secondary education and some with academic education.

Another key phrase is "Invest in the children!" *All* actors of the field say that this is what will pay off for the future. When it comes to working with children, it is necessary to distinguish between working with unaccompanied minors and children with families. When working with the latter group, it is vital to have the consent and trust of the parents/legal guardian if you want achievements. Another common and important reflection in relation to the children is that children have a sense of responsibility for their parents; they interpret, help and even give advice. Most important for newly arrived young people is a stable daily life. This means having a residence permit, permanent habitation, going to school or having a job. This security is not present in the life of many young asylum seekers or new arrivals. "I think that residential segregation is a major problem that affects us all, but children and young people more so. As things are, I think it is unclear who is responsible for the establishment of newly arrived children." (NGO, 2012).

7. Five refugees tell their stories

Maysa

Maysa's father was killed in the war in Iraq. Her older sister disappeared, probably kidnapped. Her mother wanted to save her and sent her to Sweden with the help of a smuggler. She arrived in 2002, together with one brother. At the airport the smuggler told them he was going to buy food and left them. They were accommodated in a private foster home. Maysa's mother is still alive and she has three married brothers with refugee status in Sweden. Today, Maysa has no contact with her family and she lives with protected identity since her brothers and her foster mother tried to force her to marry.

Maysa was 14 years old on her arrival. She had been to school in Iraq but when she arrived in Sweden, the foster mother, also from Iraq, did not allow her to go to school. After a few years she met a girl who told her about the Equal project "Arrival Gothenburg" and Maysa managed to join the project. There, she learned more Swedish and, thanks to the extensive civic information, she began to understand her rights. Once she had started her new life with a new identity she enrolled in adult education programme. For three years she studied at double speed and managed to finish six years of missed schooling. She is now in her last year at Gothenburg University.

Maysa would like to work within the area of social work, especially with women. One of her dreams is to write a book about her experiences as an ill-treated child and a young woman who has gone through many hardships to create an independent life in Sweden. She is verbal and speaks Swedish with no other accent than that of Gothenburg.

Maysa talks about the need to really see and listen to asylum seeking children. She was appointed a legal guardian who never contacted her but turned up at all meetings with the SMB, pretending to be there for her. Nobody noticed that she did not attend school. She did not know her rights and felt totally abandoned. She tried several times to commit suicide and it was not until she became a participant of the Equal project *Arrival Gothenburg* that she felt recognised and listened to: "they always made time to hear us out." She says that "without that project I would not be alive today /.../ I looked forward to every day, there were staff to talk to and other people with the same problems as I had. I walked into Sweden through the back door." A significant moment was when, through Equal, Maysa was invited to sit in a panel at a conference in Stockholm (2004). She realised that she could make something out of her life and that she had value as the person she is. "While waiting for asylum I always cried. When I was granted leave to remain, my journey began".

Amira

Amira is a woman in her mid-fifties. She came to Sweden together with her eight-year-old son and applied for asylum in 2002. She participated in the Equal project "Arrival Gothenburg" until she was granted asylum in 2006. She has one sister in Gothenburg, another sister and brother in London and two sisters in the US. Her mother stays with them all in turns.

Amira studied at a university in Teheran and at the end of the 1970s she took a degree in Sociology, Business Administration and Psychology. When she was permitted to stay in Sweden she wanted to become a deacon but, unfortunately, she was too old for the seminary. This was a very big disappointment. She then studied to become an assistant nurse and qualified in March 2012. She works as an assistant nurse in a home for disabled people.

Amira is a religious woman, active both in the Swedish Lutheran Church and in the Iranian congregation in Gothenburg, with 20,000 Iranians. Perhaps 1,000 of these are Christians. She explains that it is very difficult to convert. The price is very high in relation to family, friends and longing for what once was. She likes her job and feels that she is doing well and that she has much to give. She knows what it feels like to be an outsider and she knows how important it is to give care and warmth.

When Amira waited for a decision on her application her case handler told her to join "Arrival Gothenburg". She says it was a thousand times better than the Swedish lessons she had been attending: "it was the best thing that could have happened to me. I was lucky and it was a good period of my life." In this Equal project she had not only lessons in Swedish but was also given very good information about Swedish society and culture. There were many experts from various fields of society, public authorities, companies and organisations. What was most important, however, was that the personnel very consciously built trust; they created a feeling of security and hope. She points out that most refugees have lost trust and that it is essential to regain trust in others in order to be able to move on. There was always time for the participants and no questions were considered unimportant. She had not worked since completing her studies in her country of origin and her self-confidence was low. Getting the support she needed helped her to keep her spirit.

Zahra

Zahra's parents and five of her sisters and brothers left Iran ten years before she did. She married and had a daughter. The husband is an alcoholic and was violent towards her. She divorced him and then she got into trouble because her father was a political refugee in Sweden.

Zahra is a hair dresser by profession. She used to work in Iran. As an asylum seeker in Sweden she was referred to the Equal project "Arrival Gothenburg" by the SMB. She met a man she had known in Iran and moved in with him just to find out that he was a drug addict. She was severely maltreated. Due to her personal problems she did not benefit much from the programme and she feels that she was let down. She reported the man who was sentenced to prison. She got some financial compensation which she used to buy a shop. After some years she sold the shop and started to work as a care assistant.

Zahra would like to study, but the beating that she was subject to has caused severe neck problems, problems concentrating as well as headache and memory loss. She was so tired when she was granted leave to remain that she could not be happy and she says that she is still tired.

The Equal project was not designed for her kind of problem. She got support from individual employees, but she did not feel support within the frame of the project. Her opinion is that dealing with vulnerable people, projects must be ready to give support, even if the occurring problem is not within the direct mandate of the project.

Fuad

Fuad, who is a Christian, was born in Bagdad, Iraq, in 1982. He left Iraq in 2007. Up until then he had been working for a Canadian company (Waterloo University, UN Environmental programme) in the south of Iraq. Corruption was very common. Due to his refusal to participate in cheating the company, he was threatened and, eventually, his family begged him to leave Iraq before he was killed. He came directly from Bagdad to Gothenburg and applied for asylum. It was not possible for him to use his own passport leaving Iraq. In 2008 he was granted indefinite leave to remain in Sweden.

Fuad thought he was leaving Iraq for a short time but realises that it will be many years before he can return, even to visit. His parents are retired university professors. His father was an engineer and his mother was a biochemist. He has not seen them for a long time and hoped to meet them in Syria.

Fuad started to learn Swedish as soon as he arrived in the country and once he got the permission to stay, he very quickly passed the different tests. He felt, however, that it is difficult to learn to communicate in Swedish only through school. During his free time he only met other Arabic speakers. He looked for opportunities on Google and found GöteborgsInitiativet (working with Arrival Gothenburg), contacted them and was accepted as a trainee. He stayed for one year and, there, he really learned to speak Swedish properly.

Fuad has worked hard to find a position as a microbiologist. He was in contact with the PES, where he had been assigned a coach. He asked (begged) for any apprentice position just to be able to prove his skills. However, he did not have any response to any of this. His BA from Iraq was validated and judged equivalent to a Swedish university degree in microbiology. But this did not seem to help either. Therefore, Fuad decided to study for a Master's degree in microbiology at Gothenburg University. He was accepted and started in the autumn of 2011.

Fuad would like to go back to Iraq and help rebuild the country. He fears that it will be a long time before he can return safely and that, if he would return, he would once again have to go through the ordeals he endured when starting all over in Sweden. For the foreseeable future Fuad wishes to manage his studies. He comes back to the fact that he already has a degree, validated in Sweden, and also work experience with a Canadian company but that none of this seems to be of any value in Sweden. Evidently, he wishes to be recognised and able to work and be part of society. He talks about friends of his who also have academic qualification from Iraq but who have submitted to the notion that they will never be accepted, and that it is fruitless to even try. He has consciously chosen not to buy a parabolic antenna but watch Swedish TV and not to visit the café too often. Fuad does what he can to become part of society. This decision come with a price: "Many hate you, but a few good friends are enough".

As for working in the informal economy, he says that it is a trap. "You only meet with fellow countrymen and you work long hours for very low wages with little security". Then he goes on to say that people need to work and need to feel accepted. The low wage is compensated by the fact that those who are working in the informal economy also receive social security assistance. "But most people would prefer a regular job".

Fuad thinks that integration is a two-way process – you have to work hard, learn and try, and at the same time you have to be accepted and given chances. His first contact person, responsible for the introduction plan, still contacts him after more than five years if she sees a job advertisement or something else that he might benefit from. This interest for his wellbeing has helped him to cope with adversities.

Simon

Simon is a stateless Kurd, born in Syria in 1981. He left Syria in 1994 to go to Russia where he studied to become a chemist. He finished his studies and started to work. But in 2003 he was expelled from Russia and went to Sweden to seek asylum. He could not go back to Syria as a stateless person, especially since he had been politically active against the regime during his exile. His asylum application was rejected, as was his appeal, but he was stateless and therefore could not be expelled from Sweden. After a few years he applied for asylum again. In 2009 he was granted leave to remain in Sweden. During this time he was depressed for long periods of time. "It was an extremely difficult situation, to stay at home with nothing to do but to think all day long. What is going to happen to me? What am I to do? Everything around me was darkness. I had lost all hope and I was contemplating suicide." A friend told him about Caritas in Gothenburg. There he got all the support he needed. "They were the first people in Sweden who believed in me. This was what I had been missing."

"Caritas gives counselling, information about laws, finds ways to deal with your health problems, and finds lawyers. It is extremely important for the individual to feel that someone cares and gives support. If a Swedish person believes in you it makes a huge difference; most refugees feel that a rejection is the same as not being believed. It makes a big difference when you are allowed to tell your story." Simon is not sure that he would have survived without Caritas. He says that "Every day tens of discouraged people go there. They can talk to someone, participate in Swedish classes or other activities and they start to think about the future /.../ I felt new hope, like a man in the middle of the ocean would feel if someone suddenly came to the rescue."

Simon started to learn Swedish early but as an asylum seeker it was not possible for him to gain enough language training to pursue academic studies. As soon as he was granted leave to remain he dived into language studies and managed to do all tests within a year. He then went through the necessary studies to qualify as a chemist in Sweden. "In six years you forget much and, anyhow, all countries have different rules. When I read the books I recognise and remember. Apart from new developments within the field, the differences lie with the pedagogical aspects."

Although his studies have been successful, Simon is not a happy man. First of all, he is extremely worried about his only brother living in Syria. And he is tired. He says that he waited for so long and was so worn out when he got permission to stay. Then, he had to attend many meetings, make decisions about a whole range of things and start studying, and he never really relaxed or had time to be happy about the fact that he was granted permission to stay. He talks warmly about Caritas, where he continues to find support and encouragement.

Simon plans to get a job in Gothenburg, but is no stranger to moving in order to find work.

Simon did not participate in the Equal programme, but what he says about how he was met at Caritas goes well in hand with the philosophy of Equal. To see the individual, to create trust, to give time, to listen, to support on an individual basis, to support the development of hope and to empower the individual in order to create a situation where it is possible to take charge of his/her own life. He is a well-educated man who had lost hope, and what made hope return was the human aspect together with the concrete actions he met at Caritas. Without that support he is not certain that he would have had the strength to benefit from the integration programmes offered to him.

8. To see the other – a road to social participation

Once, many years ago, at an introduction meeting for asylum seekers, an overhead was shown with the following text: "In Sweden, work is the foundation".

This is true enough just about everywhere. Access to the labour market is another matter. Understandings of what it means to have a job and how responsibilities within a family concerning earnings differ. Understandings of why work is important from a solidarity point of view also differ.

The Act on Establishment Activities for Certain New Arrivals is meant to deal with such things. SFI offers support in learning Swedish; SO offers orientation about the social system, rights and obligations in Sweden; the PES offers activities supporting access to the labour market. For many new arrivals the system proposes real opportunities to establish oneself as an equal member of society and there are many who take advantage of these possibilities. Several interviewees testify that it is amazing to see for example a young woman who has previously been deprived of schooling, grabbing every opportunity to learn, and learn quickly.

Yet, as the reports from the PES to the government (June 2012) and the *Swedish Agency for Public Management* (2012:22) show the result of the establishment reform after almost one and a half years is that only just above four per cent of the new arrivals entering the introduction activities have been employed. Why is that so?

In this article we have described and analysed the reception and introduction of asylum seekers and new arrivals in Gothenburg, the second-largest city in Sweden. In this final part we discuss some of the findings in relation to the three overall questions: Under what circumstances can the vocational preparation and integration of asylum seekers and refugees be successful? What role can be ascribed to their biographies? How can quality be assured in the vocational education?

Under what circumstances can the vocational preparation and integration of asylum seekers and refugees be successful?

As previously mentioned, measures to facilitate integration into the Swedish society have been criticised over the years. The Report (2007) from the SIB passed judgement on the work of the authorities, but there has been much more radical criticism asserting that the failure of the integration policy depended on distinctions made between Swedes and immigrants, cementing the perceptions of diversity (cf. Kamali, 1997, 2002, 2008). In *The (in)visible boundaries of labour* (SOU 2006:59) eleven researchers and one expert analyse various barriers to enter the labour market. They find that discrimination is never isolated from other power relations or from constructions of "the other". This was briefly discussed in the section about validation in chapter 4, but is obviously a matter of concern throughout the whole introduction system. All structures favour some and disadvantage others. It should not be a task for the future to prove this self-evident aspect once again, but to continuously evaluate the chosen system and to develop models and methods that minimise the effects of downsides. The norm for effectiveness and ethical attitudes must be included conceptually as well as operationally within both the legal system and within all agencies, whether governmental or non-governmental. It is the task of parliament and the government to ensure equal rights through a legal system in which justice is assured. It is for the agencies to apply logos with impeccable practical skills, and with a realisation that it is the decision maker who apply the meat and blood to the desiccated skeleton which comprises the legal infrastructure, thereby giving it meaning and social relevance (Justice P.N. Bhagwati, 1995:6). The process of realising rights is contained in the context demanding discourses of self-comprehension (Habermas, 1999:118). Self-reflection (organisational, structural and individual) would, therefore, be an important tool for making the new arrival the true point of departure, cooperating over organisational borders, and searching for the mechanisms of obstruction.[67]

One way to start is to look at the recommendations of previous reports and investigations in order to see what would also benefit the current programmes of reception and introduction. In 2007 NTG Asylum & Integration published a paper with National policy proposals for the future.[68] These following proposals were based on conclusions drawn from the Development Partnerships, mainly the Equal Initiative, and they are set in NTG Asylum's reference group and steering committee:

- Organisational separation between asylum application testing and asylum reception
- Socio-economic cost benefit analyses of reception and introduction policies and measures
- Quality control and external supervision of asylum reception, development of procurement capacity and target group involvement
- Labour market placement support for asylum seekers
- Offering asylum seekers vocational skills auditing, validation and complementary training and education
- Healthcare for asylum seekers
- Civic education
- Gender perspective/equality
- Repatriation/return, dual perspective and foreign aid
- The future role for the NTG Asylum & Integration thematic group

---

67 There are many studies made about this and much literature to be inspired from, e.g. Gibney (2004), Habermas (1999), Hertzfeld (1993), Moxnes (1987), Norström (2004), Persson (2012), Povrzanovic (2001), Seukwa (2007), Söndergaard (1991).

68 www.temaasyl.se/Templates/Page.aspx?id=63 (right hand column, word document).

As we see, these proposals deal with the reception of asylum seekers. However, as so many have pointed out, there is a clear relation between the reception of asylum seekers and the introduction and integration of new arrivals. Currently, there is not much offered to asylum seekers, which in reality means moving problems from one period of the life of the individual to another period. As introduction activities are not offered until a person becomes a new arrival, we will continue the discussion from that point.

The PES, with overall responsibility for coordinating the introduction activities, is almost compartmentalised. Each local office is an entity of its own. Each unit and each officer is specialised. Calling to ask about validation, for example, meant talking to one officer for each sector. None of these officers can answer overall questions or questions about new arrivals, as they "belong" to the Establishment Unit. Criticism about making refugees a category of "others" should be taken seriously. Why should an electrician who happens to be a refugee not be part of the common validation programme for all unemployed electricians? Separating new arrivals from others looking for jobs becomes a paradox in relation to the aims of integration. It is true that many new arrivals need time and social support, but that is also true for many other job seekers and is not reason enough to create parallel structures. The new arrivals would benefit from coordination and use of the wider range of existing professional and economical resources within the PES.

The asylum seeker becomes a "new arrival" if granted leave to remain. This term is deceiving; for the simple reason that a new arrival is not new in Sweden. He or she has been through the whole process of waiting and most likely formed opinions of Sweden and Swedish society. In order to meet him/her as an individual it is thus important to be clear over what this means when it comes to making use of their former experience and education. "The period of waiting for permission to stay, sometimes for many years, could very well have been filled with informal work and non-formal VET. Then, once you are a *new arrival*, it is as if you were without experience and knowledge" (NGO, 2012).

The official goals of equal rights, responsibilities and opportunities regardless of ethnic or cultural background have to be understood from the individual point of view. People integrate into the surroundings where they spend their time and where they make friends. For most new arrivals this means the multicultural immigrant-dominated neighbourhoods, sometimes very far from the Sweden that is outlined in official documents. The cultural understandings developed there could be better reflected in the official understandings of a pluralistic Sweden. It may be hard to be loyal to "the abstract Swede", abstract people and an abstract society that is not perceived as loyal to you. And yet this dual loyalty is what is needed for the contraction of welfare.

Another basis for success is to look for competences rather than deficits. When looking for competences it is constructive to use the lifelong learning and life-wide learning concepts as well as the formal, non-formal and informal learning/ training. In a project in Huddinge, south of Stockholm, named Mira, a useful three-step model was developed.[69] The first step is working with the question: Where do I come from? Here, the full range of life experiences from the country of origin, the transit to Sweden (sometimes several years long) and the waiting period is mapped. The second question is: Where am I? – talking about now, understanding the situation and its options. The third question is: Where am I going? The latter involves formulating wishes for the future and planning the steps necessary to take.

Early integration, as suggested in the EU Council Directive 2003/9/EC, would eliminate many problems later on. Although some asylum seekers have the opportunity to work while waiting for asylum, too many are in fact unoccupied; living in cramped conditions, poor, worrying about the outcome of the application, often with deteriorating health and suffering from experiences prior to arriving in Sweden. Such trauma may be related to experiences of war, persecution, many years in limbo, sexual or other forms of abuse, loss of family, friends, home, dignity, skills and status. Certainly not all new arrivals are in a bad condition after the waiting period, but it is important that the PES introduction officer and the introduction guide are able to see the wide diversity among the new arrivals and to realise what it means to be a refugee, what the waiting period may represent, and that they are prepared to meet each individual exactly where he/she stands and not typecast as a "new arrival". Each individual has a personal history and personal prerequisites for dealing with the demands of the future.

A road to broader understanding of the society may be the methods used in the SO programme in Gothenburg. These methods build on a pedagogy that has a starting point in the factual experiences of the participants. The understanding reached through SO may well function in two ways – to learn from the new arrivals and to serve as a door opener for them. For lasting effects, however, it has to lead further in practice, e.g. to work, housing, education and participation. A reoccurring issue in our interviews is why asylum seekers and new arrivals are not naturally integrated and recognised. "They (immigrants) are everywhere and yet nowhere!" (NGO, 2012). NGOs and others also refer to a regular question from asylum seekers and new arrivals, namely "where are the Swedes?" The work of Gothenburg municipality refugee guides is one tool to introduce new arrivals into wider spheres of society and to make meetings with private native Swedes

---

69   www.mynewsdesk.com/se/pressroom/huddinge/pressrelease/view/mira-skapar-dialog-mellan-unga-flyktingar-och-samhaellet-361879.

possible. A paramount part of true integration is making friends and building social relations; new arrivals may very well have friends and family where they live. The dilemma is not that most new arrivals are isolated, as often believed, but that the full range of options for reaching ones full potential is not available without wider social contacts than family and friends, knowledge about the systems available and being addressed in a manner free of bias.[70]

A precondition for success on the labour market is health. The restrictions concerning healthcare are criticised by medical staff in many parts of Sweden. According to healthcare organisations, Sweden is one of the weakest countries in Europe when it comes to medical healthcare for asylum seekers. Early treatment is vital for reducing both suffering and cost, as well as the spreading of infectious deceases. Health problems manifest themselves as sleep deficiencies, inability to concentrate, and as lethargy, depression, and physical ailments of all kinds. Brekke (2004) examined pending asylum and showed that asylum seekers have difficulty coping with their situation because of the uncertainty that comes with the asylum procedure. When the future is uncertain, it becomes difficult to manage both the present and the past. Among other things, it becomes impossible to plan for both an acceptance and a rejection of the asylum application. Another effect on the health of asylum seekers is the uncertainty of how long the pending will be.

It is also valuable to have knowledge about post-traumatic stress disorder, PTSD, which can influence the way people act, e.g. in an interview situation (Firnhaber, 2000:49). The PES introduction officer and the introduction guide have a duty to understand that people with traumatic experiences might dole out what they relate in order to guard against a re-experiencing of the trauma in question. In cases where the interviewees protect themselves, it may seem as if the person has no feelings at all. In addition, people who are beaten with blows to the head can suffer from lack of concentration and poor memory. Neither doling out information nor putting up a shield indicates lack of credibility. It is not until the person has processed the trauma that it is possible to describe the experience with words, instead of reliving the trauma or putting up a shield.

Regarding health it is important to take into account the human and social cost of a sick person on his/her environment. In an EBO home both the host family and the family of the asylum seeker are affected when one person is ill. Children are most certainly affected, which is confirmed by both teachers and NGOs.

Moreover, health is a matter of staff welfare. In order to really see the other and to be able to maintain a holistic way to work, including not rejecting or diminishing traumatising experiences, officers and introduction guides need to know themselves and to handle their own bias. This implies a responsibility for

---

70   Cf. Arbetslivets (o)synliga murar (SOU 2006:59).

their managers to give support and provide methods for handling reactions and feelings (cf. Hawkins & Shohet, 1989; Ayalon, 1999; Norström, 2004).

Meeting each individual on a personal level is part of the duty of the PES introduction officer and the introduction guide. This, however, involves some natural difficulties. Bureaucracies are formed to handle large case loads. The sociologist Roine Johansson studied local PES offices and Social Insurance Agencies already in 1992 and found that although the ideology is to work with the individual as a whole, the complete person is reduced to "a case" (Johansson, 1992). In order to actually "see the other" the introduction officer somehow has to go against the core of bureaucracy. To enable this, the officer has to be allowed a certain space and flexibility as well as support from superiors. PES staff does not find that such support is given in a satisfactory way (Statskontoret, 2012).

An important point in the EU Directive 2003/9/EC is actually the necessity to develop training programmes for staff (Article 24). Tools to be included in such training are methods for self-reflection and handling feelings and reactions in order to stay vital and professional. These areas are mostly neglected in training, although essential for ethical reasons and for being able to fully meet the other, whatever that entails. This is in turn a prerequisite for success (the 4 per cent that so far found work within the introduction system would probably have found work anyway). It is important not to forget the introduction guides and SFI teachers in such training. They are the professional individuals in everyday contact with new arrivals and apart from being invited to training they have much specific knowledge to share.

What role can be ascribed to biographies?

From the definition of validation we know that the merit portfolio should include all formal, non-formal and informal knowledge and experience from the country of origin and the transnational period, as well as from the waiting period in Sweden. According to the evaluation of the VINN project, this is difficult (Diedrich 2011). To fulfil this aim, the PES introduction officer and the introduction guide need to go outside predominant cultural preconceptions of what knowledge and experience relevant for the labour market is, as well as of how this should be achieved. Attention must be paid to the solid experience of the informal labour market that many new arrivals may have. There are many employers offering informal work for very low pay and, according to NGOs, several thousand asylum seekers and people with no documents work under inadequate and even dangerous conditions. These experiences are not really recognised in the official system, but they constitute experience of working life in Sweden and ought to be a self-evident part of the merit portfolio within the introduction plan. In the same way, the experiences from the transnational period between leaving the country of origin and arriving in Sweden need to be recognised. This period is sometimes several years long. Many have worked in several countries, and many have been subject to slavery and trafficking. These experiences are most relevant in the planning for the future, although it takes competent staff to give support in such cases. One example is the 15 year old boy who came to Sweden after a four-year-long transnational journey. He was caught at the age of nine and kept like a slave, working for a blacksmith in Turkey. At the age of 14, he managed to escape (NGO, 2012). How do you deal with this young man? It is not only a challenge because of the difficulties associated with continuing to work as a blacksmith in Sweden, but also because it might be difficult to see beyond the slavery and trafficking experience with relevant professionalism.[71] Another Example: "People say that the Somali women do not know anything, but they certainly know how to survive – and to cook and to raise children!" (PES officer, 2012).

Developing the methods for taking stock of the total competence of a new arrival will have many positive effects. First of all, it means recognising the individual as a whole person and opening the wide range of possibilities actually at hand for him/her. For the Swedish society it opens possibilities such as development of methods for the merit portfolio, validation and training of staff, etc. It is part of widening of the common understanding of competence and skill, e.g. taking advantage of experiences of new arrivals in developments within various trades.

How can quality be assured in the vocational education?

Quality is not just a matter of the system functioning at a grassroots level. It is also about political will to listen to those with daily experience of how the system works, to learn, to put party politics aside and to allocate enough recourse for the demands to be fulfilled.

The daily activities for the new arrival are subcontracted. With the strong sectioning within the PES, it is difficult to follow up all the different services that are procured from external providers. Each officer has to monitor not only the process of the individual but also how the external provider carries out its services. There is little time for individual monitoring. Monitoring the providers' services is almost impossible, for two reasons: the first is lack of time and the other is that the local officer seldom knows the content of the many contracts

---

71   Cf. Tornborg (1984).

signed at the PES head office. Monitoring of external contractors is defined as a strong need in several of the interviews. Close monitoring would reveal aspects of the service provision that could be improved and it would aid refinement of the quality requirements in coming procurements.

The idea to introduce Pilot Companies falls into a situation where private operators have been given increasingly larger space in the production of welfare services in Sweden in areas such as schools, healthcare, pharmacy, and interpreter services. From the beginning it was mainly in a context where the public purchaser wrote a contract with the commercial services to perform certain services. A gradual shift has occurred towards the model with Pilot Companies, i.e. the consumer is free to choose between approved Companies. In a research anthology published by the *Centre for Business and Policy Studies,* SNS, the researchers (Hartman and others 2011) draw the conclusion that there is a remarkable lack of knowledge about the effects of the privatisation of the Swedish welfare sector. Based on existing research, it is not possible to find evidence that the reform of the public sector led to greater quality and efficiencies. The privatisations of the public welfare sector have not been evaluated in a comprehensive and systematic manner although it is known that there are severe problems that must be addressed. [72] Experience shows that there is a need for a regulatory framework that ensures that an equivalent quality can be maintained.[73]

"The introduction guide should have the skills to quickly assess..." (Prop. 2009/10:60). This concept of 'quickly' is not discussed and the time allocated for an introduction plan is maximised to 24 months. What quickly means has to be related to the individual. What is the educational background? What is the wish of the individual and what are the possibilities? The new arrival might be young or old, educated or not, have a profession or not, be ready to study or not. What is quick for one person might be extremely long for another. 24 months might be plenty of time or far too short a time. Analysing the concept of quickly together with PES introduction officers and introduction guides would probably be valuable in making the system more flexible. Flexibility would also help to avoid situations where "academics are forced into competing with unskilled job applicants for the scarce opportunities available for them" (Municipal officer, 2012).

Understanding the life situation of a refugee is a strong tool. Part of that tool is recognising the importance of building trust. Trust is one of the most frequent topics in our interviews. Building trust between individuals is essential as a

---

72 Results from the earlier mentioned research project *Behind closed doors* support these findings. There is a clear parallel to the situation on the interpreter market.

73 See article by former undersecretary of state Sören Häggroth (11 March, 2012) at http://fram tidensvalfard.wordpress.com/2012/03/11/vinstsyftande-aktorer-inom-vard-skola-och-omsorg/.

method of widening perspectives, building new loyalties and self-esteem, and daring to leave the smaller "safe" situation of the close neighbourhood. Those who have been through war, persecution, slavery, trafficking, waiting in camps etc., have most probably developed mistrust to any system, however benevolent (cf. Daniel & Knudsen, 1995). Waiting for a long time with inactivity and anxiety does not help. In the Equal project "Arrival Gothenburg", a method of creating trust was developed, called 5T[74]. It consisted of five points for building trust, hope and self-esteem all of which was mentioned as key factors by the interviewed refugees:

- *Trust* is created between persons. This is particularly important because it is precisely the ability to build trust that is seriously impaired by persecution, war, life in camps, etc. Listening to and confirming a person normally helps to *re*build his/her trust.
- *Time* is essential; time to listen until he/she is ready, the time he/she needs to learn and to have the strength to think about the future, time to get a letter from the lawyer explained, or to talk about personal problems.
- *Clarity* is vital when working with traumatised people. Language difficulties, concentration problems, anxiety, fatigue and many other things are in the way. It can be difficult to absorb information and to keep agreements. Lack of interpreters is a weakness in more serious situations.
- *Accessibility* is another necessity. For those asylum seekers who have problems with time perception and emotions such as anxiety and fear it is of crucial value if he/she has someone to talk to as soon as possible when problems arise.
- *Faith in the future* is perhaps the most difficult aspect of 5T. Faith and trust go hand in hand.

Coordination is a key word. Coordination internally within the PES and with all other actors is of importance, not forgetting the NGOs who carry much responsibility for the welfare of asylum seekers and new arrivals, counselling, offering language training and social orientation, activities for children and elderly, etc., thus supporting people socially, health-wise as well as preparing for work. NGOs also provide support for the many refugees who have lived in Sweden for years, maybe working or without knowing how to find their way to learning the language. Also, if you have waited for years for a decision and have attended these classes, you are already prepared when finally admitted to the "official" SFI and SO.

Asylum seekers bring with them a wide range of skills and experiences from their countries of origin and from their transnational movements; an enormous

---

74 Tillit, Tid, Tydlighet, Tillgänglighet och Tro på framtiden.

gift of knowledge flows into the country every day. To take full advantage of this at an early stage seems like a particularly good idea.

The Ministry of Labour in Finland, responsible for the reception of asylum seekers, launched a study, LATU (2008), on the reception conditions for asylum seekers in Finland. The aim was to analyse the services provided, the costs incurred in this process, and to:

- Develop quality and productivity in refugee work by using the EFQM model
- Create a cohesive and economically sustainable operating model for the services offered at the reception centres
- Productise services and develop work processes
- Create clear gauges and indicators in order to compare refugee camps' functional productivity
- Prevent marginalisation – promote empowerment

The study was a continuation of the project *Operative profitability of the reception of asylum seekers* that the Ministry of Labour began in 2002 to create uniform conditions at the 15 reception centres for asylum seekers run by the state, municipalities or the Finnish Red Cross. It included the development of performance indicators in the reception centres in Finland where most asylum seekers live. EBO is permitted, but because of the cost, few choose this option. The report *Change is a permanent state – Services provided at the reception of asylum seekers and the costs incurred* (LATU report 2008) shows that the statutory services, which according to the EU Directive 2003/9/EC are to be provided at the reception of asylum seekers, are available in all reception centres. It was noted that asylum seekers have a remarkable number of psychosocial symptoms. To develop preventive psychosocial support, in order to minimise mental-healthcare costs was therefore seen as important. Other important areas to develop were counselling services and opportunities to work and study. In addition to the availability of activities and cost effectiveness, quality development was seen as something that has to be ongoing. LATU divided the refugee process into five categories: Accommodation, Acute care, Social services and income security, Services for children, young people and families with children and Social participation and empowerment. Interpretation and Legal Aid was established by support Services. The LATU report points out that " the asylum seekers have decided to seek a new future in a new country; regardless of where the future is, you cannot return to the past" and develops two more services separately from the asylum reception services: Successful start for inclusion for granted residence permits and Decent return or Dignified repatriation. It was furthermore seen as important that reception centres should develop their reporting and documentation systems since many problems were due to the different ways of recording costs by the different agencies maintaining reception centres.

276

Taking into consideration the large number of asylum seekers choosing EBO in Sweden, in Gothenburg far from the office of the SMB, and because of the lack of activities, training, work and practice for most of the asylum seekers, it would be advisable to look at the Finnish study and develop some form of quality assurance systems also in Sweden. As understood by the UNHCR (2003), the spirit of the EU directive 2003/9/EC is clearly built on an understanding of the human and economic benefits of including asylum seekers in normal activities from their arrival. The model for quality assurance and monitoring of asylum reception, developed within the project LATU, meets the requirements of such a system well.[75] It could well be developed to include control and development of EBO in areas such as health and child care, occupational and vocational activities. "Seeking asylum is an intermediate stage in the life of the individual. The client should be supported through this difficult stage of life with well-adapted measures" (LATU report 2008).

Finally, we think that it would be worthwhile to go back to the above mentioned proposals from NTG Asylum & Integration, to evaluate and take stock of those suggestion that would support the development of the current system, especially proposals supporting early integration of asylum seekers.

---

75 The project builds on the EFQM (European Foundation for Quality Management).

Appendix 1
Statistics on a national level

Immigration/Emigration to/from Sweden 2000-2010 – including Swedes returning/leaving

Total number immigration: 872,000, whereof Swedish citizens 167,000.
Total number emigration: 433,000, whereof Swedish citizens 231,000.

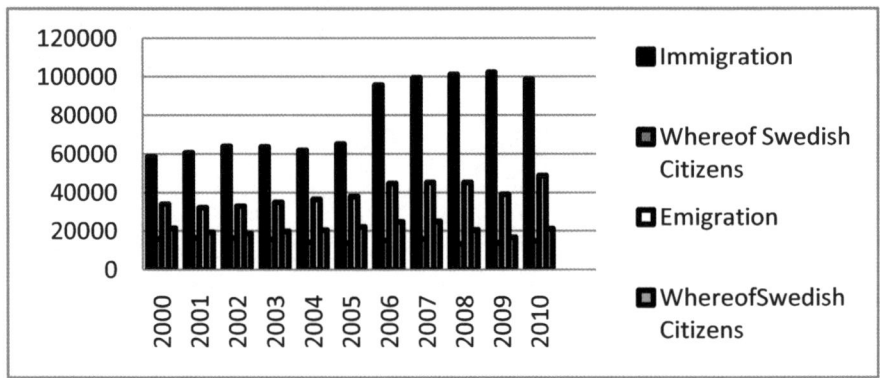

Source: Immigrantinstitutet/SCB (www.immi.se)

Immigration to Sweden 2000-2011 – categories

All categories: Refugee related immigration, family reunion, work permits, students, adopted children, and EES-agreements. Total number: 897,000 individuals.

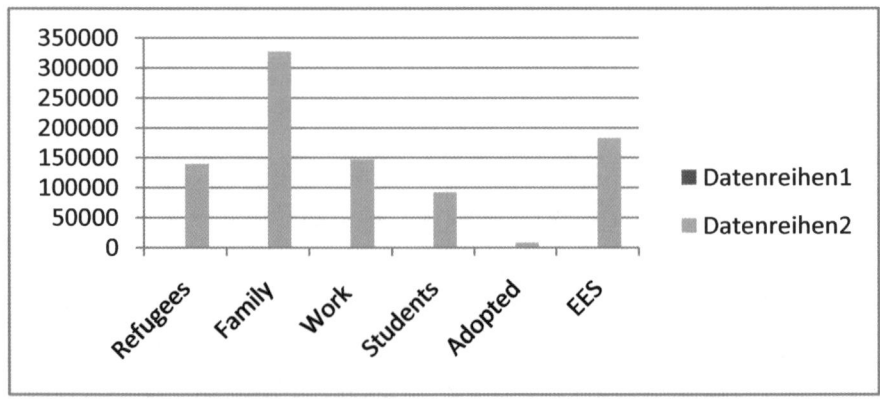

Asylum seekers by citizenship 2000-2011

Bulgaria	3991
Yugoslavia (former) :	62387
Kosovo [1]	5 047
Poland	145
Rumania	2005
Russia	12082
Eritrea	8438
Ethiopia	1602
Somalia	29472
Uganda	461
Togo	125
Cuba	290
Chile	634
Peru	601
Afghanistan	13839
Bangladesh	1407
India	953
Iraq	61 137
Iran	9534
China	1209
Lebanon	3654
Pakistan	1208
Sri Lanka	499
Syria	5858
Turkey	4484
Stateless/Unknown [2]	13857
Other countries	71 413
Total	316332

1) From 2008 Kosovo included
2) From 2007 Serbia
3) Majority Palestinians

Asylum seekers arriving in Sweden 2000-2011

Total number: 316, 300 (203,900 male and 112,400 female. 228,000 adults and 87,500 minors whereof 13,500 unaccompanied). *Estimated* number of asylum seekers for 2012 is 44,000.

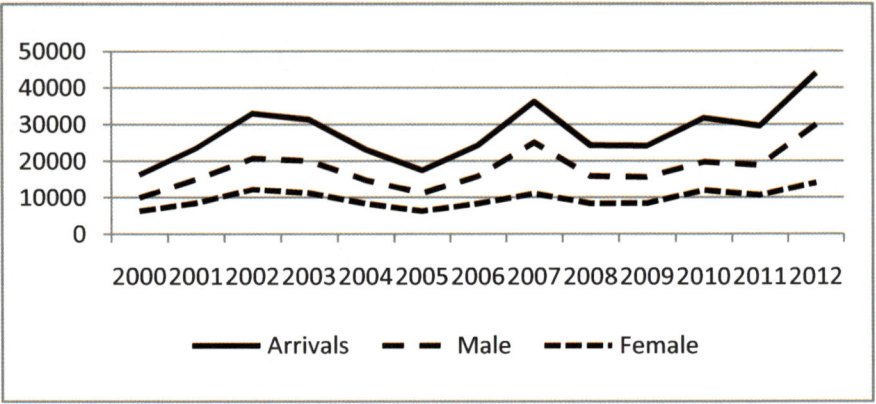

Source: SMB

Asylum seeking minors arriving in Sweden 2000-2011

Total number: 87,500 minors whereof 13,500 unaccompanied minors.

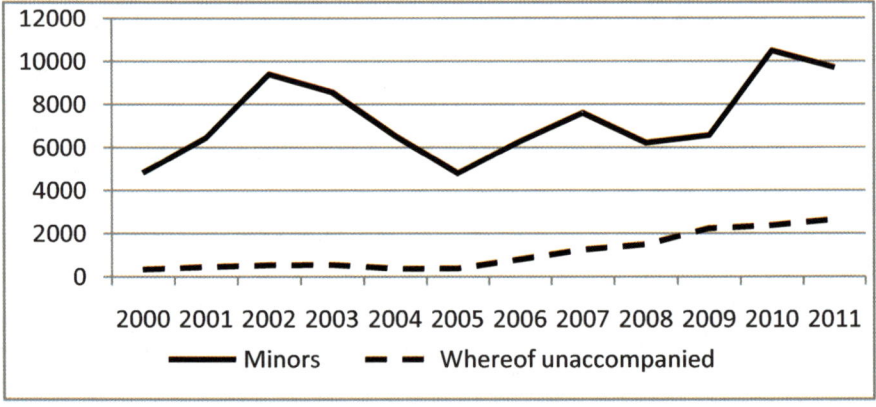

Source: SMB

280

Asylum seekers to Västra Götaland 2000-2011

Total number 66,000 (41,000 male, 25,000 female. 46,000 adults, 20,000 children, whereof 2,000 unaccompanied minors).

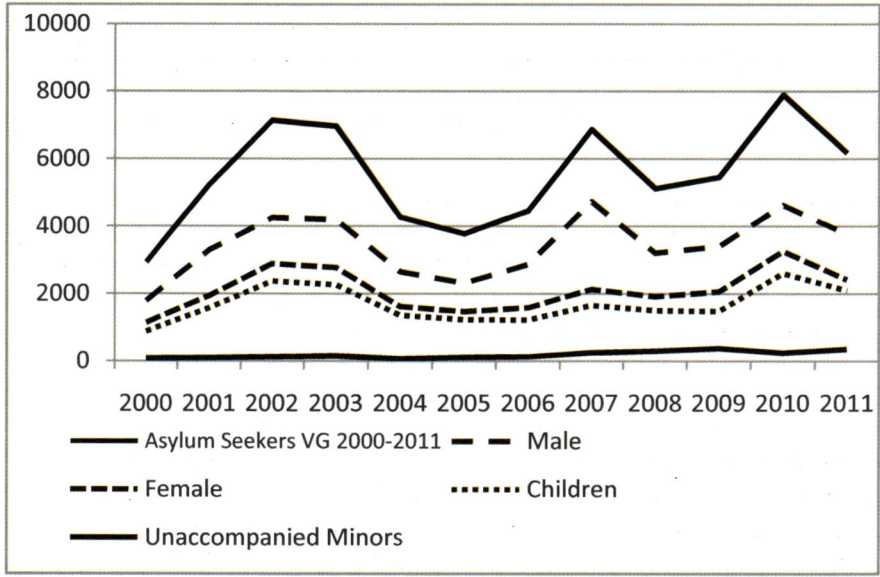

Source: SMB

Asylum seekers granted leave to remain in Sweden 2000-2011

By category
Total number 139,000 individuals

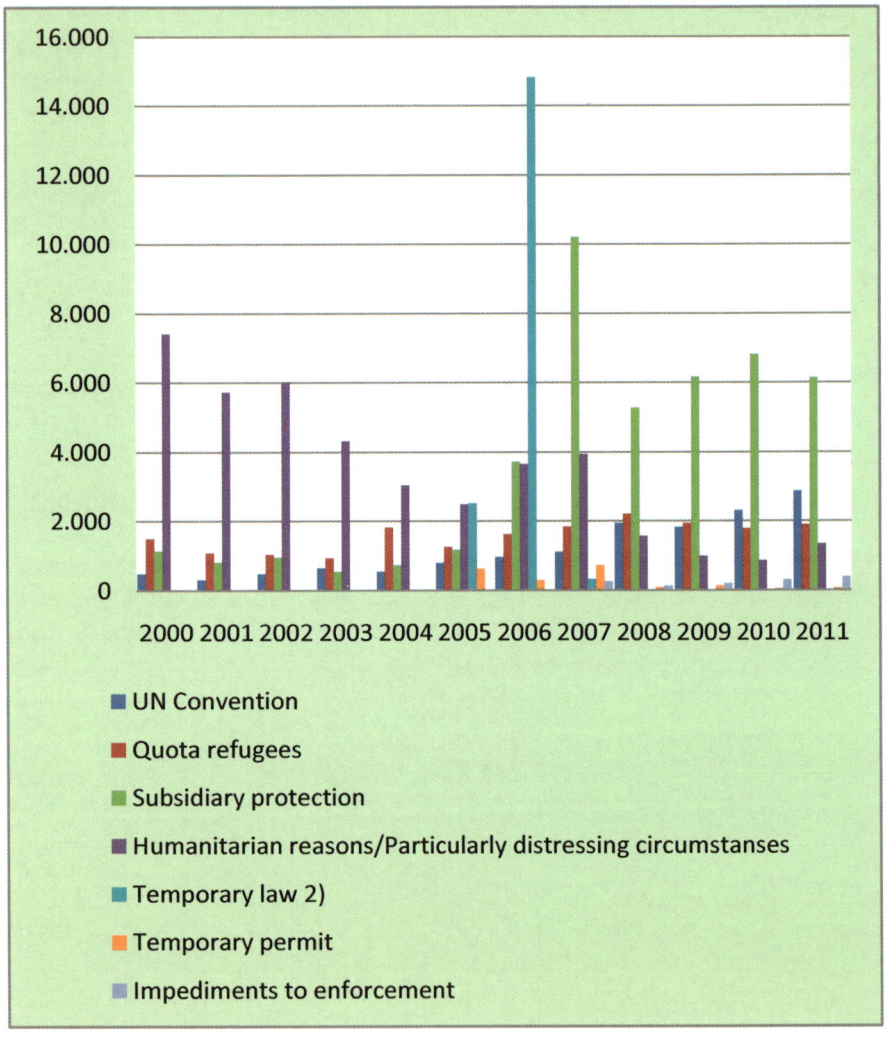

Source: SMB
1 Humanitarian reasons until March1, 2006. Thereafter Particularly distressing circumstances
2 From October 1, 2005 to March 31, 2006

Appendix 2
The districts of Gothenburg

The municipality of Gothenburg consists of 10 districts. Each district is divided into a number of areas. The majority of new arrivals live in Angered (areas: Hjällbo, Lövgärdet, Gårdstensberget, Hammarkullen) and Gothenburg East (areas: Bergsjön West and East).

Place	Inhabitants	Born in other country than Sweden [%]	Middle income (2010) SEK	Ill health – Reimbursed sick days per person	Paid employment [%]	Openly unemployed or in programmes [%]	Families with income support [%]	Qualified for high school [%]	Higher education [%]
Gothenburg municipality	520 374	22,8	242 550	25,1	73,9	6,7	6,9	83,6	
Districts (nr of areas)									
Angered (11)	48 780	49,0	179 800	36,4	56,2	12,8	20,4	69,0	26,8
Gothenburg East (6)	45 170	41,2	171 200	36,3	57,8	11,4	16,0	68,4	35,4
Örgryte – Härlanda (12)	56 880	13,7	264 200	18,9	80,8	4,8	3,2	87,9	60,8
City center (9)	58 270	17,4	259 800	16,1	76,2	4,2	2,4	89,5	67,0
Majorna-Linné (9)	62 480	13,3	258 100	23,5	78,7	5,3	3,8	92,3	64,5
Askim – Frölunda – Högsbo (12)	54 800	16,7	271 700	25,2	76,7	5,5	4,8	90,1	53,0
Gothenburg West (13)	51 600	14,8	304 700	21,8	80,7	4,9	4,8	90,8	52,7
Hisingen West (9)	51230	24,8	250 200	25,8	74,0	8,0	9,3	80,9	38,6
Lundby (7)	42 430	21,0	240 100	23,5	76,1	6,0	6,2	82,4	48,6
Hisingen North (8)	47 550	23,0	243 700	28,2	76,9	6,5	5,2	88,3	35,2

Samhällsanalys och statistik, Göteborgs stadsledningskontor
Göteborgsbladet 2012 (http://www4.goteborg.se/prod/G-info/statistik.nsf)

Lessons learned:
Recommendations on the European level and conclusive remarks

Maren Gag, Paul McGill, Eva Norström, Maria Omodeo, Sarah Jane Pretty,
Maike Schröder, Louis Henri Seukwa, Claudia Zaccai

Within the European partnership project of EduAsyl, various educational and professional backgrounds of refugees and asylum seekers in four European cities have been analysed and the local contexts of the respective VET systems have been evaluated as to whether they consider the particular educational needs of refugees. Based on that, a number of hurdles and success factors could be identified, which, after careful analysis, have proven crucial to the development of refugees' educational and professional careers. The case studies compiled in this book comprehensively explore the difficulties refugees and asylum seekers face in European cities, while also revealing that, for the most part, the cities involved in this project hardly meet the minimum standards to ensure this group's vocational integration in the European member states. This applies not only for refugees *with a precarious status who have been living in the receiving countries for a long time, but is partly* also true for recognised refugees (e.g. Italy).

Regarding the sometimes significant historical, economic and structural differences between the European cities examined here, a certain scepticism may be justified when it comes to the question of integration and of how to achieve full harmonisation according to the EU Council Directive 2003/9/EC of 27 January 2003, laying down minimum standards for the reception of asylum seekers as well as for the promotion of access to education and of participation in employment and VET. The contexts in the research cities vary considerably and it can be shown that the provision of long-term support programmes tailored to the specific needs of refugees and asylum seekers is of particular significance in protecting an extremely marginalised and vulnerable group of people and in developing innovative project approaches on a sustainable basis.

With reference to this context, the following conclusions can be formulated as recommendations on how to facilitate access to education and employment for refugees and asylum seekers in Europe:

1. Developing target group-specific local support programmes for refugees and asylum seekers to pilot tailor-made concepts and to institutionalise and strengthen different forms of cooperation between the actors in the labour market, the VET systems and refugee organisations.

Traditionally cities and metropolitan areas have been centres of attraction for refugees, migrants and asylum seekers, as they can expect to find some members of their community there, or because of already existing family networks, or just because the possibilities to find a job or training programme or to study are better there. The cities and municipalities in the member states should recognise this reality and include this extremely marginalised migrant group in their integration policies. The reconstruction of the educational careers analysed here has shown what could also be highlighted during the research period associated with EQUAL: For refugees and asylum seekers, the success of asking for education and of getting access to it depends on whether their life situation is comprehensively considered. In order for them to successfully attend training programmes, their legal status needs to be adjusted, while also ensuring their financial security. Apart from that, comprehensive social support programmes, an improvement of the living conditions and an optimum of medical care are required (Brekke 2004, Schroeder, Seukwa 2007) i.e. a so called holistic approach is needed.

In fighting multiple discrimination against refugees and asylum seekers, working in networks has proven efficient, as could be shown in the network approach during EQUAL. The interaction between refugee organisations, educational bodies and school institutions on one hand, and companies, employment offices and government departments on the other hand, allows the implementation of an integrated social space approach that is tailored to the life situation of refugees. This form of networking and cooperation within one system helps to build bridges to reach the target group and to facilitate access to training and qualification for them. The diversity of actors involved here contributes to handling the complex requirements, which go hand in hand with a strategy to implement the results on a sustainable basis and thus also require training programmes for multipliers and capacity building in the civil society.

2. Developing and testing monitoring concepts that will ensure a regular education- and integration-related reporting on the life situation of refugees.

As the case studies in the four cities have clearly demonstrated, the data available on the life situation of refugees – both quantitative and qualitative – are insufficient. The objectives as set by the EU in the strategy of Europe 2020 focus on the *social inclusion* of vulnerable and disadvantaged groups. The introduction of monitoring systems that are compatible with the interests of the EU will help uncover discrimination, improve the structure of education and support pro-grammes in the cities and municipalities of the member states as well as educational planning, and it will also contribute to a better understanding of how education in transnational spaces could look like for this group. This allows to analyse the efficacy of European VET policies and to adapt the systems of the VET institutions in the European member states where necessary in such a way as to address the life situation and educational needs of refugees.

3. Adjusting structural imbalances in the European member states and their labour markets by means of a "fair" harmonisation strategy in order to give refugees and asylum seekers the opportunity to develop their full potential and to be able to participate in education, training and employment.

According to EU statistics, about 23 million people today are unemployed and about 113 million people are living on or below the poverty line and are at risk of social exclusion. Against the background of demographic change, however, there is a growing lack of qualified personnel to be observed for the European labour market. Many problems have become worse in the course of the financial and economic crisis[1]. Regarding this development, the proposed regulation for implementing the European Social Fund (ESF) 2014-2020, thus focuses on fighting social exclusion and poverty. Since the proposed regulation, if adopted, would mean to spend at least 20% of ESF funding on social inclusion measures, for migrants and marginalised communities, for instance, while at the same time there is still considerable room for improvement when it comes to the target group-specific development of educational systems in the member states, synergy effects could be achieved when combining the support measures in the VET systems with comprehensive programmes for fighting poverty in the regions. Especially for the economically weaker countries, this would mean that even the limited financial means available could contribute to the successful integration of refugees and asylum seekers. The imbalances in the reception of refugees, which are the result of the closed-door policy adopted by the EU towards the influx of refugees and which are to be observed in some member states due to their geographical location, however, cannot be overcome with it.

---

1   European Commission (2012): Europäischer Sozialfonds (ESF)/European Social Fund 2014-2020, proposed regulation.

4. Explicitly including the target group of refugees and asylum seekers in European support programmes of the next ESF funding period, focusing on transversal aspects, in particular.

Regarding the development of the labour market in the European countries, a polarisation of employment with rising wages for highly qualified professionals and falling wages for unskilled workers can be noticed[2]. At the same time, demographic change and the ageing of the population in the European member states will result in a massive lack of qualified workers. In other words, the European member states cannot afford to ignore this enormous potential in (young) asylum seekers and refugees for training and employment systems. As the case studies indicate, only by explicit support measures is it possible to keep the structures developed during the experimental project of EQUAL active (example of Hamburg). Consequently, previous experience contributes to making sure that this group is explicitly supported as a target group in the member states and regions, as it is extremely marginalised and as such tends to be ignored by traditional VET and integration policies. Accepting the living costs of refugees as part of the co-financing of ESF measures may accelerate the process, while transnational cooperation on the European level may lead to a mutual learning effect and to a qualitative improvement of common European standards and benchmarks. Regardless of what exactly future EU regulations on European programmes will look like, it is also in the responsibility of the member states to ensure this group's participation. When taking into account that the minimum standards for education and employment as laid down in the directive 2003/9/EC of 27 January 2003 have barely been met in the European member states, the development of national and/or regional programmes should also address considerations as to whether the respective measures for this target group are feasible. The example of Germany has shown that there are enough possibilities for the member states to set their own focus and that the implementation of a federal programme may yield reasonable results[3].

---

2 European Commission (ibid.)

3 Lessons learned – Cooperation between stakeholders on the European level:
SaviAV (Social inclusion and vocational integration of Asylum seekers and Victims of human trafficking) – This network consists of 11 partners (ESF managing authorities and intermediate bodies) from six member states and is coordinated by the German Ministry of Labour and Social Affairs. Its aim is to enforce the human rights of trafficked people and to contribute to a dignified standard of living for asylum seekers by identifying emerging issues and policy gaps and by influencing policy take-up and structures in this field. Advice, education and vocational training are the topics under the asylum seeker strand. This network intends to promote good practices in education and training models through lobbying, exchanges and study visits.

Insted of a conclusion: cloudy future for asylum seekers and refugees with regards to their integration into the European educational and labor market

In the current ESF period, asylum seekers and refugees were much less visible, and in these days we already ask ourselves what will come in the next ESF period 2014-2020. Not much is sure at this moment. In its proposals, the Commission refers to migrants, disadvantaged and vulnerable groups in general, but the group of refugees is not mentioned specifically.

There is a risk of creaming off those migrant groups who might be useful for countries competitiveness. Such an evolution would certainly lead to negative consequences of which we will name only two: at first asylum seekers and refugees as specific target group could simply disappear on the integration agendas of many EU member states, or their special needs could not more being paid the necessary attention that the complexity of their situation requires with regards to integration process. Secondly the available treasure of knowhow and best practices in dealing with the integration of refugees and asylum seekers and their further development could just be abandoned with considerable negative impact in the pedagogical management of integration issues of this target group whose ongoing presence in EU countries is absolutely certain.

This would be shortsighted and counterproductive since the causes of flight such as natural catastrophes, wars, poverty, and bad governance etc, are largely structurally determined, and the EU, as one of the wealthiest, most stable, and structurally sound regions in the world, continues to constitute a preferred destination for many refugees from crisis areas despite its rather repressive Asylum and refugee policies. Considering the treats that could generate such a negative trend, it seems to be useful to stress out here definitely how important the positive achievements in the integration work with this specific target group is for the whole area of migration and Integration. Our final thesis is that given the complexity and multiplicity of their marginalization, working for the integration of asylum seekers and refugees into the European educational and labor market today offers great opportunities for pedagogical and social innovations which could be transferable for the integration of other disadvantaged migrants groups.

References

Arbetsförmedlingen (2012): Nyanländas etablering – reformens första år (2012-02-22).

Ayalon, O. (1999): Creative means toward psycho-social aims of reconciliation. Tivon: Nord International Trauma Consultancy, Israel.

Bhagwati, P. N. (1995): The Role of Judiciary in Legal Aid. Legal Aid In Crisis. The Present and The Future. Presentation vid World Legal Aid Conference, Kuala Lumpur, Malaysia. Organiserad av "Bar Council Malaysia" i samarbete med "the Law Faculties, University of Malaya" och "the International Islamic University", Malaysia.

Baumgarten, B.; Lahusen, C. (2006): Politiknetzwerke – Vorteile und Grundzüge einer qualitativen Analysestrategie. In: Hollstein/Strauss (Hg.) (2006), S. 177-197. Wiesbaden.

Baur, W.; Mack, W.; Schroeder, J. (Hg.) (2004): Bildung von unten denken. Aufwachsen in erschwerten Lebenssituationen – Provokationen für die Pädagogik. Bad Heilbrunn

Beckmann-Schulz, I. et.al, passage gGmbH (2007): EQUAL LANGUAGE. Manual on Second Language Training with Asylum Seekers and Refugees. Hamburg.

Beckmann-Schulz, I.et al., passage gGmbH, Koordinierungsstelle Berufsbezogenes Deutsch (2011): Qualitätskriterien interaktiv. Ein Leitfaden zur Umsetzung von berufsbezogenem Unterricht Deutsch als Zweitsprache. Hamburg.

Beier, B. et al. (1993): Altona und Ottensen. Hamburg.

Bethscheider, M. et al. (2010): Positionspapier. Weiterbildungsbegleitende Hilfen als zentraler Bestandteil adressatenorientierter beruflicher Weiterbildung. Zur Relevanz von Deutsch als Zweitsprache und Bildungssprache in der beruflichen Weiterbildung. Frankfurt/Main.

Bourdieu, P. (1983): Ökonomisches Kapital, kulturelles Kapital, Soziales Kapital. In: Kreckel, R. (Hg.): Soziale Ungleichheit, Soziale Welt, Band 2, Göttingen, S. 183-198.

Bourdieu, P. (1991): Physischer, sozialer und angeeigneter physischer Raum. In: Wentz, M. (Hg.): Stadt-Räume. Frankfurt/Main, S. 25-34.

Brekke, J.-P. (2004): While we are waiting. Uncertainty and empowerment among asylum-seekers in Sweden. Oslo.

Bundesministerium für Arbeit und Soziales (2011): Nationaler Aktionsplan zur Umsetzung des Nationalen Integrationsplans. Abschlussbericht des Dialogforums 3 „Arbeitsmarkt und Erwerbsleben". Bonn.

City of Hamburg, Behörde für Schule und Berufsbildung, Institut für Bildungsmonitoring (2009): Bildungsbericht Hamburg. Zusammenfassung 2009. Hamburg.

Daniel, E. Valentine & Knudsen, J. C. Red. (1995). Mistrusting refugees. Berkeley, Los Angeles, London.

Diedrich, A. (2011). Uppföljning av VINN-projektet. Gothenburg: School of Business. Economics and Law. Gothenburg University.

Engels, D. (2006): Lebenslagen und soziale Exklusion. Thesen zur Reformulierung des Lebenslagenskonzepts für die Sozialberichterstattung. In: Sozialer Fortschritt, Heft 5, S. 109-112.

Englmann, B.; Müller, M. (2007): Brain Waste. Die Anerkennung von ausländischen Qualifikationen in Deutschland. Augsburg.

EU Commission (2001): European Governance. A White Paper. Brussels.

Fager, S.; Gag, M. (2007): Vocational guidance for migrants in Germany: a partnerships model. In: Greco Silvana; Clayton, Pamela M.; Janko Spreizer, Alenka: Migrants and Refugees in Europe: Models of integration and new challenges for vocational guidance. Milano.

Firnhaber, R. (2000): På minerad mark – i exilen? Flyktingar med särskilda behov i mötet med ett oförberett samhälle. Beskrivningar från ett antropologiskt-integrativt perspektiv. Socialmedicinsk tidskrift. Nr 1, 2000. Göteborg: Svensk socialmedicinsk förening.

FLUCHTort Hamburg Plus, passage gGmbH (2010): WIR SIND HIER! Portraits von Hamburger Flüchtlingen und Bleibeberechtigten auf ihrem Weg in den Beruf. Hamburg.

Gag, M. et al. (2011): Migration, work and education under transnational conditions of life – educational biographies of migrants, refugees and asylumseekers from the perspective of different European countries. In: dies. (Eds.): Globalisation and Opportunities: Vocational Education for Transnational Careers. Radom, 22-97.

Gag, M.; Schroeder, J. (2011): Refugee Monitoring: Vorschläge zu einem Pilotvorhaben am Beispiel der Stadt Hamburg.- Monitoring und Bildungsberichterstattung auch für Flüchtlinge. In: http://www.fluchtort-hamburg.de/fileadmin/pdf/Konzept_Refugee_Monitoring_Hamburger_Kontext.pdf.

Gag, M.; Schroeder, J. (2011): Refugee Monitoring. Vorschläge zu einem Pilotvohaben am Beispiel der Stadt Hamburg. Presented in a „Werkstattgespräch" (seminar) June 22nd, 2011 in the Patriotischen Gesellschaft von 1765 Hamburg.

Gag, M.; Schroeder, J. (2012): REFUGEE MONITORING. Zur Situation junger Flüchtlinge im Hamburger Übergangssystem Schule/Beruf. Berichterstattung. Herausgegeben von der passage gGmbH, Hamburg.

Gibney, M.J. (2004). The Ethics and Politics of Asylum. Liberal Democracy and the Response to Refugees. Cambridge.

Gomolla, M.; Radtke F.-O. (2002): Institutionelle Diskriminierung. Die Herstellung ethnischer Differenz in der Schule. Opladen.

Gustafsson, K., Norström, E. & Fioretos, I. (2012). Between Empowerment and powerlessness: Separated minors in Sweden. In: New Directions in Child and Adolescence Development 3/1/2012 p. 65-77.

Habermas, J. (1999): "Kampen för ett ömsesidigt erkännande i den demokratiska rättsstaten". In: Gutmann, Amy (ed) Det mångkulturella samhället och erkännandets politik. Göteborg.

Hartman, L. (ed.) (2011): Konkurrensens konsekvenser. Vad händer med svensk välfärd? Stockholm.

Hawkins, P. & Shohet, R. (1989): Supervision in the helping professions. Open University Press.

Herzfeld, M. (1993): The Social Production of Indifference. Chicago, London.

Holgersson, H. (2011): Icke-medborgarskapets urbana geografi. Göteborg.

Honigfabrik (1988): Einwanderer – Einwohner – Einheimische. Ausländer und Inländer in Wilhelmsburg. Dokumentation zur Ausstellung. Hamburg.

Hunt, P. (2007). Implementation of General Assembly Resolution 60/251 of 15 March 2006 entitled "Human Rights Council". Report of the Special Rapporteur on the right of everyone to the enjoyment of the highest attainable standard of physical and mental health. Addendum. Mission to Sweden. Human Rights Council. Distr. General. A/HRC/4/28/Add.2. February 28, 2007.

Institut Arbeit und Qualifikation (2009): Wirkungen des SGB II auf Personen mit Migrationshintergrund. Duisburg.

Ioannidou, A. (2008): Governance-Instrumente im Bildungsbereich im transnationalen Raum. In: Hartz, Stefanie; Schrader, Josef (Hg.): Steuerung und Organisation in der Weiterbildung. Bad Heilbrunn: S.91-110.

Ioannidou, A. (2010): Steuerung im transnationalen Bildungsraum. Internationales Bildungsmonitoring zum Lebenslangen Lernen. Bielefeld.

Isoplan Consult (2005): Weißbuch Flüchtlinge und Asylbewerber/innen im Saarland 2004. Erstellt im Rahmen der Entwicklungspartnerschaft SEPA, ein Projekt der Gemeinschaftsinitiative EQUAL. Saarbrücken/Berlin.

Johann Daniel Lawaetz Stiftung, Univation Institut für Evaluation, Wirtschafts- und Sozialforschung (2011): Evaluation des ESF-Bundesprogramms zur arbeitsmarktlichen Unterstützung für Bleibeberechtigte und Flüchtlinge mit Zugang zum Arbeitsmarkt. Abschlussbericht. Hamburg, Köln, Kerpen.

Johansson, R. (1992): Vid byråkratins gränser: om handlingsfrihetens organisatoriska begränsningar i klientrelaterat arbete. Lund.

Kaas, L.; Manger, C. (2010): Ethnic Discrimination in Germany's Labour Market: A Field Experiment. IZA Discussion Paper No. 4741 – http://ftp.iza.org/dp741.pdf.

Kamali, M. (1997): Distorted integration : clientization of immigrants in Sweden. Uppsala: Centre for Multiethnic Research. Series: Uppsala multiethnic papers, 0281-448X; 41.

Kamali, M. (2002): Kulturkompetens i socialt arbete: om socialarbetarens och klientens kulturella bakgrund. Stockholm.

Kamali, M. (2008): Racial discrimination. Institutional patterns and politics. Hoboken: Taylor & Francis Series: Routledge Research in Race and Ethnicity, 2.

Khosravi, S. (2010): 'Illegal' traveller: an auto-ethnography of borders. Basingstoke: Palgrave Macmillan.

Kreisausschuss des Landkreises Hersfeld-Rotenburg (2010): Lohnende Integrationsarbeit mit Flüchtlingen. Arbeitshilfe für die Verwaltungspraxis. Kreis Hersfeld-Rotenburg.

Länsstyrelsen (2011): Utan hälsa ingen etablering – hälsans roll i flyktingmottagandet. Stockholm: Länsstyrelsen. www.lansstyrelsen.se.

Lennartsson, R. (2007): Mellan hopp och förtvivlan: erfarenheter och strategier i väntan på asyl: en etnologisk undersökning om situationen för asylsökande i eget boende i Västmanland och Uppsala län. Stockholm: Nationell Temagrupp asyl, integration inom gemenskapsinitiativet EQUAL, 2007.

Moxnes, P. (1987): Ångest och arbetsmiljö. Hur organisationen påverkar personalen. En fallbeskrivning. Stockholm.

Neumann, U. et al. (Hg.) (2003): Lernen am Rande der Gesellschaft. Münster.

Norström, E. (2004): I väntan på asyl. Retorik och praktik i svensk flyktingpolitik. Umeå: Borea.

Norström, E. & Gustafsson, K. (2010): To Receive With Grace – The Reception of Separated Asylum-Seeking Minors Arriving in Sweden, In: Diskurs Kindheits- und Jugendforschung 2010:2. p. 159-167.

Norström, E., Gustafsson K. & Fioretos I. (2011): The Interpreter – a cultural intermediary. Behind closed doors. – The importance of interpreting for the rule of law and for integration, with special focus on separated minors. Lund: www.tolkprojektet.se

Parreira do Amaral, M. (2006): The Influence of Transnational Organizations on National Education Systems. Frankfurt am Main.

Persson, A. (2012): Ritualisering och sårbarhet – ansikte mot ansikte med Goffmans perspektiv på social interaktion. Malmö.

Povrzanovic Frykman, M. (ed.) (2001): Beyond integration. Challenges of belonging in diaspora and exile. Lund.

Radtke, F.-O. (2003): Integrationsleistungen der Schule. Zur Differenz von Bildungsqualität und Beteiligungsgerechtigkeit. In: Vorgänge. Zeitschrift für Bürgerrechte und Gesellschaftspolitik 163, 23-34.

Sachverständigenrat deutscher Stiftungen für Integration und Migration (2011): Migrationsland 2011. Jahresgutachten 2011 mit Migrationsbarometer. Berlin.

Sager, M. (2011): Everyday clandestinity: experiences on the margins of citizenship and migration policies. Lund: Faculty of Social Sciences, Centre for Gender Studies, Lund University.

Schroeder, J. (2002): Bildung im geteilten Raum: Schulentwicklung unter Bedingungen von Einwanderung und Verarmung. Münster.

Schroeder, J.; Seukwa, L.H. (2007): Flucht Bildung Arbeit: Fallstudien zur beruflichen Qualifizierung von Flüchtlingen. Karlsruhe.

Schroeder, J.; Thielen, M. (2009): Das Berufsvorbereitungsjahr. Eine Einführung. Stuttgart.

Sennemark, E. & Moberg, A. (2009): Dialog i centrum. En utvärdering av samhällsinformationen till nyanlända flyktingar i Göteborgs Stad. Gothenburg.

Sennemark, E. & Moberg, A. (2010): Dialogen fortsätter. Utvärdering av samhällsinformation till nyanlända. Gothenburg.

Seukwa, L.H. (2006): Der Habitus der Überlebenskunst. Zum Verhältnis von Kompetenz und Migration im Spiegel von Flüchtlingsbiographien. Münster. New York. München. Berlin.

Seukwa, L.H. (2007): Soziokontextualität von Kompetenz und Bildungsprozesse in transnationalen Räumen. Der Habitus der Überlebenskunst. In: Diskurs Kindheits- und Jugendforschung 2 (2007) 3, S. 295-309.

Seukwa, L.H. (2007): The Ingrained Art of Survival. The Nexus between Competence and Migration as Reflected in Refugee Biographies. Köln.

Sigvardsdotter, E. (2012): Presenting the absent. An account of undocumentedness in Sweden. Uppsala: Kulturgeografiska institutionen, Uppsala universitet.

Socialstyrelsen (2010): Social rapport. Stockholm: Socialstyrelsen.

Söndergaard, H. P. (1991). "A psychiatric view of refugee policy". In: En framtida flykting- och immigrationspolitik. Slutrapport från seminarium i Lund den 7 november 1990 och konferens i Stockholm den 5 december 1990. Arrangerade av Forum för Etnicitets- och kulturmötesstudier, Lunds universitet och Svenska flyktingrådet. Stockholm: Svenska flyktingrådets rapportserie nr 1-1991:150–153.

Statistical Office (Amt für Statistik) Berlin Brandenburg (2010): Results of pilot study on indicator development and monitoring 2005-2008. 3. Bericht der länderoffenen Arbeitsgruppe „Indikatorenentwicklung und Monitoring" der Konferenz der für Integration zuständigen Ministerinnen und Minister. Berlin.

Statskontoret (2012): Etableringen av nyanlända. En uppföljning av myndigheternas genomförande etableringsreformen. Rapport 2012:22.

Swedish Migration Board Annual Report (2009).

Tornborg, R. (1984): Jacobs stege. In: Är lagom bäst? Om kulturmöten i Sverige. Norrköping.

UNHCR (2003): UNHCR annotated comments on Council Directive 2003/9/EC of 27 January 2003.

Viitanen, K. & Tähjä K. (2012): Undocumented Lives. Available in September 2012 as an Electronic book. In September 2012 this book will be also available in English as an electronic book. In September 2012 this book will be also available in English as an electronic book.AvAaadd

Voges, W.; Jürgens, O.; Mauer, A.; Meyer, E. (2003): Methoden und Grundlagen des Lebenslagensantzes. Bremen.

Willke, H. (2001): Systemtheorie III: Steuerungstheorie. Stuttgart.

Womack, J. P. & J. D. T. (2003): Lean thinking: banish waste and create wealth in your corporation. London.

Zeitschrift für Erziehungswissenschaft 7. Jg. (2004): Heft 1. Schwerpunkt: Transnationale Bildungsräume.

Internet sources

www.arbetsformedlingen.se/Globalmeny/Other-languages/New-in-Sweden.html – The Pubic Employment Service.

Häggroth, S. (2012): Framtidens välvärd inom vård, skola och omsorg http://framtidensvalfard.wordpress.com/2012/03/11/vinstsyftande-aktorer-inom-vard-skola-och-omsorg.

Integrationsverket (2007). *Integrationspolitikens resultat. På väg mot ett samlat system för uppföljning och analys vid 16 statliga myndigheter.* Integrationsverkets rapportserie 2007:05. www.temaasyl.se/Documents/IV/integra tionspolitikens%20resultat.pdf.

www.asylumscotland.org.uk/asylumstatistics.php.

www.botkyrka.se – Municipality of Botkyrka.

http://www.bridgesprogrammes.org.uk.

www.digitalasparet.se/eng/index.htm.

www.digitalasparet/safir/index.htm – lexin.nada.kth.se/lexin/.

www.dn.se – Dagens Nyheter (Daily paper).

www.equalityhumanrights.com/uploaded_files/research/refugees_and_asylum_s eekers_research_report.pdf.

www.equalworks.co.uk/resources/contentfiles/3540.pdf.

www.equal-works.com.

www.esf.se/sv/english – ESF.

www.fastighets.se/home/fast2/home.nsf/1407cbf214ec3e18c125712a003458ae/4 fc95637772d94d1c1257427002f69d0?OpenDocument – Fastighetsfolket Nr. 3 (2008). *Städarna som inte finns*.

www.fcfp.se – The Swedish Trade Unions Center for Undocumented Migrant Workers.

www.forsakringskassan.se/sprak/eng – The Swedish Social Insurance Agency.

www.gp.se – Göteborgsposten (Daily paper).

www.glasgow.gov.uk/en/YourCouncil/Atlas.

www.icar.org.uk/?lid=9982.

www.ilascotland.org.uk/ILA+Homepage.htm.

www.ilpa.org.uk/infoservice.html.

www.ingenillegal.org/no-one-illegal-world-without-borders.

www.insidehousing.co.uk/care/one-in-four-glasgow-asylum-seekers-are-destitute/6522282.article.

www.lattlast.se.

www.lo.se/home/lo/home.nsf/unidView/943717B4077AAF1AC1256E4B00336 29C.

www.meritea.se.

www.mynewsdesk.com/se/pressroom/huddinge/pressrelease/view/mira-skapar-dialog-mellan-unga-flyktingar-och-samhaellet-361879 – Mira, Huddinge.

www.migrationsverket.se/info/443_en.html.

www.parliament.uk/briefing-papers/SN01908 – Melanie Gower, Asylum seekers and the right to work – Commons Library Standard Note, 7 November 2011.

www.refugeecouncil.org.uk/policy/briefings/2009/caseresolutionsupdate.

www.refugeecouncil.org.uk/Resources/Refugee%20Council/downloads/briefing s/nia_act_02/ed_1_dec02.pdf.

www.regeringen.se – The Government.

www.rosengrenska.org – The Rosengrenska Foundation.

www.sahlgrenska.se/upload/SU/omrade_barn/BUP/Flyktingbarnteamet/PM_asyl _flyktingar.pdf.

www.scb.se – Statistics Sweden.

www.scotland.gov.uk/Topics/People/Equality/Refugees-asylum/.

www.scottishrefugeecouncil.org.uk – Gareth Mulvey, Refugee Integration in Scotland, June 2011(p. 9-10).

www.skolverket.se – The Swedish National Agency for Education.
www.socialstyrelsen.se – the National Board of Health and Welfare.
www.tco.se/Templates/Page2____2319.aspx.
www.temaasyl.se – the National Thematic Network on Asylum & Integration in Sweden.
www.temaasyl.se/Templates/Page.aspx?id=3004 – LATU (2008). Slutrapport.
www.tolk.mariestad.se – The Interpreter Agency in Mariestad.
www.tolkprojektet.se – Interpreter Research.
www.undocumentedlives.com.
www.vardforalla.se – Member of the International Federation of Medical Students' Associations.
www.vardforpapperslosa.se – Right to Health Care-Initiative.
www.valideringstolk.se.
www.8sidor.se/start.

Parliamentary Press and other Public Prints

Ds 2003:23. Validering m.m. – fortsatt utveckling av vuxnas lärande.
European Parliament and Council Directive 2003/9/EC of 27 January 2003.
Bürgerschaft der Freien und Hansestadt Hamburg, Mitteilung des Senats an die Bürgerschaft: Maßnahmen zur Umsetzung der Reform der beruflichen Bildung in Hamburg. Drucksache 19/8472 vom 18.01.2011.
Gothenburg City Committee for Adult Education. Protocol 2012 (§ 60 Projekt 101, dnr: 0046/12).
Gothenburg City Council (2010-12-9). Protocol 13, § 11 Dnr 1017/10. Implementation of a new organisation for municipal refugee reception in Gothenburg. Document 2010 nr 180.
The Swedish Migration Board. Protocol VCA nr 223/2011 of December 19, 2011.
Prop. 2007/08:147 Nya regler för arbetskraftsinvandring.
Prop. 2009/10:60, Nyanlända invandrares arbetsmarknadsetablering – egenansvar med professionellt stöd.
SFS 1982:763 Hälso- och sjukvårdslag.
SFS 1986:223 Förvaltningslag.
SFS 1994:137 Lag om mottagande av asylsökande m.fl.SFS 2007:996 Förordning med instruktion för Migrationsverket.
SFS 2008:344 Lag om hälso- och sjukvård åt asylsökande m.fl.
SFS 2008:962 Lag om valfrihet hos Arbetsförmedlingen.
SFS 2010:197 Lag om etableringsinsatser för vissa nyanlända invandrare.

SFS Lag (2010:536) om valfrihet hos Arbetsförmedlingen.
SFS 2010:800 Skollag.
SOU 2003:89 Asylsökandes förmåner under mottagandet.
SOU 2006:59 Arbetslivets (o)synliga murar. Rapport av Utredningen om makt, integration och strukturell diskriminering.
SOU 2009:19 Aktiv väntan – Asylsökande i Sverige.
SOU 2010:16. Utredningen om samhällsorientering för nyanlända invandrare.
SOU 2011:48. Vård efter behov och på lika villkor – en mänsklig rättighet.

Contributors

Margherita Buchetti has graduated in Modern Languages at University of Florence in 2010.From 2010 to 2011 she worked as Italian teacher at the "Associazione di Mutuo Soccorso"

Rita Cardini got her Master's degree in Political Sciences – International Relations from the University of Florence in 2010. She has worked as intern on research projects concerning international migrations, refugees and asylum seekers at the National Research Center (CNR) in 2010 and at NGO COSPE in 2011.

Dr. Pamela Clayton was a Research Fellow at the University of Glasgow and managing Director of Anniesland Research Consultancy Limited. She passed away at the beginning of 2012. May her soul rest in peace.

Daria Franceschini got her Degree in Economy for developing countries from the University of Florence in 2008. She collaborated with Cospe on a research project on refugees and asylum seekers in the Florentine territory. Now she works as italian teacher for migrants at NGO Cospe.

Maren Gag is a staff member in "Migration and International Cooperation" at passage gGmbH and directs the network project FLUCHTort Hamburg Plus (SAFE HAVEN Hamburg Plus).

Eva Norström (PhD) is an independent researcher, retired from Lund University in Sweden. Her current research deals with the use of interpreters in meetings between representatives of the public sector and migrants, and its importance for the rule of law and for integration. Web: www.evanorstrom.se

Maria Omodeo – Graduated in Oriental Languages and Literature at the University of Venice. She worked for years in People's Republic of China, in programmes of cultural exchanges. Since 1990 she works in the NGO COSPE, as responsible for the educational projects in Italy for preventing discrimination in schools and in the society. In collaborating with the didactic équipe of COSPE, has managed many projects funded by the European Commission and has contributed to the implementation of several multimedia teaching materials in the field of interculturality and multilingualism promotion

Dr. Joachim Schroeder is Professor at the Faculty of Education Sciences at the Universität Hamburg

Dr. Louis Henri Seukwa is Professor at the Faculty of Business and social Sciences at Hamburg University of Applied Sciences

Chiara Trevisan got her Master Degree in Social Sciences – Social Services from the University of Florence in 2011, while she collaborated with Cospe on a research project on refugees and asylum seekers in the Florentine territory. Now she is working in an educational farm, planning and managing activities for children.

Claudia Zaccai is professor and chair of "Migration Studies" and "Development Anthropology" since 2003 at the University of Rome, "La Sapienza".